CELEBRATING
THE STITCH

CELEBRATING THE STITCH

Contemporary Embroidery of North America

BARBARA LEE SMITH

The Taunton Press

Front-cover: detail of *La Noche de las que Brillan* by D.R. Wagner (the full piece is shown on p. 99). Photo by Robert Hollis.

First printing: June 1991
Printed in the United States of America

A THREADS Book

THREADS® is a trademark of The Taunton Press, Inc.
registered in the U.S. Patent and Trademark Office.

The Taunton Press, 63 South Main Street, Box 5506,
Newtown, CT 06470-5506

Library of Congress Cataloging-in-Publication Data

Smith, Barbara Lee.
    Celebrating the Stitch : contemporary embroidery of North America
  Barbara Lee Smith.
        p.   cm.
      "A Threads book"—T.p. verso.
      includes index
      ISBN 0-942391-39-X
      1. Embroidery—United States—History—20th century—Themes,
  motives. 2. Embroidery—Canada—History—20th century—Themes,
  motives   I. Title.
  NK9212.S64   1991   91-8961
  746.44' 0973' 09045—dc20   CIP

Dedicated with love to Mel and our families.

FOREWORD

around the world, museums thrill their visitors with exhibits of royal and religious garments from the past that are gloriously embellished with embroidery. But in the 20th century, without the patronage of popes and potentates, stitchery and embroidery are known to most as the homely needle skills used by our grandmothers to decorate pillowcases and tea towels.

Unlike older nations, the United States has no single strong tradition that dictates style or application of needlework. Instead, artists who have mined the expressive possibilities of needle and thread have forced us to look at embroidery in new ways. They, like others who have chosen materials and processes long associated with the crafts (rather than painting canvas or carving marble), show us that stitchery can add, literally, another dimension to art. Whether they tell stories with their stitches or rely on pure color and texture for abstract imagery, these artists compel us to look and invite us to touch.

Acceptance as artists has not been easy for those makers, or for other craftspeople who have used their talents to create functional objects or purely expressive ones. The optimistic years of the 1950s stimulated craft industry. New ideas began to be accepted. Yet for skilled embroiderers, opportunities lay in the embellishment of functional things—two-dimensional clothing, handbags, church vestments. It was not until the 1960s that artists using a variety of textile processes enjoyed the great freedom that Barbara Lee Smith has documented in this book.

In that decade the international tapestry biennials in Lausanne, Switzerland, were inaugurated. They began to give visibility not only to fabric pictures woven on a loom, but also to a spectrum of textile techniques, advocating artistry in three dimensions and on a grand scale. And on a popular level, outrageous embroidery embellished the blue jeans of the hip counterculture, leading the way (along with the ubiquitous tie-dyed T-shirts) to the wearable-art movement of the next decade.

By the 1970s, Ed Rossbach, teaching at the University of California at Berkeley, had creatively explored the structural techniques of knitting, crochet and basket construction. His own work and that of his students proved that textile art was not limited by process. Others, like Sheila Hicks, continued the investigation of ancient Peruvian textiles that had influenced another important weaver, Anni Albers. Dorothy Liebes was integrating reeds and metallic ribbons into her woven space dividers, infusing them with the vitality of unorthodox but vivid color combinations. Still others examined the potential of knotless netting from New Guinea, Scandinavian cardweaving and other exotic textile processes.

Across the country, artists were discovering that textile structure could be a creative end or a mere starting point for further embellishment. The surface-design movement united various dyeing techniques—many borrowed from Asia—with beadwork, heat-transfer printing, silk screening, fabric collage and on top of it all, the age-old processes of needle and thread.

Barbara Lee Smith has done more than merely examine this art and its evolution. She also takes us to meet the artists, to know them and their creative processes. Through her eyes and her words we can begin to understand not so much how art is made, but why artists have chosen needle and thread to express themselves. Her insight as a practicing artist is invaluable to our understanding of the artistic maturation of contemporary embroidery. Her choice of artists embraces those whose work is essentially flat and others who embroider surfaces that they have already made three dimensional. Her choices include pure embroidery, canvas work (needlepoint) and combinations of stitchery with other techniques such as appliqué and quilting.

The sources of inspiration for these art objects are equally diverse, whether they are the narrative traditions of tapestry and painting, the pattern and texture of a fabric's surface, the remembered traditions of needlework, or the vivid colors and rhythms of urban living. Art museums and galleries have slowly begun to recognize that art is not limited by medium, only by the individual artist's creative application of material and technique. But until art historians revise their texts to embrace the crafts, museums will continue to discriminate against art in fiber, wood, glass, clay and metal.

Antique textiles from other cultures are exhibited in art museums and galleries, but only quilts have gained museum recognition among contemporary textiles. That has come about in the past 20 years. Maybe the next 20 years will give contemporary embroidery the recognition that it deserves.

Lloyd E. Herman
Director, Cartwright Gallery/Canadian Craft Museum
Founding Director, Smithsonian's Renwick Gallery

Acknowledgments

hile working on this chronicle of late 20th-century North American embroidery, I was reminded of one of its worthy ancestors stitched over 900 years ago, the Bayeux Tapestry. Worked in a vigorous manner in words and pictures covering a band of cloth over 200 ft. long, it tells the story of the Norman Conquest in a work intended for celebration at the Cathedral of Bayeux. Like a tapestry made over time, this book, also intended as a celebration, developed a life and character of its own. It became a bit of a conquest as well, and my acknowledgments, which relate the history of its making and the many people involved, could fit around a room just as the Bayeux embroidery did.

Christine Timmons, senior editor of books at The Taunton Press, helped me do battle with words, pulling on my reins with commands written in the margins of my manuscript like "Boil," "Toss" and the much-dreaded "Huh?" She helped define the character of this work and was generous in her words of encouragement while gently leading me through the process of making a book. Rebecca Caldwell came in fresh, near the end of the project, to add her editorial expertise to this creation of words and image. Pam Purrone's eye for detail and cheerful willingness

to discuss changes were much appreciated. A special thanks to Donna Pierpont, who worked tirelessly on promoting the idea for an exhibition connected with the book. the staff at The Taunton Press had been consistently supportive, enthusiastic and professional, and I'm honored to be associated with the. My thanks all of them.

It took months of accumulating information and ideas before *Celebrating the Stitch* began to take form. A number of people and organizations were helpful: Sandra Dunn at the Crafts Resource Centre of the Ontario Crafts Council; Pam Godderis and Connie Jefferess, each of whom were helpful with information on Canadian resources; the Slide Library at the American Crafts Council was very useful; and the Council of American Embroiderers was generous in lending me slides and related materials from the "Needle Expression" exhibits. The late Diane Itter, who was encouraging and supportive in the early stages of this book, paved the way for me with a number of artists included here. Gunnel Teitel helped me at the Metropolitan Museum of Art.

I appreciate the assistance of the Helen Drutt Gallery, the HoltHaus Gallery, Julie: Artisans' Gallery and Wittenborn & Hollingsworth, Ltd., for their help in locating the artists they represented. Mary Dritschel, independent curator, also helped me locate artists. My thanks to Cynthia Boyer not only for allowing me to use photographs of the Mariska Karasz work she owns but also for lugging it to be photographed.

Stitched through this tapestry are some constants, those whose helpfulness and support are much appreciated: B. J. Adams, who was my guinea-pig interviewee and who later returned the favor by interviewing me; Stephen Thurston, who posed some intriguing questions early in the project that helped me to focus on what I wanted the book to say; Dot Woodsome, who listened to and helped with all manner of trivia without grumbling; the late Margaret Bowman, whose joy in creating as much as she could in her lifetime I'll always cherish; and my fellow fiber friends of the S and B clan who shared so much. One of that group, Nora Lou Kampe, deserves special thanks for transcribing hours of interviews and wading through piles of notes; her reactions to and thoughts on the book were truly valuable. She is always a lady, even with a pair of wolves at her feet.

My thanks to Constance Howard, MBE, who had nothing directly and everything indirectly to do with this book. She turned this American embroiderer around many years ago, and I have never been the same since.

I am grateful to Lloyd E. Herman, director of the Cartwright Gallery/Canadian Craft Museum in Vancouver, British Columbia, and of the Smithsonian Institution's Renwick Gallery, for all he has done for crafts over the years, for his discerning eye and for his thoughtful foreword to this book.

To each artist who supplied information, illustrations and names and addresses of other artists, I am deeply indebted. Many of you have become true "phone friends," sharing your time and talents as well as the secrets of your craft. When I began this book my aim was to deepen the public's understanding of contemporary embroidery. As I worked with each of you my goal shifted slightly, since I felt a responsibility to be true not only to the art of embroidery but also to the artists who embroider. I have great admiration for your ability to bring art out of needle, thread and fabric to chronicle your life and times just as those embroiderers of the Bayeux Tapestry did. I hope this book serves each of you well.

To my family: Mark Smith, the true writer among us, for his encouragement and moral support; Lee Lanou and Amy Novak, whose enthusiastic support has reached me from too far away; and Randy Lanou, whose keen eye for visual detail never ceases to amaze me. I am both grateful for your help and proud of you all. And finally, thanks to Mel Smith, a man of few but well-chosen words and good humor who knew I could do this project well before I was convinced. I am happy for every interruption that made the months at the Word Farm fly by.

CONTENTS

INTRODUCTION

MARISKA KARASZ
Larsen and Lace

1950s, #7038; 70 in. by 20 in.; handmade paper, antique lace; embroidery, collage; detail below. (Collection of Cynthia Boyer; photo by Fredde Lieberman, Silver Spring, Maryland.)

he art of making marks on cloth with thread, stitching color, texture and structure, is the essence of embroidery. It is an ancient craft, possibly derived from the appreciation and repetition of a row of regularly worked stitches by one of our ancestors binding skins together to make a garment. It has been extolled in many generations as the embodiment of fashion and the finest of gifts, an essential skill for "marriageable" ladies in many cultures, and it has been invested with importance in the service of church and state. Conversely, the art has suffered through periods of scorn and was reviled as one of the more useless crafts—a frivolous and repetitious plugging of holes.

In the last 30 years, however, embroidery in the United States and Canada has quietly kept pace with the changes in the art world. These have been exciting times for embroidery, ranging from the richly decorated hippie jeans and the

exploratory, ropy, barely spun, fibrous "stitcheries" of the 1960s to the research-laden, historic and ethnic-oriented documents of the 1970s and 1980s. This has been a time of recreating the medium, a simultaneous acknowledgment of the work of the past and an exploration of the new.

Contemporary embroidery has wit and bite. It is heavily symbolic and allusive. It is folksy and simple or densely figured and purposely obscure. It is cool and serene or passionately political. Recent work may strive for technical excellence or abandon technique completely. By placing importance on color and image, many embroiderers de-emphasize stitches and their myriad variations and treat the threaded needle like a paint-laden brush.

Many significant changes have occurred over the past three decades, and my own experience has followed this period of change. Introduced to embroidery by my mother and sister, I enjoyed it as a traditional pastime for many years. Then in the early 1960s, I saw books by artists Mariska Karasz (see her work on the facing page) and David Van Dommelin in the local library that suggested possibilities for exploring a technique I had already acquired. These ideas seemed fresh and exciting to me, and more important, I could pursue them within my own time and space. Later, a short article on machine embroidery caught my eye, and I learned as much as I could about it on my own. I moved from the 1960s to the 1990s as I patched and stitched jeans, collected enough boxes of heavy yarns to keep many moths happy, went back to school to earn degrees in art and finally felt secure enough to rename my sewing room the "studio." Out in the community a few teachers taught "traditional" crewel work, stressing fine technique and patterns from the 18th century. The rest of the field, emphasizing design and ex-

perimentation, was lumped under the heading of "contemporary." I learned from the former and joined the latter.

In England there was a much earlier movement to unite embroidery with contemporary design. An important influence on many embroiderers in the United States and Canada was Constance Howard, MBE, who was then principal lecturer at Goldsmiths' College School of Art in London. First her book, *Inspiration for Embroidery* (see the Bibliography on pp. 225-227) and then her lively presence challenged and encouraged us on this side of the Atlantic to explore and expand our understanding of embroidery.

As more people became reacquainted with embroidery, the need for classes and workshops in technique and design developed. Schools and universities did not meet these needs, so a network of organizations grew, many calling themselves "guilds" after the traditional artisans' trade organizations. They sponsored (and still do) classes, lectures and workshops for their members. National associations, with membership in the thousands, assisted in both the educational and organizational needs of the smaller guilds and provided correspondence schools and national exhibitions to help educate the public. It was through these organizations that I received my training and developed my skills as a teacher.

Every region produced its pioneers who were tremendously influential. In the West and Southwest, Martha Mood's animals and people stitched with a wealth of detail were well-known and loved. Nik Krevitsky's strokes of color and light, seemingly random stitches of line over line, gave many artists permission to try abstractions. In the East, Dorothy Ruddick created poetic forms over a ten-year hiatus from painting. Illi-

nois artist Virginia C. Bath (work shown at left, top) continues to contribute unique combinations of lace and embroidery and documented historic textiles in her books. Chicago artist Claire Zeisler (work at left, below), known for her monumental knotted sculptures, uses detached buttonhole stitches to create tiny, fetishist objects. Katherine Westphal, living in California, prints and stitches extraordinary garments. Dominic DiMare, also of California, uses thread as a singular element as well as to tie and bind, combining it with wood, feathers and paper to construct mystical and ritualistic objects.

A few colleges began to recognize embroidery within their home-economics or art curriculum. One particularly influential program in the United States was at Indiana University. There, in the late 1970s and early 1980s, a talented and imaginative group of students meshed with an innovative faculty to produce extraordinary results. With former students like Tom Lundberg, Renie Breskin Adams and Susan Wilchins now teaching in university art departments around the United States, the program has a continuing influence. The late Diane Itter, whose glorious sense of color and form influenced many, was then a graduate assistant. There are more Indiana connections, and many are found in this book, whose works display a strong emphasis on color, a respect for traditional textiles, a refined technique and an idiosyncratic imagery. Other influential schools in the United States that have encouraged individual expression with a needle include Cranbrook Academy of Art and The School of the Art Institute of Chicago.

In Canada, the guilds were primarily responsible for educating their members, inviting first English embroiderers, and then a few American embroiderers, to join Canadian teachers in leading intensive workshops. There has also been a continuous tradition of ecclesiastical textiles and group projects for churches, schools and hospitals, which has kept a fine technical tradition alive.

Many artists trained in other techniques have been drawn to embroidery. Some, particularly printmakers, became allergic to the materials of their chosen technique. Some were moved by feminist concerns to work with fabric; others found it difficult to paint or sculpt while tending young children. For many, it was a chance discovery that fit their philosophical, aesthetic and physical needs. Unintimidated by the weight of embroidery's tradition, they have begun to treat needle and thread in new ways, to connect previously unrelated materials and processes and to make their own rules as they progress.

There has been a blurring of boundaries, a remarkable convergence of techniques within the fiber medium: embroidered quilts, surface-design techniques worked over and under embroidery and threads embedded in and stitched on handmade paper. Imagery has kept pace with these changes. Symbols suffuse a surface with layers of meaning. Samplers that once displayed quiet sentiments are now aflame with passionate prose; traditional cross-stitched Jacks and Jills are replaced with machine-embroidered life-size nudes. Precious gardens remain, but they may be full of tangled weeds. Embroidery has matured and now resists categorization. *Celebrating the Stitch* is a product of and testament to these changes.

ABOUT THIS BOOK

The chapter headings in this book, like exhibition titles, are a "categoryless" means of organizing, hinting at what is within and intending to allow for expanded rather than contracted thinking about the work. And, as in any group exhibition, the work of one artist may strike a more responsive chord when it is compared with a nearby work of another artist. Each work is actually filled with "Light and Shadow" and is a "Poem and Portrait," revealing "Mysterious Messages" from "Within and Without" and ultimately "Celebrating the Stitch."

The work of nearly 100 artists living in the United States and Canada is included, and there is discussion of both why and how they do what they do. The longer profiles are based on lengthy interviews; the indented paragraphs are direct quotes from the artist, a firsthand account of their work. The shorter profiles include quotes from the artist's statements. The "Thinking about..." and "Trying out..." sections that follow each chapter treat issues common to making art: generating ideas, relating to materials and techniques, dealing with blocks to creativity and staying in tune with the work. In "Thinking about...," the artists speak from experience, and in "Trying out...," they offer exciting challenges for the reader to explore. At the end of the book you'll find a list of artists and their home towns. (To maintain a certain amount of privacy, I did not include the addresses or phone numbers of the artists.) If you wish to contact a particular artist for commission work, the town and state will give you a starting point. Notes that reference previously published material can also be found at the end of the book.

What the artists say about their work is very important, but as the great photographer Margaret Bourke White asserted, "In the end, it is only the work that counts." This book is about the images contained within it, magical works that often appears effortlessly made, the works that challenge and confront us, works that affect and inspire, works that make us forget their humble materials, yet simultaneously celebrate them. Whether it is with the speed of the machine-powered needle flying across the fabric or the deliberate pace of the hand guiding the thread through the needlepoint canvas, the ancient craft of embroidery has been transformed in the late 20th century into an innovative, imaginative and inspiring art form.

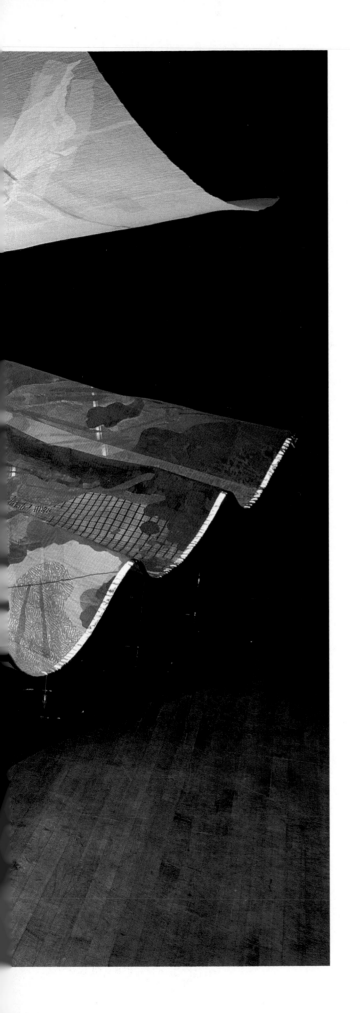

LIGHT AND SHADOW

CAROLE SABISTON

Planets proceeding at an orderly pace, debris tumbling haphazardly through space, flying carpets providing transport to the past, the future or the place of one's dreams—these are the images of Carole Sabiston. Images about movement.

Silent travel is Sabiston's focus. She challenges herself to make visible the highly predictable movement of planets, the random movement of the stuff we have discarded in space and the elusive movement of the wind. She sees tension in the motion and constants of the natural world, citing for example the horizon, the "imperceptible line between ever-changing constants of sky and sea; limitless, infinite." Directional movements punctuate her speech as she talks of the "vertical of growth; the circular of planet, season and seed; and the diagonal of wind, rain and clouds."

Using the dynamic elements of the natural world, she forms otherworldly designs. She is keenly aware of the forces of nature, particularly as they affect islands, on which she has spent most of her life. Born in England, she emigrated with her family to Canada when she was a child and remembers well the voyage by boat to Canada—"two weeks of constant horizon." In the 1960s she spent a year living on the island of Ibiza, Spain, and now her home is Victoria, British Columbia, on Vancouver Island. There is no island insularity in her viewpoint, however, for she thinks in global, even cosmic, terms.

Sabiston's work reflects a dynamic energy consistent with voyages through time and space.

Take Off: Point of Departure and Mode of Travel

Overleaf: 1988; 12 ft. by 16 ft. by 16 ft.; fabric assemblage. (Photo by Jeff Barber.)

Flying into Delos (on the facing page) takes us into the past. She recalls a trip by boat to the ancient Greek island of Delos, and projects herself there:

> I wanted the idea of actually flying into history. Delos was the spiritual home of the ancient Greeks. It's a very small island, and at one time it was a sacred city. No one could give birth there, women had to leave during their menses, no one could be ill there. It's just all ruins. The history is so evocative, it's bouncing all over your skin. It was the most magical experience. That stayed with me, and a few years later I did the work.

Flying into Delos consists of four panels, forming a montage of Sabiston's mental transport to the island. The first panel depicts an offshore approach to the island emerging from an azure sea. Hills and ruins are depicted in the second panel, and the last two panels zoom in on the poppies glimpsed in the lower corner of the second panel. The last panel, with its focus on the oversized flowers, provided special pleasure for Sabiston. "After I had done the piece it occurred to me that it was Georgia O'Keefe's hundredth year. That coincidence was a wonderful topping."

An additional element cements the relationship of each panel to the next and further engages the viewer's eye. Diagonal bands create repetitive dynamic lines that divide the space, reflect colors from top to bottom or from one panel to another and lead the eye on a merry chase around the work. She explains:

> A few years ago it just came to me as one of those little "eurekas" that if I cut a piece off the assembled design and turned it upside down, I would get a reflection. A lot of the work I had done in the past was in a sense reflecting one image to another, like using the positive and negative of both sides of fabric within the same piece. I realized I could reassemble the pieces, reverse the strips, have the image I wanted and also have something else.

Flying into Delos

1988; 6 ft. by 22 ft.; fabric assemblage; detail at right. (Photo by Jeff Barber.)

Sabiston's work calls to mind the energetic movements of modern dance. Color and image soar across her surfaces, a characteristic she attributes to her early training in classical and contemporary dance. In fact, she came very close to choosing a career in dance rather than in the visual arts:

> Everything I do is still geared to dance, though it's not a conscious thing. It's in my bones and it's in my muscles. It's probably one of the reasons that I like working large. It's much like choreography; I often jokingly call it textile aerobics. I have these huge things on the floor and I have three other people in different corners to lay things down, and it's really like talking the piece down through cooperative movement. That's closely related to dance, where you have a team working toward a deadline.

Sabiston's assemblages consist of layers of fabrics of all varieties and sizes, composed on a heavy ground fabric, overlaid with net and all held in place with a wide zigzag machine stitch. This sandwich of backing, colored bits of fabric and neutral-colored net sounds simple enough, but technically it is extraordinarily demanding.

There are demands made by the sheer size of the work. Her largest work to date was a 100-ft. high sunburst for the opening ceremony of Expo '86 in Vancouver, British Columbia. Sizes of other works vary, but all average at least 20 ft. in one direction. Pieces must be worked in sections to accommodate the space between the needle and the body of the sewing machine. Her sewing machine, an industrial Pfaff, has a 12-in. space, almost twice that of a standard machine; although

Costumes designed for Kaleidoscope Theatre for Youth production of *Merlin*; 1980; swan wings: Ethafoam, cotton, elastic. (Photo by Carol Sabiston.)

Designing for the theater

Most of Carole Sabiston's works are intended to hang close to a wall, she has also designed installation works, such as *Take Off: Point of Departure and Mode of Travel*, (see p. 6) that are dramatic in scope and scale. These pieces remind her of the transformation of a space when a circus comes to a small town and of the magical changes occurring when the tent goes up. She has also designed works for the larger arena of the theater. She says:

"The motion, invention, illusion and magic of theater have been with me all my life. I studied classical ballet and acting until I was eighteen years old, and now I'm designing sets and costumes for opera *(The Magic Flute* and *Madama Butterfly*, among others), dance (a 35-ft. silk dragon) and children's theater (the Kaleidoscope Theatre for Youth in Victoria, British Columbia, which travels all over the world).

"Much of the designed elements for masks, puppets, props, costumes and sets combine fabrics, mostly cotton and silk, with bamboo and Plexiglas. These materials are usually interdependent. Fabric, that mundane, flexible and unbreakable medium, often improves with use, acquiring wrinkles and patina. The designs must be interchangeable from one illusion to the next. I try to make them look spontaneous, immediate and even childlike.

"Form and structure for sets are minimal to allow for maximum multiperformance use and to facilitate quick set-up and strike [take-down] for itinerant performances. Remember the small town when the circus visits!"

that still allows a maximum of only 28 running feet of rolled-up work.

An additional technical challenge is created by the need to work in sections of a manageable size. The piece must be assembled whole, cut apart and reassembled without distorting the fabrics or the design. Sabiston has developed a working order that meets these needs.

First, she draws the position of the sections on a heavy Pellon backing. Next, fabrics, from large shapes to tiny snippets, are laid out "in one go." This part cannot be handled alone, and here she is aided by assistants positioned at the corners to make sure each piece of fabric is settled and smoothed into place. Once the work is laid out, all the pieces and the overlaying net are pinned with glass-headed pins. Those first positioning lines that had marked the sections are by now covered by the bits of fabric, so it is necessary to remark their placement by laying string over them. Sections vary from 10 in. to 30 in., but average around 24 in. wide.

Using the string as a guide, she cuts out the sections. Each section is machine sewn with a wide zigzag stitch, which holds the fabrics and net to the Pellon ground. Smaller strips are now cut from these wider sections, which ultimately will form the diagonal bands seen in most of her work. These strips are about 6 in. wide at the outset, but with 4 in. allowed for seams, only 2 in. are left visible. Once cut, they are either reversed in place or worked into another panel of the same piece. Now that it is cut apart, the whole piece must be put back together. Technically, the matching and seam-making must be exact.

With 4 in. lost every time a strip or section is cut and resewn, Sabiston must consider how this will affect the design. For example, an oval, laid on its side, can become a circle if its midsection is cut and removed. Sometimes she compensates by designing with the potential distortion in mind. She may start with a distorted rectangle, for example, which will become a square once it is cut and sewn. Other times she risks the results, preferring to see what happens when the work is cut and seamed.

A line is suggested where contrasting colors meet in the indentation formed by a seam. Like the slightly shadowed corner of a room where two walls meet, the seams reveal the workings of the piece. "I have always left my structure visible; I don't try to hide it. I suppose it's like contemporary architecture, like the Pompidou Museum in Paris. The structure is visible; all the conduits are on the outside."

Architectural comparisons come easily to Sabiston, since she frequently deals with architects for her large-scale work. About half of her work is commissioned for a specific site, and each new space presents its own visual and potential technical challenges. She approaches the designs for the spaces in various ways. Sometimes she simply wonders how to cover the area, or sometimes the image comes first and then techniques must be developed to create that image. "I love the challenge of bringing technique and image together."

For work of such size, she needs a large studio and the occasional aid of several assistants. Sabiston and her assistants work in a 1,200-sq. ft. space in the building that also houses her husband's book shop. In addition to the assistants who help with the initial assembling, one assistant, Elizabeth Anderson, does all the machine stitching. Sabiston commends her technical expertise and also appreciates having her near to react to new ideas. Another inherent characteristic of Sabiston's experience in the collaborative arts of dance and theater is the ease with which she works with assistants, sharing ideas. Sabiston, however, is the work's choreographer, presiding over each step of its production.

The floor of her studio is white linoleum with small squares, which are useful for lining up the work as it is assembled on the floor. She revels in the all-white space, which excludes all color except for works in progress and folded fabrics, arranged by hue and stored in see-through wire-mesh bins. "I need to see the fabrics all at once. It's nice when I start a piece; it helps to find my palette by bringing them all out. And I can easily see when I don't have a certain area of color, and then I can hunt for it."

Sabiston buys fabrics wherever she can find them. She shops for color first and buys mostly lightweight materials. "I like to go to theatrical places and buy awful stuff—you want to tap dance your way over the rainbow in it." No fabric is ever wide enough, even 72-in. nets, but with judicious planning at the outset and the use of the seaming technique, she makes any width work. She buys one or two yards at a time, preferring to have variety over quantity.

The appeal of fabric for Sabiston is in its mundane quality, and she recognizes that cloth is often less accepted in the art world because of that quality. "Because you wear it, it's not romantic or mysterious. If you work with egg tempera or glass, that's mysterious. I made a very deliberate choice to work with something very accessible and ordinary. Now, I don't worry about acceptance, I just do my work. I use a lot of everyday things like mattress ticking, and clothing labels are often embedded in the work."

There is another connection with fabric beyond its ordinariness. "I've always thought of the recycling process: things that were never thrown away. I suppose that comes out of the original quilting idea. Every square inch was to be reused. I keep fabrics right down to the smallest pieces."

Sabiston tries to avoid fabrics that have a special connotation. "In the early days I used a lot of velvet. The comment on the work was always, 'your work is so sensual.' The hell with that! That wasn't what I wanted at all. I wanted people to get beyond that and look at what the work is saying." She finds fewer prejudices now about fabric, and her work is certainly well accepted. In 1987 she was awarded Canada's top craft honor, the $20,000 Saidye Bronfman Award for Excellence in the Crafts, administered by the

Spatial Possibilities:
The Blush Pink Planet

1988; 18 ft. by 15 ft; fabric assemblage. (Collection of 4 King Street West, Toronto; photo by Carol Sabiston.)

Canadian Crafts Council. In addition to the boost that such recognition gives, the award freed her for more travel and time to work toward another solo show.

Sabiston works in a series when she is not doing commissions. Designs for personal work are usually sketches no larger than 3 in. by 5 in. She uses minimal color in her sketchbook, indicating only where strong colors will go. She approaches the actual assemblage with a freewheeling attitude, which allows for changes along the way.

More advance planning is needed for commissions. After seeing the space where a commissioned work will be hung and getting an idea of what the client wants, Sabiston develops ideas, starting with color. For a large lobby space in Toronto's financial district, she did three works based on planets, calling the series *Spatial Possibilities*. "Here I was in these tall, richly dark buildings. Everything was grey, and my first reaction was to bring in color." For this commission she did three watercolor renderings, about 20 in. by 30 in. each on Arches paper, cutting them into strips and reassembling them to illustrate how the finished works would appear.

One of the three, *The Blush Pink Planet* (shown on the facing page), looms over a stratosphere filled with flying carpets, patterns of brightly colored floating astral objects, a dotted cube and ribbonlike forms. Sabiston sees metaphors in these atmospheric elements of fantasy, escape and freedom. Bisecting diagonal lines pit light against dark at regular intervals and add to the movement across and around the work. The decorator-color names Sabiston chose as titles for each work—blush pink, harvest gold and ruby red—hint at the fantasy world of interiors, of inner space ("spatial possibilities"), as well as the infinite possibilities of outer space.

Some commission processes are not quite so easy. Frequently the client wants too many choices and too many changes. "Once that starts, you lose the piece, you lose the feeling." If choices of designs are requested, Sabiston saves her strongest preference for last. "I've gone through all the process of designing, and I know the ideas. I present my strongest idea last and say that this is the one I feel is right, and they usually go with that."

Occasionally, Sabiston's personal work literally comes off the walls to take over a room. The installation piece *Takeoff: Point of Departure and Mode of Travel* (shown on p. 6) is one of many works inspired by places the artist has lived or visited. In this work the landscape itself becomes a flying carpet with yet another patterned carpet riding upon it. *Takeoff* pictures a loosely interpreted aerial view of the area between Victoria and Vancouver over the Gulf Islands, which include the American Gulf Islands. The carpet flies over the spinning earth joining Canada and the United States as part of the same landscape. "A thin red line represents the border line that goes through the water. From where I look southward we see the peninsula. There is a very close symbiotic relationship."

As an installation, the work can be altered for different sites. "This piece is also a very theatrical piece. It relates to my work with itinerant actors and performances, the idea of 'when the circus comes to town' making a small moment of magic." The 12-ft. by 22-ft. carpet is draped on Plexiglas rods of varying heights, establishing the illusion of the carpet in motion, flying through space. Suspended, apparently weightless, above the carpet is a diaphanous 12-ft. by 20-ft. cloud-filled "atmosphere."

Sabiston's work moves from past to future. Flying carpets soar through outer space or over familiar territory. They provide the possibility of returning to a much-loved place or of being projected into the unknown. Assemblages of mundane fabric, remnants, the "fragments of society," unite through her vision the earthly world and the vastness of space.

RISË NAGIN

Cloth, despite its apparent fragility, is an amazingly transformable medium, and as such it evokes a range of powerful responses. It can be both delicate and strong, elegant and coarse, long-lasting and disposable, comforting and frightening. It is the stuff of relaxation and ritual, parade and masquerade, sweater and shroud.

Cloaking potent, primitive imagery in delicate diaphanous fabrics and fine, refined sewing, Risë Nagin takes full advantage of the contradictory nature of cloth. Elegant fabrics give form to an inner landscape of fearsome symbols.

Nagin is well aware of the paradox her work presents. She delivers a strong message in a subtle, almost subliminal way. The works, she says, have "really lush surfaces, and they can be very seductive. People look at that and don't think about what else is going on, which can be to my advantage if I use it well. I can exploit the contrast; it's a way to do something more expressive of things emotional."

Although Nagin consciously manipulates her medium, she refrains from manipulating any sort of message, preferring not to pin too specific a meaning to her symbols. She refers instead to a statement by Picasso, in which he recalls his response to seeing African masks for the first time:

> Men had made those masks and other objects for a sacred purpose, a magic purpose, as a kind of mediation between themselves and the unknown, hostile forces that surrounded them, in order to overcome their fear and horror by giving it a form and an image. At that moment I realized that this was what painting was all about. Painting isn't an aesthetic operation; it's a form of magic designed as a mediator between this strange, hostile world and us, a way of seizing the power by giving form to our terrors as well as our desires. When I came to that realization, I knew I had found my way.[1]

Nagin's images disturb, but the lush fabrics that form them cast their own inviting spell. She describes the effect she strives to achieve and its hoped-for response in the viewer:

> I don't know if this was conscious or if it was because I always enjoyed this quality in paintings, but from far away you get a sense of the strength of the piece that pulls you in, and you look closer; when you look closer there are all these other things going on, so that you don't tire of it. The more you look, the more you see. When I'm working on a piece, I take a lot of pleasure in the sensuality of developing a strong image with complex surfaces, and I hope the viewer will experience some of that same involvement. I want to achieve a sense of intimacy between the work and its audience, and to establish a connection between the content, form and technique.

Once that bond is established, Nagin feels that a work will speak for itself to those who linger before it. Although she is hesitant to explain specific symbols in her work that evolve intuitively, she shares some thoughts about the motifs and meanings of one particular piece (shown on the facing page):

> Gate is about rites of passage. There are references to death and rebirth as a person passes from one stage in life to another. On the journey to the gate one experiences difficulties, intense and sometimes painful, which must be confronted and dealt with. Passage through the gate occurs when something is shed and a new life is begun. We all experience something that corresponds to such a passage, and in that sense, Gate deals with those aspects of heroic mythology that apply to each person's life.

The dark, dirty yellow, bright turquoise and blood-red fabrics in Gate do not appear at first glance to be pieced; they look painted with shimmering glazes. Nagin has a painter's eye, sensibility and training, all of which help her achieve some of the unusual effects with her favored medium, fabric.

Adding to the paradox inherent in Nagin's work is a sense of immediacy, which belies her labor-intensive technique. Though it might appear to have come together in moments, a work's composition may in fact take weeks. Nagin finishes only three to six works a year. She accepts the labor-intensive aspect: "It's like painting. I'm sure Lucien Freud and others spend hours on their works."

Construction begins only after making many sketches, none bigger than 18 in. by 24 in., some in pencil, others in gouache. She traces the sketch on tracing paper and enlarges the work using an Artograph projector, which takes much of the figuring and labor out of the enlarging process. This provides a cartoon.

Nagin begins by assembling the fabrics she will use. She stains white silk organza with acrylic paints, treating the fabric as if it were watercolor paper. Working over a large piece of plastic stretched over her work table, she wets the organza, then saturates it with color. She may have to repeat the color washes three or four times to deepen or intensify the color. Another fabric that stains well is a lightweight polyester felted fabric that reminds her of rice paper. She frequently employs commercially dyed sheers and other fabrics, being more concerned with the effect than whether she applied the paint herself. She also layers fabrics to achieve a new hue, a sheer blue over a green, for instance, to produce a rich blue-green. "It gives depth to the color; I do things like that to make the color deeper or to manipulate the reflecting qualities of the fabric surface."

Exile: House and Mountain

1989; 54 in. by 81½ in.; silk, polyester, rayon,
nylon, cotton, paint; staining, piecing,
appliqué, quilting, embroidery, hand stitching.
(Courtesy of Helen Drutt Gallery, New York
City and Philadelphia; photo by Lockwood
Hoehl, Pittsburgh, Pennsylvania.)

After staining some fabrics and selecting others, Nagin is ready to sew. She starts to hand-piece the work in lap-sized sections. She assembles small pieces, pinning, basting, sewing and pressing, moving from section to section without any particular system, although she usually starts near what will be the center of the finished work.

Nagin rarely strays from the original sketch, except for some color changes she might make as the work progresses:

> When the cartoon is made, any revisions in composition are worked out. Once that's in place, I don't change the basic structure of the piece very often. However, sometimes when the piece is under construction, I will see areas where I need to add or take out something. I may have to change the color a little bit. Some-

times what worked in the small drawing won't work at a large scale. The color always intensifies immensely in fabric. Everything becomes richer. I make necessary adjustments as I go along, but the basic composition usually stays much the same as when it began.

The edges of the fabrics are treated in different ways: sometimes they are turned under and blind-stitched, or they may be secured by a herringbone stitch or occasionally left to fray. Nagin uses other bits of embroidery, running stitch, French knots and couching (see the Glossary on pp. 216-221) primarily as line or pattern elements. Her recent subject matter lends itself to a looser treatment, "more like drawing on top of the fabric, then just allowing it to do what it's going to do." She uses a variety of fabrics and does not adhere to any rules about lining up the grain. In fact, she prefers the appearance of the sheers when they are layered without attention to the grain. The finished works hang softly from a dowel run through a sleeve in the back if they are opaque, or from Velcro® attached to the wall if they are transparent. She weights the bottom with drapery weights.

Despite intense planning, some works do not develop quite as Nagin expects. She comments on *Exile: House and Mountain* (on the facing page), which, unlike most of her pieced works, is appliquéd on a sheer blue background:

> This is a good example of a piece where I had to make a lot of changes in the color. I worked from a rather loose color maquette. I started with the lower left half of the piece, then figured out how I wanted to layer and construct the greys in the top sky sections. I moved to the central panel and worked the section where the house and mountain shapes actually appear and then began working on the right side, where, once scaled up, the color began to get really intense. At this point I saw that the right side was so much stronger than the left that the composition had been thrown off. The major elements in the dark blue left panel could not balance the intensity of the yellows and heavy reds on the right. My original plan had been to make those circles much more subtle, but I ended up brightening the color and floating the round shapes to pull it all back into balance.

Nagin's vocabulary of symbols has grown and expanded over time, but earlier works still reflect that sense of mediation between intuitive perception and considered expression. In an earlier series, Nagin used the kimono as her canvas. She was spending a lot of time on the Pennsylvania Turnpike at one point, and the works in this series were based, she says, on "perceptions of the whole roadway. They are landscapes over time." As Nagin drove between Pittsburgh and Harrisburg, where her husband was working, she made mental notes, which she would record in thumbnail sketches upon arrival. The finished works are about "perception and light; how one sees things in motion and time, and how one

Fog Area

1985; 56½ in. by 64½ in.; silk, cotton, acetate, polyester; layering, piecing, appliqué, embroidery, hand stitching. (Photo by George Erml, New York.)

recollects them. *Fog Area* (above) is definitely an attempt to evoke a certain kind of light." She chose a kimono form for these works because it encloses the wearer just as a car encloses its occupant. She realized the kimono as a cylinder, designing the back before the front, then resolving the two sides so that the design flowed around the work. She will consider using the kimono shape again "when the images want to go back on a body."

It has been something of a leap from the lush, subtle beauty of *Fog Area* to the raw power of *Exile: House and Mountain* and *Gate,* but Nagin was ready for the change. *Gate* is, in fact, all about change. It reflects a moving away from the intellectual, formalist composition to a more intuitive process, a rite of passage, that ultimately reveals much more of the artist within the work.

JANET LESZCZYNSKI

Tracings V

1988; 3½ in. by 3½ in.; cotton floss on cotton; embroidery. (Photo by Steve Grubman.)

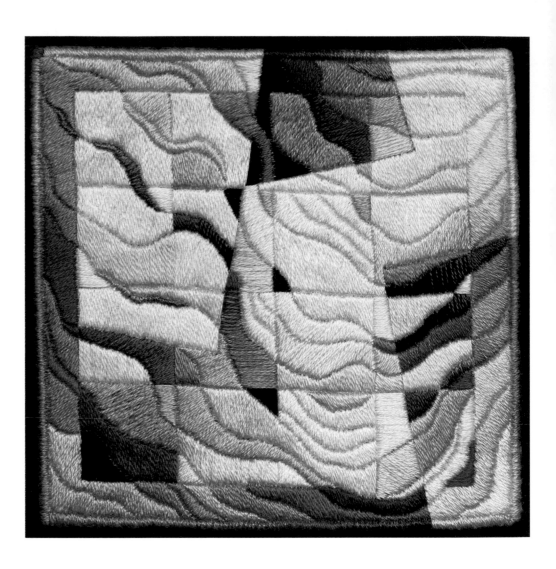

Minute and delicate, yet richly colored, the embroideries of Janet Leszczynski are about fantasy and escape. She shares her thoughts on her work and her working process:

> It has always been my desire to draw the viewer into the private world of my art and offer an alternative and refuge from the reality of daily living. The small scale of my work demands concentration in order to be experienced and encourages an intimacy.
>
> I began stitching in 1979 as a response to the limitations I was experiencing with weaving. Stitching allowed me the freedom of working on an open format, applying my stitches as a painter would a brush stroke. Nonetheless, my early embroideries were influenced by my weaving experience. Weaving designs based on grids and patterns were transformed into embroideries where the imposed structure of weaving could be broken or eliminated. Geometric forms and their placement into systems metaphorically expressed the structures and rules of life. I worked to modify and soften these elements through the use of sensuous color, subtle gradations and interruptions in the established systems. With time the pieces

became more open and atmospheric. Unstitched areas dominated the surface.

My current work carries elements from the past—use of color, gradations, interest in pattern—yet takes on a smaller format and new visual elements. These pieces are entirely covered with embroidery. Geometric forms are replaced by literal subjects, hands, figures, celestial objects. These subjects are abstracted and out of proportion.

Because of the minute size of the work I was concerned that they might appear as small self-contained images lost or dominated by their surroundings. To expand and integrate the work, literally and psychologically, I've created stitched borders that surround and frame the central narratives while allowing the story to move into the border.

These more concentrated pieces have become extremely meticulous and the process more obsessive. The stories they tell of flights and dreams are the antithesis of process and technique.

I begin working by becoming at peace with myself. I need solitude and concentration. I often have gentle instrumental music as a background to ease me into an awareness of my emotions. With paper and pencil in hand I express feelings and ideas with sketches and words in a kind of free-association exercise. A stack of papers containing other sketches, ideas and images is within reach to offer stimulation. I accumulate anything that appeals to me—an image from a magazine, a phrase heard on the radio. At some point I examine the finds on a more intellectual level to understand my attraction to them, but during the designing process I trust my intuition.

Once I've determined the theme of a piece, I work out a sketch to scale. A pencil drawing indicating the light and dark intensities is completed. I transfer the outline of the drawing to stretched cotton fabric. With my palette before me, I choose single strands of DMC floss and apply a simple satin stitch. I don't predetermine the colors. I allow for the discovery of color as I work.

Within Reach

1989; 3¼ in. by 3¼ in.; cotton floss on cotton; embroidery. (Collection of Sarah Nichols; photo by Steve Grubman.)

As I'm working, the minute scale allows me to focus all of my attention within an unadulterated viewpoint. Distractions are few because there is little within my sight other than the work and my tools—my hands. Although I take care in working out a piece in advance, the piece evolves during the process. The finished embroidery is always different from the original drawing.

I find the actual stitching a discovery process. I'm continually excited by new color relationships and the transformation of an idea from a flat black-and-white drawing to a rich and real stitched surface. The embroidery becomes an entirely new and different experience.

CAROL D. WESTFALL

Using paint, embroidery and computer printouts of weave structures to form her collages, Carol D. Westfall pays simultaneous homage to textile traditions and 20th-century technology. She writes: "My current work evolves from the American crazy-quilt tradition. I use embroidery to amplify the textile sources in the imagery."

Crazy Quilt II

1988; 60 in. by 42 in.; paint, paper; embroidery, collage. (Photo by Susan Kahn.)

BIHK Series III

1988; 22 in. by 30 in.; lithography, collage, embroidery. (Collection of Maureen Bassett; photo by Susan Kahn.)

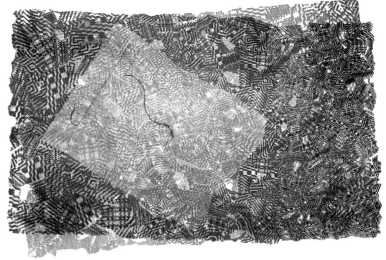

Patricia Malarcher

Westerly

1988; 48 in. by 66 in.; Mylar, fabric, mixed media; appliqué, machine stitching. (Photo by D. James Dee.)

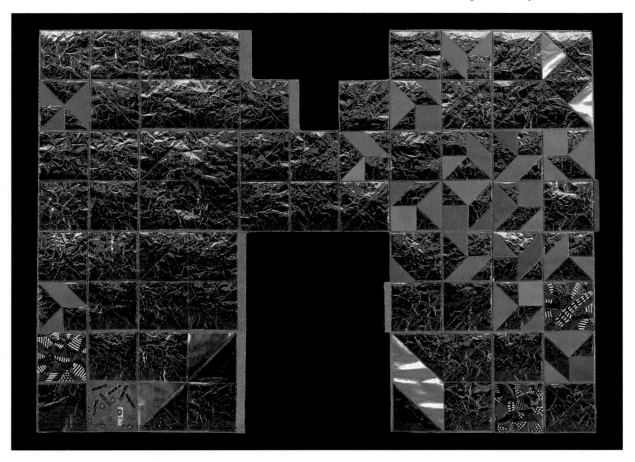

Sunlit paintings, reflections of street lights on a rainy night, silver trucks on a turnpike—they all contain the common denominator of light that inspires Patricia Malarcher. To capture, manipulate and reflect light, Malarcher incorporates large amounts of Mylar, a space-age reflective material. She builds mirrored surfaces that interact with light, color and movement. She explains her interest:

> I've always been attracted to paintings that have light in them. I remember going to the Spanish Museum in New York when I was in high school. They had paintings that seemed to be full of sunlight, which filled my mind, and I thought about them for years.

Rainy nights and looking at street lights reflected in the street are exciting to me. I do a lot of driving now up and down the New Jersey Turnpike. I love those silver trucks on the highway, and I think about them as I drive. They're mystical presences. I've always wanted to do a series of works inspired by the backs of trucks. I haven't done it yet, but I've been thinking about it for years.

There is a sureness about Malarcher's art based on years of study, thought and practice. Trained in painting, she remembers that early on she was conscious of trying to give a sense of illumination to her work. Her first textile work was done in the late 1950s. She saw an exhibition of fabric banners by the students of a well-known graphic artist of the time, Corita Kent, and was impressed with the "spirit in them that was so compelling to me that I really wanted to work with fabric. I felt there was a freedom there, of working without having a style imposed on you, an ability to experiment freely."

Malarcher explored working with wool but was frustrated by the fact that it absorbed light. She began to add bits of colored threads, raffia and metallics to contrast with the wool. Some Mylar left over from making Christmas cards intrigued her, and she began to play with it, exploring its possibilities, first treating it like paper, using a hole punch to create random patterns, then handling it like fabric and sewing on it. Before she began to work with Mylar, her work was, she says, "typical of the experimental work of the 1960s, stuffed and dimensional." She tried to work out geometric designs, but once stuffed, all the hard edges of the works were lost and "all my geometry just collapsed." Mylar could do what fabric could not: it had enough body to make a pyramidlike unit and could hold its own without being stuffed. The structural capabilities of Mylar, not its illuminating qualities, were what first drew Malarcher to it.

It was not an easy material to tame, but in the process she made some discoveries. Mylar creases easily and holds the crease; however, Malarcher wanted to keep it flat. She began to work in 8-in. to 12-in. units to avoid folding the material as she sewed on it. If air were captured under the Mylar, it became puffy. Topstitching solved the problem and kept it flat. She developed a process working with preconstructed units, arranging them on a backing and stitching them in place. In other words, she was reproducing the time-honored process of making a patchwork quilt. "It wasn't quilting to quilt, but to solve a technical problem. I felt like I was reinventing the wheel. Then I found the quilting patterns on the surface of the Mylar made it more interesting while it solved the physical problems. The light-reflecting quality became more ambiguous and made it appear warmer." By looking for a technical solution in a new ma-

terial, she discovered both a means to manipulate the light that appealed to her and a new working process in building her works from pre-assembled units.

Due to its size, geometric structure and the resulting outline, Malarcher's work has a strong, formal architectural quality. *Westerly* (on page 21) was assembled from squares combined to create a shape around a doorlike space. Two large columns connected by a small bridge give strength and structure to the work. The crushed and quilted Mylar has a similar appearance to the type of glass used in many large buildings that reflects light and distorts the passing images of clouds or people. "These pieces change with changing light, and the more elements that are in them, the more change occurs. At certain times of day, the silver almost recedes and the color can take over."

Not only the light, but also the architectural image is important to Malarcher. "I've always thought of my work in connection with glass buildings, of building units." The "unit construction," which has become her working method for large pieces like *Westerly,* involves constructing the squares without a finished product in mind. "Sometimes I'll just think of a way of breaking up a square geometrically and will make some units with that configuration, and sometimes I start with pieces left over from another work. I use geometry a lot; I'm fascinated with geometric relationships."

Once she has constructed sufficient units, she arranges and rearranges them until a new form emerges. "I move from a very conscious measured way of working to a sort of assembling, like making a set of blocks. Then I get to a point where I let my unconscious take over a bit and try and find an arrangement that resonates and seems right at that particular time. I have a sense of needing a feeling of wholeness with them."

The individual units are assembled on a backing of artist's linen, which is about equal in weight to the Mylar. Some portions of the units are painted with acrylic on primed canvas. Oddly enough, these bright, flat areas look less textile-like than the crushed or quilted nonfibrous Mylar. Using a secondhand portable Singer sewing machine, Malarcher machine stitches the linear elements. Once the composition is arranged, each unit is then sewn individually to a heavy artist's canvas. The canvas backing must be strong and heavy enough to keep the work flat when hanging. Velcro® strips are attached at the top and adhere to a Velcro®-covered board for mounting. Irregularly shaped pieces are either weighted or have a metal bar running through the widest portion to help hold the shape.

The unit-construction process builds in opportunities for flexibility and change as the work develops. Thus, Malarcher could add some surprises to *Westerly*. "The question I was posing for myself was, 'If I had a strong enough pattern, how much incongruity could I introduce?' So there are a few little pieces, done with felt pens, that are absolutely out of context." One of Malarcher's assets as an artist is this willingness to push the limits of a successful piece, testing its strength and, in the process, testing her own.

As Malarcher has experimented with Mylar, her thoughts about it have changed. "At first I used it to solve design and structural problems. Then I began to see it more as a metaphorical thing, how it seemed possible to use the Mylar and see it as a kind of a skin or armor. In a number of pieces I did, there was a sense of the Mylar being peeled away and showing something underneath." She began to see that working in Mylar was also connected with working in cloth. "It was almost like icons of traditional textiles, and I guess that hit me when I was showing slides and someone commented that I was showing a traditional quilt pattern. Of course, I didn't know that it was a traditional quilt pattern! Then I rather liked the idea that it was an icon of the quilt. The prayer rugs that I've done [shown above] are also part of a long tradition, illuminated things with spiritual connotations."

Malarcher's smaller, private work requires changes in scale as well as changes in approach from the larger, commissioned work. Her current series of prayer rugs, an ongoing exploration, illustrates her thoughts on these differences. "I think the smaller works are probably freer, and I

Prayer Rug #3

1987; 10½ in. by 7½ in.; Mylar, fabric, thread; appliqué, machine stitching. (Collection of American Embassy, Oman; photo by D. James Dee.)

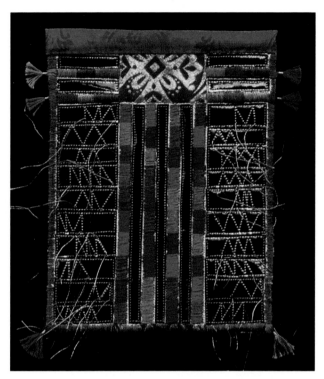

find that here I can try some things that I might not try on a larger scale." She uses more metallic and cotton threads in these small works, which are inspired by traditional textile prayer rugs and illuminated manuscripts. In some of the prayer rugs she used color photocopy transfers of photographs of graffiti on Mylar. "It actually looked like the calligraphy in manuscripts. When you break up graffiti into tiny segments it becomes absolutely magical looking."

Whether large or small, these works embody a ceremonial, almost liturgical quality. Perhaps it is the shimmer of light, the rich colors that change as they are reflected in the silver Mylar, or the recycled trim from old vestments, which form part of the surface of the prayer rugs. Whatever the visual elements, a sense of spirit pervades. "I went to parochial school when I was a child," says Malarcher, "and we seemed to spend a lot of time sitting in church. Just sitting there in that dim building, I made my first aesthetic judgments. There was a lot of mosaic and gold; there was a certain feeling, a certain quality of place that I think is somehow imprinted in my mind."

Malarcher sees making art as a process of discovery. "I feel that I design best when I can let the materials, the units that I make, guide me. I find that I discover things that I could never have created on paper. If that discovery isn't there, the labor part is more apparent. I've always tried to find ways to make the work interesting up to the very end. This was one of the things I found in painting; you're always interacting with that unknown up until the end. And that's why I make my pile of things and why I don't quite know what it will turn out to be."

New direction for a space-age medium

Patricia Malarcher discusses Mylar, a distinctly 20th-century material:

"Mylar, a metalized polyester film, was developed by DuPont Corporation for the skin of the lunar space module. It is now made by many companies, but the term 'Mylar' has become almost like a generic name to describe the product.

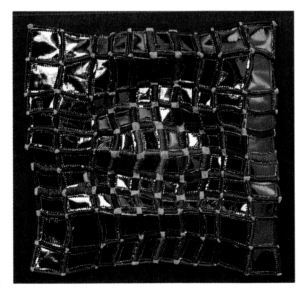

Wrizzle Wrazzle

1984; 8 in. by 8 in. by ¾ in.; Mylar, linen, cotton thread; machine and hand stitching. (Collection of Douglas and Maria Gravel; photo by D. James Dee.)

"It comes in many forms and weights and in combination with other materials. One form of Mylar is a drawing material that's almost parchmentlike and very translucent. There are two types I use most frequently: one is laminated to vinyl and the other, heavier one is laminated to cloth. The thinnest kinds, such as the kind that party balloons are made out of, tend to be perforated too easily by the sewing machine. The vinyl-backed variety is easiest to work with on the machine (I tend to use the longest stitch on my machine). It is an expensive material, but since it doesn't ravel and I can use every bit of it, there is no waste."

When working with a new material, part of the challenge is to discover its potential and the many ways to use it that were never intended by the manufacturer. There is no tradition dictating a certain treatment or handling. The artist-explorer gets to make the rules.

Malarcher has tried a variety of approaches to Mylar. She has rubbed steel wool on the surface to cut down the shine. While it is possible to buy a matte-finish Mylar, she prefers to create her own, less even finish. She has crumpled it like paper, making wrinkles that reflect light in many directions. Its surface can be silkscreened, painted or used as a base for photocopying.

In *Wrizzle Wrazzle* (at left), Malarcher cut Mylar into small irregular pieces that she then sewed to linen, leaving about ¼ in. between the pieces. She sewed over the ¼-in. space, stitching into the Mylar on each side with a tight satin stitch. This distorted the fabric and added a sense of dimensionality. Like broken pieces of a mirror, *Wrizzle Wrazzle's* distorted surface reflects light in all directions. Malarcher sees possibilities for this experiment in building units for larger pieces.

Artistic potential is found not just in new ways of handling the material, but in new ways of perceiving it. Malarcher has imagined Mylar in a totally different form. It is impressive to think of a fabriclike substance used on a vehicle for space travel. It is even more amazing to imagine the ability of the artist's mind to make leaps of the imagination, connecting this space-age material with age-old textiles—prayer rugs and quilts—and sending them in a new direction.

ERMA MARTIN YOST

Mojave Mirage

1989; 36 in. by 36 in.; paint, cyanotype; fabric assemblage. (Courtesy of Noho Gallery, New York City.)

The sunbaked colors, metallic textures and fractured imagery of Erma Martin Yost's patchwork assemblages allude to tradition and evidence innovation. Yost grew up in a rural Mennonite community where the tradition of quilts ran deep, and her artistic training was in painting and ceramics.

She and her husband, photographer Leon Yost, share a passion for Native American rock art, petroglyphs and pictographs, and for many years they have journeyed to the Southwest from their home near New York City to research and document these painted or incised images. Her constructed works, which echo the imagery of the Southwest and the inspiration of her quilting ancestry, become very personal statements through her unusual methods and materials for marking cloth. Yost discusses her work:

> Over the last few years my work has developed into a series entitled *Sacred Places*. These are assemblages of quilt patches, cyanotypes, fetish objects and drawings. Decorated with beads, bones and feathers, these patterns of expansive skies over landscapes inhabited by shamans and animals form places that allude to prehistoric rituals and ceremonial celebrations. These are places of protection, of power for the hunt, of healing and fertility.

Kiva Visions

1989; 38 in. by 41 in.; molding paste, cyanotype, paint; fabric assemblage; detail at bottom. (Courtesy of Noho Gallery, New York City; collection of Ned and Lucinda Stoll.)

Each work is constructed like a traditional three-layer quilt, but I print and paint most of my own fabrics, using the cyanotype photographic process, acrylic and metallic paints and acrylic molding paste. Then I embellish the fabric with metallic stitching.

I first taught myself the cyanotype process when I wanted to incorporate cloud images into my work. After I printed my first few clouds from negatives, I tried solargrams—laying an object on a sensitized fabric surface and exposing it to sunlight. Then came simple, dense drawings on tracing paper that were used as negatives. The juxtaposition of all these different realities posed endless creative possibilities to me—a photo of a cloud next to a solargram of a feather, next to real feathers, and so on. I like the visual surprise of such images when mixed in with commercially printed or hand-painted fabrics.

Acrylic molding paste is the thick substance used on the surface of *Kiva Visions* [shown at left]. The brand I use is Utrecht, which is available at my local art-supply store. This commercial product, about the consistency of gel medium, creates a tactile surface that can be smooth and fluid-looking or quite craggy, depending on the method of application. I apply it directly to the fabric, and it dries to about 1/16 in. thick. I collect different trowels, found objects, fabrics and laces that can be pressed into the wet paste. I immediately remove the object so that only the impression remains. The effect is something like that of a fossil.

When the molding paste is dry, I build up layers of metallic paint, which on a rough surface suggests the mineral-like qualities of rock and earth, the makings of foundations. I use Liquitex acrylic metallic and iridescent paints and also metallic powders that can be mixed with polymer-gel medium. When applied smoothly and glazed with iridescent paint, the paste can take on an ethereal quality.

I try to avoid stitching over the paste-covered surfaces with the machine, though sometimes it's unavoidable. In order to have a surface on which to machine stitch, I block off squares or rectangles with ½-in. tape before applying the molding paste. When the paste is dry and I'm ready to assemble the shapes, I cut through the tape, leaving ¼ in. of plain fabric. Sometimes I leave areas within the squares uncovered with paste, or even scrape some of the paste off, so I can stitch more easily in those places.

My works are mounted on linen that is stretched and framed in a 2½-in. deep mahogany box frame. This is not only to protect the work, but also to present a feeling of a special object, such as an icon or a ceremonial object.

ANNE McKENZIE NICKOLSON

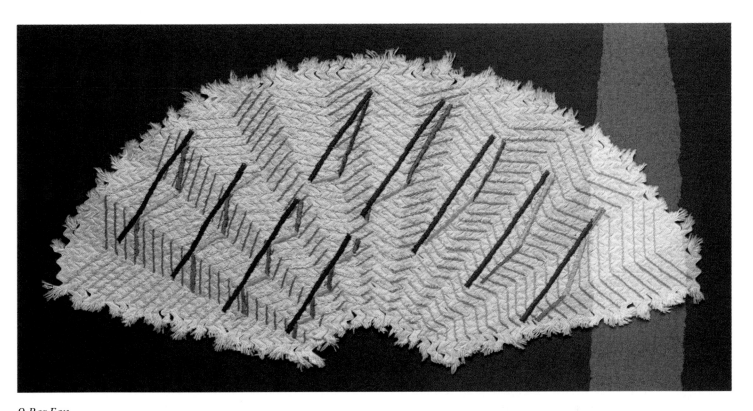

9-Bar Fan

1983; 6½ in. by 14 in.; cotton rickrack; piecing, airbrushing, embroidery. (Photo by Susan Kahn.)

Anne McKenzie Nickolson is interested in both the background fabric and what is stitched into it. She plays with illusions of space, stitching shadows or the glint of light on water. She explains:

> My current work explores the tension between pictorial space and the textile surface. The surface is both defined and challenged by patterns worked into the fabric and by shapes applied on top of the fabric.
>
> The imagery is abstract and plays fancifully in space. Patterns in the fabric may lift up and move forward, or they may hide behind other shapes. Shapes may appear solid and three-dimensional or they may be transparent and ephemeral. The image that results can appear flat at times or as a deep space at other times.

Lines and shapes seem to float, dancing around each other.

> Generally, the pieces are hand-dyed, airbrushed and hand-embroidered, although I occasionally use other techniques such as painting, appliqué and beadwork. The process that I use to develop each piece can be described as "organic." While certain phases or parts of a piece can be sketched or designed on paper, the final product becomes clear only as each of its parts is realized. There is a sort of dialog going between myself and each image that I create in response to each phase or step of the working process.

'Sconset

1989; 19 in. by 19 in.; cotton poplin, dyed fabric, threads; airbrushing, embroidery. (Photo by Pierson Photographics.)

The tactile nature of the fabric is accentuated by the use of embroidery. At the same time, the embroidery contributes to the creation of a complex pictorial space. I aim to keep these visual ideas in balance in each of my pieces.

For some years I used rickrack as the background fabric. The rickrack was hand stitched, caught with a whip stitch only at the points. This continued up one line of rickrack and down the next, resulting in a fabric that could be spread apart with your fingers to reveal the slits. In *9-Bar Fan* [shown on p. 27] the rickrack all goes vertically and does not fan out.

I take a very functional approach to embroidery. The needle goes up, the needle goes down, and that's really all you need to know about embroidery technique. The question then becomes what kind of line do I want to make? And I figure out how to make it. The result of this philosophy is that I use very few stitches. These stitches and my reasons for using them are fairly specific:

Satin stitch creates a solid bar of color. *Seed stitch* makes for a pointillist type of shading. *Running stitch* creates a quick dotted line, similar to one I use in drawings. *Stem stitch* makes a smooth, slightly heavy line around curves. *Back stitch* produces a solid, thinner line. *Surface satin stitch* blocks in very large areas of color, and the floats are all on the top with only very tiny stitches on the back. The result is a very "thready" looking solid color. Sometimes I use long stitches at an angle to tie down the long floats, which works visually like crosshatching.

Long and short stitch makes very solid, dense areas of color. *Cross stitch* relates directly to the woven grid of the linen fabric, sometimes crossing intersections and sometimes freely worked, weaving along with the linen. *Couching* shades areas of long satin stitch or long and short stitch; it also ties down long floats as in *'Sconset* [at left]. *Herringbone stitch* serves as an open and more decorative stitch. *Overlapping herringbone* provides a solid bar of color, but it also has a subtle zigzag line and a woven texture to it. *Beadwork* decorates. The beads are threaded, then couched down every so often. *Machine stitching* is something I use minimally and only when I want a straight, repeated line.

I don't use a hoop when I'm working on a small piece of fabric, nor do I use one at the edge of a piece of fabric or for long continuous lines that are more easily stitched with the needle going down and up in one stroke. The rest of the time I do use a hoop, and my favorite is an adjustable frame with 24 in. to each side. It has wing nuts at the corners and fabric strips, or "aprons," tacked on the inside edges of the square. I pin the textile to the aprons and tighten the tension. It presents a large area to stitch, so it doesn't have to be moved very often, and it distorts the textile only minimally. I can lean it from my lap to the edge of the table and work with one hand below the textile and one hand above, which makes the embroidery go pretty quickly.

A few embroidery stitches

Some of the stitches Anne McKenzie Nickolson discusses generate interesting visual textures. *Herringbone* in its simplest form is regularly spaced with some of the ground fabric showing. *Close* or *overlapping herringbone,* as its name implies, is worked solidly. Depending upon the angle of the first and last stitch made, it can begin or end with a point or a straight edge.

Surface satin stitch covers only the front of the fabric and uses less thread than satin stitch. Nickolson crosses long, surface satin stitches with others at an angle to achieve a cross-hatched effect. She used tiny couching stitches in the gold/yellow areas of *'Sconset* (on the facing page) to tie down the long floats of surface satin stitch. (For other stitches Nickolson discusses, see the Glossary on pp. 216-221.)

HERRINGBONE STITCH

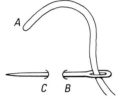 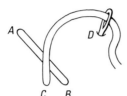 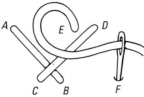 

1. Bring the needle and thread out at A, insert the needle diagonally at B and, just to the left of B, draw out at C.

2. Next, insert the needle diagonally down at D.

3. Emerging at E, stitch diagonally down to F.

4. Continue working across in this manner.

CLOSE HERRINGBONE

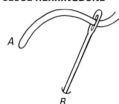 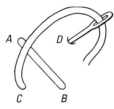 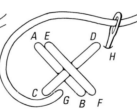 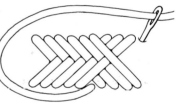

1. Bring the needle and thread up at A and insert needle diagonally down at B.

2. Draw the needle under the fabric, coming out at C (under and in line with A), then stitch diagonally up to the right at D (above and in line with B).

3. Come up at E, next to A, then stitch diagonally down to F, just to the right of B.

4. Come up at G, to the right of C, and stitch diagonally up to H, just to the right of D.

5. Continuing along, the line forms a solidly worked band of close herringbone.

SURFACE SATIN STITCH

   **Variations**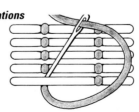

1. Working with the fabric stretched in a frame or hoop, bring the needle and thread up at A and down at B, drawing a short stitch under the fabric and out at C. Then insert the needle at D.

2. Bring the needle up at E and continue working back and forth to cover the area with surface satin stitch.

Surface satin stitch, overlaid with a second layer of surface satin stitch at 90° to it, creates a crosshatched effect.

In couched surface satin stitch (see 'Sconset on the facing page), couching stitches tie down the long floats of thread.

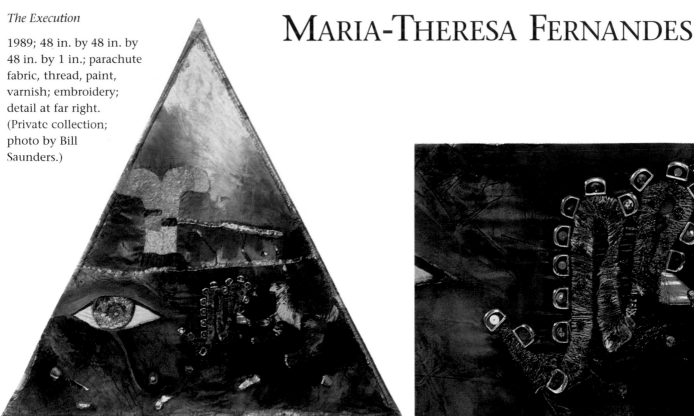

The Execution

1989; 48 in. by 48 in. by 48 in. by 1 in.; parachute fabric, thread, paint, varnish; embroidery; detail at far right. (Private collection; photo by Bill Saunders.)

MARIA-THERESA FERNANDES

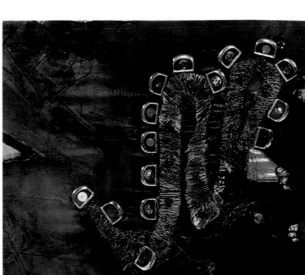

Maria-Theresa Fernandes's exuberant work is composed of brilliant color, abundant textures and magical imagery. Her rich collages combine many diverse materials such as inks, varnish, paint, glitter and metallic threads with drawings, handmade paper and hand embroidery, as well as machine embroidery on taffeta and parachute nylon. Her works radiate energy, and they reflect her strong spirit.

Every piece Fernandes creates is in some way autobiographical. She has even incorporated her clothes and shoes in large-scale works. Symbols tell her stories and convey the meaning of events in Fernandes's life during the time of a work's creation. The traumatic end of a friendship and a subsequent trip to Egypt combined to inspire *The Execution* (above) and *The Conversation* (on the facing page) Borrowing on ancient Egyptian symbols, Fernandes reinterprets them with her own instinctive twist. A cat deity, Bastet, is central to both works: as a listener and observer in *The Conversation* and as the serpent's attacker in *The Execution*. Fernandes's cat is col-

ored "a passionate red," an apt metaphor for the passion that generally prevails over reason in her work. "I don't know what symbols I'm going to use," she says. "It's intuition."

Whatever the private meaning for Fernandes, these works present a rich surface for viewing. They are large, measuring 4 ft. on each side; the triangular shape alludes to one side of a pyramid. Both hand embroidery and machine embroidery fill in shapes as well as outline them. She works without a hoop in the machine, finding the frame too restricting, and prefers to stiffen and collage the fabrics and paper with Stitch Witchery (a fusing agent). When the embroidery is completed, she adds glitter, buttons and beads.

The painting, done with Dr. Martin's inks, goes on after the embroidery. This seems like a technical impossibility, but Fernandes makes it sound simple. "The painting is always last. I bring the work together by the colors, putting on layers to see the richness." She varnishes one side of the work, sometimes the front, sometimes the back, which softens the colors and makes the fabric translucent. The finished piece is stretched over a metal armature and can be hung on the wall or suspended in front of a light source. Against the opaque background of a wall, the colors seem very strong and the embroidery is less prominent. When a piece is propped in a window or lit from behind, the fabric takes on a glowing quality and the embroidery and glitter come to life.

A strong sense of place melds with the strong sense of self in each of Fernandes's works. It may be conveyed in a small scene within a larger, abstract work, or by an inlaid or applied drawing, a postcard or a bit of embroidery suggesting a garden. *Egyptian Symbols* (shown on p. 32) is like the journal of a traveler. Fernandes draws, embroiders and adds postcards to a large sheet of her handmade paper, all of which capture the adventures of the touring artist. Perhaps Fernandes's sense of place arises from the fact that she has led an international life. She says she feels that perhaps she doesn't belong to any one country. She was born in Nairobi, Kenya, lived and studied in England, worked in Ireland and has lived in various parts of the United States. She is drawn to big cities. She enjoyed living in Baltimore but when she decided it wasn't big enough, moved to Detroit and now has a studio in a converted school building. She comments that her wandering style of life, combined with the profusion of jewelry and vintage and ethnic garments she enjoys wearing, have led people to think she is a gypsy.

Fernandes's studio actually resembles a nomad's colorful camp. It is a riot of color and texture. Here and there are large embroidered and painted screens, some with welded frames, some made from recycled window frames complete with layers of peeling paint. A large installation suspended from the ceiling resembles a tent, brilliantly colored, painted, appliquéd and positioned to invite peering within where there is more painting and embroidery. Racks of vintage clothing and spectacular shoes, part of her collection, take up one corner. In another corner are tables for drawing, painting and sewing. Her works on paper, drawings and embroideries cover the walls. Propped in the large windows are the triangular Egyptian pieces with sunlight glowing through them. The effect of the entire studio is like one of her freewheeling collages.

The Conversation

1989; 48 in. by 48 in. by 48 in. by 1 in.; parachute fabric, thread, paint, varnish; embroidery. (Photo by Bill Saunders.)

The artists Fernandes most admires also share this freedom of approach to materials: David Hockney especially for his drawing, Lucas Samaras for the variety of materials he uses and Robert Rauschenberg for his assemblages of fabric, drawing, painting and printing. Each of these artists works with many materials and techniques, using them as they are needed with no interest in labeling or categorizing. Fernandes also refuses the limits set by categories. She equates embroidery with drawing and finds just painting too limiting. "When you embroider, you have the contrasts of surface textures and you can take the work so much further."

Fernandes has an impressive background in art training, a degree in art from the Manchester College of Art and Design in England and a graduate degree from the Cranbrook Academy of Art in the United States. She credits Gerhardt Knodel, the chairman of Cranbrook's fiber department, as an influence. She explains, "One day when I had been there for two years, he said, 'You know, Maria-Theresa, you put all these

Egyptian Symbols

1988; 24 in. by 42 in. by 2 in.; handmade paper, mixed media; embroidery. (Private collection; photo by Bill Saunders.)

things on you—a brooch here and a bracelet there—and they go together. Why don't you do that with your work, because you are like a collage, the putting together of everything. You should push that idea.' So that's when I began working on all these things."

An early interest in embroidery grew from watching her mother, who did traditional Indian embroidery, and led her to study embroidery in both England and the United States. Fernandes applauds the English for their advanced, university-level embroidery courses and can't understand why there are so few university programs in the United States. "In England there were four or five people just in an embroidery department, one teaching drawing, one machine embroidery and so on." She also misses the large industrial Irish and Cornelli sewing machines available in Great Britain. But she welcomes the freedom in the United States to work without rigid guidelines and to exhibit in fine-art exhibitions.

Freedom is certainly at the core of Fernandes's approach to making art. She has an insou-

ciant manner regarding rigid rules of embroidery. Her threads are not secured neatly on the back, and her mixtures of paint, ink, drawing, embroidery and varnish would make an archivist blanch. But being outside the boundaries is essential to her work. She relates a story about a series of early works done when she was hospitalized for an extended period with arthritis. They were "gloomy pieces." A friend kept them for her while she was convalescing, and when he returned them she discovered that he had trimmed all the threads from the front of the works. "It was horrifying!"

Traditional assumptions exist for Fernandes to question. Why must edges be straight? Why can't the fabric pucker? Why not leave tears and holes and threads on the surface? Why not varnish the fabric to make it stiff and translucent? Why be precise? She declares, "I hate things that are perfect." In her work she bends, breaks and occasionally demolishes the rules of the past, and it all makes perfect sense.

SCOTT ROTHSTEIN

Night View

1985; 7 in. by 9 in.; silk embroidery on silk. (Courtesy of Helen Drutt Gallery, New York City and Philadelphia; collection of Dr. Marcia Meckler; photo by Gary McKinnis.)

In Scott Rothstein's early work, stitches dart like minnows across a still lake. In one series, *Night View* (at right), Rothstein works fields of dots in one or two strands of one-ply silk. In more recent untitled works, he uses up to 12 plies of silk in 2-ft. long strands, varying colors and hand plying as he stitches. He incorporates other elements like long pine needles, small wooden sticks and broom bristles with the embroidery. To begin a work, he first covers a heavy 2½-in. stretcher with a layer of black cotton for strength, then stretches a fine black china silk over the cotton, stitching through both fabrics as he works. The finished works are matted with white silk and framed. Rothstein writes about his work:

> In 1978 I constructed a piece that was 2 in. square and was surprised to discover that a work so small could be engaging. Since then, my stitched silks (with few exceptions) have been made within a 10-in. by 15-in. format. Technique is not of major interest to me. Although I have a traditional training in fibers, technically these pieces are experimental.

> I work with fiber because of its color possibilities. There is a luminous color quality to the silk I use that cannot be found in other conventional art materials. With silk, the color in my work is more like light than pigment.

> There have been many influences on my work, among them the paintings of Malevich and Rothko, the Aymara weavings of Bolivia, and the Noh costumes and Mingei textiles of Japan.

Untitled

1989; 13 in. by 14 in.; silk embroidery on silk. (Courtesy of Helen Drutt Gallery, New York City and Philadelphia; photo by Gary McKinnis.)

CLAIRE M. STARR

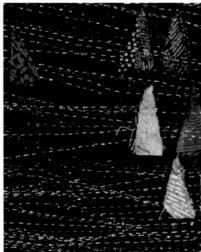

Landscape I

Far left: 1986; 21 in. by 16 in.; metallic thread, cotton fabric; appliqué, embroidery; detail at left. (Photo by Matthew Starr.)

Small bits of shiny fabrics and traces of metallic lines illuminate the dark ground in Claire M. Starr's works, suggesting the night sky, which is for her a major source of inspiration. She discusses her inspirations, techniques and materials:

> The imagery in my work relates to the night sky. I have been deeply influenced by astronomy. Within the pieces themselves, I attempt to set up a tension between color, line and shape, so that each is essential to maintain the equilibrium of the whole. I think of the stitched line as the drawn line. In some of the work I have attempted to use the embroidery as one would use pastels, that is, blending one color over another.
>
> My work is constructed of many fabrics: metallics, chiffon, tulle, rayon and cotton. One restriction I have is that the material not ravel or shred excessively, because I like to work with exposed edges. However, I consistently use cotton fabric for the background.

All of my pieces are hand sewn and constructed without the use of a machine or glue stick. I prefer to use silk thread when I appliqué because it's very smooth. For embroidery I use metallic thread, buying whatever brand is available that's suitable for a hand-sewing situation. Metallic thread is prone to twist off its core, so I use a fairly short length. It is also important to make the knot carefully since it loosens easily. I like to use a very thin needle with a small eye for all my sewing. It gives me better control and passes through the fabric smoothly.

When a piece is completed, a framer prepares stretcher bars covered with black linen. The piece is tacked with short pins directly to the linen-covered surface. The stretcher bars are designed to combine with a Plexiglas box for framing.

Each piece evolves from an idea or image generated by previous work. There's no drawing or preconceived design that I follow. My studio is set up with a large work table placed across the room from a wall. The wall is covered with white cotton over Homasote boards. The background fabric is pinned to the wall, and I develop the piece directly on it, laying on pieces of fabric and evaluating them. I don't begin to sew until I'm satisfied with the final form. When all of the pieces have been sewn down, I begin to embellish the surface with metallic thread. I do a lot of ripping out.

BARBARA LEE SMITH

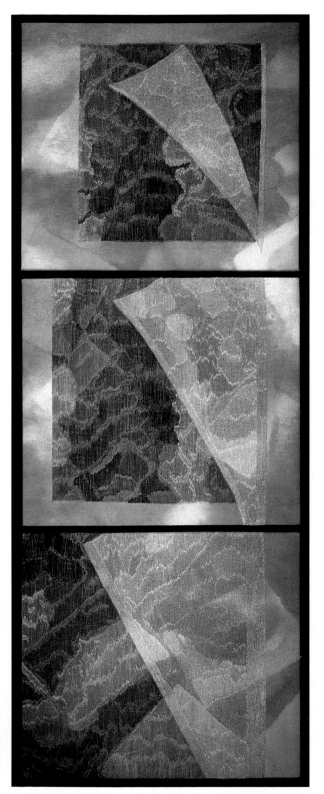

New Leaf

1989; 65 in. by 24½ in.; textile pigment sprayed on cotton/silk fabric, cotton, rayon and metallic threads; machine embroidery; detail on p. 40. (Collection of Mr. and Mrs. Donley Klein, Marietta, Georgia; photo by Steinkamp/Ballogg, Chicago.)

I am grateful to B. J. Adams (whose profile appears on pp. 202-207) for turning the tables, or the tape recorder, on me. Through the interview transcripts I could "see what I had to say," which proved very helpful.

A page, edged in gold, is turned. Reading from top to bottom, new information is revealed, the picture expands and the color becomes richer. *New Leaf* (at left), made during the writing of this book, is a wordless, visual homage to language. Until this work emerged, I had not given much thought to words or books as inspiration for my work, though reading, writing, teaching and conversation certainly consume much of my time. I would have listed music, architecture and nature as the major influences, each nourishing some segment of whatever it is that occasionally emerges and merges in a creative act.

Words and writing speak for my cerebral side, helping me to see what I'm thinking before I ever begin a new series of work. My intuitive side has its origin in music. Born with "a good ear," I learned to read music before I could read words. I still think in musical terms: themes and variations within a series; brooding, nighttime nocturnes; pizzicato dots that punctuate the stitches. While I gave up playing an instrument years ago, my musical training seems to have produced a visual voice.

An interest in architecture also inspires me. I am fascinated by doors and windows, which function as frames for light and shadow. Frames visually connect interiors and exteriors for me, which can also correspond to the inner and the outer self. Nature offers up color, light, shape and line, while words, music and architecture—man-made forms—provide structure.

Simply described, my work it is a painting on fabric with machine embroidery superimposed on it. Nothing is ever that simple, however, but by way of example, I will try to recreate the thoughts and processes that led to *New Leaf*. I had not intended to spend much time in the studio while researching and writing this book, but an invitation to be part of an upcoming exhibition was the catalyst for some intense work. Many ideas whirled in my head, and by writing them down in my notebook, I could see that references to pages ("leaves") were frequent. The triangular form of the turned page that I sketched related to sail-like shapes I had used in the past. The idea of getting closer visually, as each panel of *New Leaf* does, also related to the in-depth interviews I was doing with the artists for this book. Gold edges added a new texture and also connected me to the old volumes I own that my parents collected and treasured.

X

1989; 44 in. by 36 in.; textile pigment sprayed on cotton fabric; machine embroidery. (Collection of James W. and Louise Barber; photo by Steinkamp/Ballogg, Chicago.)

Nature usually provides me with color ideas, and frequently I note color combinations I observe as I travel. Oddly enough, even thinking about where I will be going will set my mind toward mixing colors in anticipation of what I will find. Nature, once-removed, in the strange and striking blend of greys, umbers and violets of a ceramic pot by Harvey Sadow, set me on a course for choosing the palette for *New Leaf*. I came across the photograph of Sadow's work while researching a trip I would soon be taking to Australia. When I read that he had made it while in Australia, I studied it all the more carefully. I experimented with these colors, and anticipating the sandy beaches and the sky that I would soon see led me to add some blues to the palette. I was ready, then, to paint the heavy cotton/silk-blend fabric that I use.

The steps of the process wherein I actually begin to manipulate my materials show evidence of the same interplay of intuition and intellect. Unlike the "inspiration" stages, the steps followed in the technical part of the process remain fairly consistent from one work to the next.

For spray painting my work, I use Euro-tex, Lumière and some of the aptly named Primal Glow textile paints, first diluting them with water or an extender. Pigments or paints coat the surface of the fiber and, unlike dyes, do not chemically become part of the fiber. However, the paints are lightfast and colorfast, and, for my purposes, considerably easier to use than dyes. I spray the diluted pigments on, one layer of color at a time, using a hand-operated sprayer from the hardware store. (I spray water through it to clean it for each new color.) Like watercolors, the pigments are transparent, so each time a new color is added it changes the surrounding colors, which causes some built-in risks and surprises. Once the painting is complete, I press the fabric and pin it on the wall in my studio. It takes three to five days for the pigments to set before I can mark the work for embroidery. In the interim, I do a lot of staring and sketching.

I had already done some sketching for *New Leaf*, but there is always the need to refine sketches once a painting is complete. There may be areas of light and dark in the painting that I want to reinforce, strong areas I want to emphasize and weak areas to correct. The movement in the painting must work with the movement planned for the embroidered areas.

Once I have selected the final sketch, I enlarge it freehand on the painting, using a marking pen whose ink can be removed with water. Next, I begin to select threads, choosing colors and values based on the effects of light and transparency I am aiming to build into the work. I select and stitch all the darker areas, then I imagine what would happen if the colors in the painting and embroidery were washed over by bright sunlight, choosing, then, these lighter colors and stitching them.

Threads are chosen primarily for color, the glowing and transparent effects I aim for, and also for their compatibility with the fabric and the machine-embroidery stitch. For a machined whip stitch, a very loose bobbin thread is pulled to the surface by a stronger top thread, whipping around it on the fabric surface (see the sidebar on p. 38-39). The viewer's eye optically mixes the colors of top and bobbin thread, blending the different hues or values.

Between the optical mix of hues and the sheen of the Natesh and Madeira rayon threads, which I always use on the bobbin, a glowing color results. These threads come in an enormous range of colors, a palette that provides me with literally hundreds of options. I use sewing thread or machine embroidery thread on top. The fine rayon thread slides easily through the heavy fabric, and its density enables the completed whip stitch to stand up straight, making a thick surface texture. I move the frame forward and back under the needle, so that the rows are vertical and parallel.

As I push or pull the fabric, ending or beginning each run of a row of stitching, tiny dots are formed that run counter to the vertical lines and punctuate the surface. They form a visual counterpoint, outlining the areas that have been stitched, adding subtle shapes to the surface. I change the color of thread—top, bobbin or

The pleasures of machine embroidery

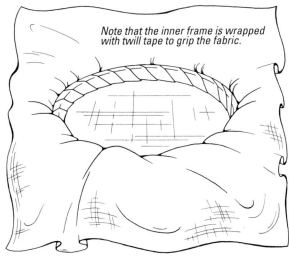

Note that the inner frame is wrapped with twill tape to grip the fabric.

The fabric is set in a hoop so it will rest flat on the bed of the machine. While keeping pressure on the inner ring so it won't pop out, grasp the fabric and pull it taut, working all around the hoop so the fabric is stretched evenly. Tighten the screw in the frame until it squeaks.

Like riding a bicycle, machine embroidering is awkward at first, and you might feel a little foolish and uncomfortable until you get the hang of it. But once you have acquired the knack, you'll be able to travel to uncommon places, exploring all the way. It's not so farfetched to compare a physical activity like biking with machine embroidering, because each involves skill, coordination and working in rhythm with a machine. Both are done best when the mind is concentrated and the body relaxed. It takes practice to learn the basics of machine embroidery; about 20 hours seems to be the norm.

Hand embroidery has been around for centuries; machine embroidery is a relative newcomer. Machine embroidery developed a bad reputation over the years, partly because it was marketed as a "quick" way (done on a treadle machine) to imitate hand embroidery. The treadle machine promised a certain speed and control, and while some instructors made lovely samples, few others had the patience or inclination to do much with it. The machine was used for constructing garments and domestic textiles. There were some early practitioners in Europe, but it was not until the 1960s, in connection with the resurgence of interest in embroidery, that machine embroidery began to come into its own, not as imitation anything, but as a unique tool for producing line, texture and structure.

A number of artists have discovered the challenges of machine embroidery, including several featured in this book. Artists who work with the machine often think of it as a

both—about every three to five minutes. I use a Bernina sewing machine with a knee-operated presser-foot lifter, which allows me to use both hands for removing the old top thread and rethreading a new one.

Once the embroidery is complete, the work is pressed, stretched and stapled over padded, sealed plywood. Behind the plywood I attach a slightly smaller frame. This hidden frame, painted black, makes the work appear to float on the wall. Much of my work is composed of modules, and each section is intended to hang about an inch or two apart.

I enjoy designing for and working with modules, and it fits my interest in the layering, additive process. I can use as many modules as I need to build a wall of work, and separating them slightly allows the work to integrate with the wall. Since the designs have many diagonals and the paintings are full of romantic, flowing lines, the additional horizontal and vertical straight edges of the modules add a contrasting structure. It is easier to work in smaller sections with the machine; they are less cumbersome to frame and pieces stack for shipping or carting off to a show.

drawing tool. In addition, people just learning to work with "free-motion embroidery" (with the fabric stretched in a frame, the presser foot removed and the feed dogs lowered or covered) find that ease of drawing is its first appealing characteristic. Experienced sewers expect a nice, even 12-stitches-to-the-inch line and are uneasy approaching the naked needle minus its protective presser foot. They are sure that the machine was made only to sew seams and construct things. Machine embroiderers use those functions also, taking advantage of the strong seam lines and power of the machine to construct large and small works, sculptural and flat.

In art terms, machine embroidery seems more akin to the spontaneous quality of watercolor than the time-consuming aspect of oil painting. One benefit of seeing the work grow quickly is that it is easier to stay in touch with the idea that initiated the work and gauge sooner rather than later whether that idea is working. If it is not, however, machine embroidery is next to impossible to rip out,

which might prove daunting to some. Frequently, it is easier to start afresh or to cover the offending section in some way, probably inventing some new possibilities in the process.

The machine might indeed free the artist to treat the work with a lighter touch, to see making art as a process of exploring rather than a process of producing. A playful approach is important with the machine; an afternoon of experimenting just to see what you and the machine can do together is fun.

Machine embroidery does not require a specialized machine; any home sewing machine in good working order is fine. The important elements are being able to move the fabric freely and keeping the fabric flat against the face plate at the point where the needle pierces it so that a stitch, the linking of top and bobbin thread, can be formed. All else is variation on a theme.

There are many ways to secure the fabric so that it moves easily and the stitch is formed and many books that explain the techniques (see the Bibliography

on pp. 225-227). However, here are some basics:

A wooden hoop with a screw adjustment is essential for most machine embroidery. In a reversal of the way fabric is stretched for hand embroidery, a machine embroiderer keeps the inner ring, wrapped in twill or cotton tape to grip the fabric, on top. This makes the taut fabric flush with the bed of the machine. The embroidery is worked within the stretched area; the hoop is moved to new areas as needed.

It is important to lower the feed dogs (the "teeth") or to cover them. See the instruction book that comes with your machine under "embroidery" or "darning." Make sure the free arm cover is in place, if the machine has one. Start with a new needle, slightly larger than that used for normal sewing (a 90 or its equivalent), and remove the presser foot.

Once the presser foot is removed, remember to raise the presser-foot lever when threading the top and lower it to sew. That lever controls the upper tension, and it is easy, without the presser foot in place, to forget to raise

In *X* (on p. 36), only two modules form the work, but cutting the otherwise asymmetric composition in the middle enhanced the visual tension between the two halves. The colors and superimposed shapes in this work were also inspired by my imaginings about Australia.

Words begin the process, and while I let go of them in the midst of making a work, invoking my intuitive skills, they return with the selection of a title. Usually a name attaches itself to a piece while I am working, but if not, it may arrive after a dream. Other titles are borrowed (shamelessly extracted) from a line of poetry or music, or from

right out of the middle of an aphorism. I like ambiguous titles, which suggest that the work is open to interpretation.

I work on one piece at a time, concentrating on it completely until it "feels" right and is finished. I rarely return and rework a piece, since I see each as a step in a continuing process. This philosophy is contained in the title of a work I did some years ago, *Drawing the Line,* which is based on a gem of an aphorism by H. L. Mencken, who summed it up nicely: "Art, like morality, consists of drawing the line somewhere."

and lower it. (If you get a tangle on one side of the fabric or the other once you begin, chances are you forgot one of those steps.) Using sewing threads for practice, run the machine at a comfortable speed, not too fast, but definitely not too slow. However, move your hands, which are resting within the hoop guiding the fabric, at what may feel like a slower than normal speed. ("Fast foot, slow hands.")

One good way to begin is by writing your name. If the stitches look too long, the thread breaks or you see the needle bending, you are either running the machine too slowly or pushing the fabric too fast or both. Dot the "i's" and cross the "t's," noting the easy rhythm of making the line. Trim the threads as you go. This is good discipline, because it is easy to get caught up in the momentum of machine embroidery, and trying to cut away the threads that have been sewn over a few times is extremely difficult.

Try changing colors, adding a second or third color to the sampler. If the bobbin thread is showing a bit, loosen the top tension slightly. Try using the stitch-width adjustment, noting how the line varies from narrow to wide and back again. Also note how a smooth line (satin stitch) or jagged line (zigzag stitch) is formed depending on how quickly you move your hands in relation to the speed of the machine.

Loosening the bobbin tension won't produce a strong seam, but it makes an enchanting texture on the top of the fabric. Working with the material face down and

a heavier thread on the bobbin produces a strong line, a visual force to be reckoned with when the work is turned right side up.

You've now done at least half of what machine embroidery is all about. All the rest is variation, depending on the kind of fabric (dense, loose, printed, plain, natural, synthetic), thread (metallic, machine embroidery, sewing, perle cotton, rayon), tension (balanced or purposefully out of balance), gadgets (darning foot, walking foot) and the ideas, which begin to come as you feel more at ease with the machine.

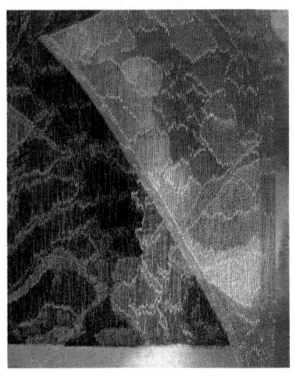

A detail of New Leaf *shows the tiny dots of rayon thread pulled up from the bobbin to form the whip stitch; full photo, p. 35. (Photo by Stainkamp/Ballogg, Chicago.)*

MACHINE TENSIONS

Top (spool) and bobbin thread at normal (equal tension)

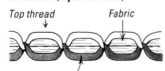

Sewing machines are designed to sew seams with an evenly balanced, normal top thread (spool) and bobbin tension.

Loose bobbin and/or tight top

Machine embroiderers manipulate tensions to produce different textures. A loose bobbin and/or tight top tension brings the bobbin thread to the fabric surface to form a whip stitch. It is also possible to thread perle cotton or other heavier threads on the bobbin, then turn the fabric face down and stitch a cordlike line (cable stitch).

Loose top and/or tight bobbin

Loose top and/or tight bobbin tension brings the top thread to the back of the fabric. This is useful to create a very smooth edge in satin stitch. But taken to extremes, it can jam the bobbin — a result of forgetting to raise the presser foot when threading the top or forgetting to lower it when sewing.

What inspires an artist? What initiates the urge to explore? The sources are as many and as varied as the people who are challenged to make art. Artists speak of a constant need to be aware and receptive, to allow ideas to invade their imaginations. A word, an object, a dream or a drawing may be the catalyst that will compel an artist into action.

Ideas are captivating, but they can be slippery if not quickly seized and recorded or made visual in some form. Artists speak of their sketchbooks, repositories for these ideas made visual, as if they were an extension of themselves. Within these pages are drawings, diagrams, words, phrases, experiments and notes for grand or humble plans. For some artists, a camera substitutes for a pen in their sketchbooks as a means to record, define or explore.

Many artists cite the difficulty of too many ideas and, consequently, the need to make choices. They note that it is often easier to create within self-imposed limits; to begin with what is nearby when reaching for the sky. Here are comments by some of the artists interviewed on what inspires them and how they translate idea into action.

CAPTURING THE IDEA

Justine Vaughn: "I get inspiration from just about everywhere. It's essential to take a good notebook along—it's a good reference and a stimulus for down times."

Merrill Mason: "My notebook is a lot of tear out, tape in and stick in; pictures that I've seen that interest me and postcards of show openings with the artist's work on the front; lots of quotes and ideas, words that I like; titles."

Tom Lundberg: "There are times when I've kept a written dream diary. Do it long enough and it becomes a habit. A sketchbook is important. Taking a lot of snapshots or a lot of slides is definitely the best, the closest thing I have to a diary."

Wilcke Smith: "I think that what helps when I begin a work is my folder of titles. I have pages and pages of them. They're just little snippets that I hear or read. A lot of them come from books on mythology and that kind of thing. Sometimes I don't really know what the titles mean; they're just there to direct me. It's possible that I may not stick with a title; I may change the name of a work when it's done. Something may happen midway into the piece, when it begins to do something more interesting. Then I'll just go back and work up that title another time, maybe years later.... A good habit (which I have to force myself to do) is this: first thing in the morning, even before breakfast, I come in the studio and jot a few things down and write it up later."

B. J. Adams: "If I can't decide what to do, I go back over all my notes, exercises and sketches, and I'll often find an idea to develop or to push me in a direction. A teacher once suggested that I just jump in, rather than spending a lot of time planning a composition. However, sometimes the composition comes back to haunt you when you just jump in."

Kimberly Izenman: "I do a lot of sketching before I start an embroidery. The inspiration for the subjects and backgrounds often comes from entirely different sources. Most of my subject matter is taken from nature and has no symbolic meaning. I do small drawings from nature or photographs, or I just play with shapes that interest me."

COURTING INSPIRATION

Mary Snyder Behrens: "What interests me most are color and composition. That's what's most important to me to make the piece work as a visual whole. It's working with grids, juxtaposing things asymmetrically, matching things up."

Wilcke Smith: "When do my ideas flow the easiest? Probably when I'm not sitting at the drawing board. On an airplane. In the shower. When I'm not forcing it. In the middle of the night when I awaken or just as I'm falling asleep. If I'm just blanking out my mind, I'm thinking about designs.... What inspires me to begin a work? I just can't wait to get at it. It's such a build-up. It's a bursting out, really, of too much to do, too many ideas, too many ways I want to go, too many experiments I want to make, too many things I want to try, too many materials I want to put together. I don't have a problem starting. I have a problem sorting out and directing myself strongly on one route and getting rid of the 'too much's'."

Justine Vaughn: "Most often the best ideas strike late at night before I fall asleep or while I'm working on another piece. If I don't plan a piece completely, I'm freer to make creative decisions along the way. Because of this, my studio is always in chaos. When it's too messy, I take the time to clean it up; it's like cleaning my mind, and I'm able to focus again.... Also, I never give up on an accident. It will eventually work into a piece."

Merrill Mason: "When I was a printmaker, I worked with a group of people in a shared studio. I felt we should have a banner over the door that said, "Transformation of mistakes is the path to beauty." Somehow it would encourage this business of feeling that you have the freedom to experiment and never quite know when some error is going to turn out to be a serendipitous mistake. It is going to expand you in a way that you wouldn't have thought to do on your own."

Robert Burningham: "I've used cassette tapes of synthesizer, computer and contemporary music to assist me in thinking about texture, color and design, which I relate to stitchery."

Joan Schulze: "I'm interested in the crinkling of the paper, the collaging of all the little things that I've been collecting. I like the process of sitting with paper and pencil; it feeds me somehow. I like those drawings that I do; I have a couple of them on my wall. They may never get to be done in a piece, but I like them as drawings. That will be good enough."

Mary Bero: "Every idea is worth a try—to find it, watch it, experience it, develop it and thereby have a relationship with it."

Patricia Malarcher: "I tend to work on little things and big things at the same time, and I also try to have some things that are just to play with. Sometimes they develop and sometimes they don't. Sometimes those things never see the light of day; they're never looked upon by eyes other than mine."

Tom Lundberg: "I have ideas, but they'll be proved by the working rather than the talking."

ILLUSTRATING RULES

Caroline Dahl: "Come up with a 'Rule of Life' and illustrate it both with words and images. It should be something fairly common and obvious, and by virtue of these characteristics, humorous. Things like 'Never march behind the horses,' 'Always keep the curtain inside the tub,' and 'Never leave the main road' come to mind."

PLAYING WITH PAPER DOLLS

D. R. Wagner: "Cut a bunch of photos out of the newspaper and make up a series of panels where the people in the news photos are talking or interacting with each other. Then, instead of thought balloons, cut out objects from the paper and use them to fill what would be words. Let these images keep getting more complex and dense until you find something that helps you to compose. This never fails if you use your imagination in what the nature of these conversations could be. Stories can develop with just objects as the subject. Sports pages are good for extreme gestures. A lot of the time sports gestures look like samurai or Kabuki postures. Try it."

LEARNING FROM A MASTERPIECE

Renie Breskin Adams: "Do embroidered studies of famous paintings. People come with a mindset about a certain geometric, decorative way of working with stitching, and if they take their rules from a famous painter rather than from a stitchery book, they'll find that they have to stitch erratically. So that's a good way to break a mindset. Do a little cartoon with tracing paper on the painting and transfer that to fabric. Any limits are placed by the master painter. Use any kind of threads.

"This can be done with nature too, with a photograph, or better, with a natural object. For example, what people think is a plain grey rock, upon close inspection, may have craters and little objects attached to it. Doing color studies from nature gets people experientially involved in color rather than relying on theory or coming up with just the bright colors on the color wheel."

MAKING POSTCARDS

Joan Schulze: "Getting started in the studio is often difficult, so the following is an idea generator for me. I also use this when I've run dry or when I'm bone tired but don't want to leave the mood I've created in the day's work:

"I'm a constant clipper of magazines, newspaper headlines, funny juxtapositions of images and words and whatever is my latest obsession. These are semisorted in various boxes and trays along with leavings from my work, little bits of things that I collect as I travel, and an odd assortment of paper and photographs that I feel I can cut up. They are the source for some of my best postcards (or 'Mail Art' as many seem to call it).

"Surrounded by all this ephemera, I get to work cutting and pasting to make postcards. I'll send them to family and friends either that day, or lay it in my future file. Most times I spend less than an hour and find that I have entered into the spirit of working in the studio. Other times I find the images so enthralling that I realize it's lunch time, and I'm still at it.

"There are some which have triggered quilt ideas, others the start of a poem. I think it is the simple, unaffected nature of the idea 'postcard' that lets me find new ways of looking at things in a spontaneous and speedy manner. My friends seem to like what I send and often marvel at the ability of the U.S. Post Office to deliver the mail, hanging threads, dangling participles and all."

GALLERY

DENISE BEAUDIN
Le lion d'or

1988; 54 in. by 36 in.; gold thread
on plastic sheet; embroidery.
(Photo by Jean-Pierre Beaudin.)

MARY G. FRY
Gold Leaf

1987; 12 in. by 10 in.; linen fabric
and cotton threads dyed with
Inkodye; images worked in
counted-thread stitches; gold leaf
applied to linen and some of the
threads. (Photo by Patricia Lambert.)

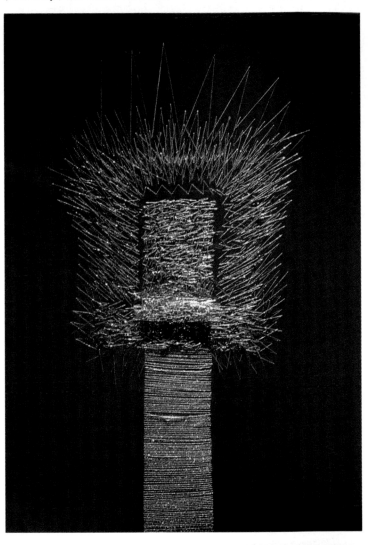

JANET PAGE-KESSLER
Daylilies

1990; 34 in. by 68 in.; cotton
fabric, blends; machine appliqué,
machine embroidery, machine
quilting, painting. (Photo by Janet
Page-Kessler.)

KIMBERLY IZENMAN
Dragonfly Moon

1988; 3½ in. by 3½ in.; 27-count linen, cotton floss, china silk, Balger blending filament, Mylar, Natesh rayon threads; body and wings stitched in tent stitch, wings and eyes overstitched with Mylar, outlined in backstitch or stem stitch, background worked in artist's version of laid work: stranded cotton threads laid vertically, held with seed stitch. (Photo by Kimberly Izenman.)

CARYL BRYER FALLERT
Life in the Margins I

1988; 17 in. by 26½ in.; hand-dyed cotton; machine stitching, quilting. (Private collection; photo by Caryl Bryer Fallert.)

LINDA H. KONYA
Two Boys in Eden-Hveragerdi, Iceland

1981; 9 in. by 12 in.; perle cotton on linen, shisha mirrors; embroidery, needle lace and needleweaving. (Photo by Linda H. Koyna.)

"One of my favorite shops to visit in Iceland was a beautiful little nursery/produce market/gift shop/art gallery/cafe. This piece was inspired by a photo I took of my two oldest boys, age two and five at the time, looking down the main aisle of the nursery at the profusion of plants."

ELIZABETH TAYLOR
November Sunshine

1986; 57 in. by 57 in.; padded, quilted squares strung into a grid on monofilament thread and overlaid with a needle-lace grid in *pointe d'Angleterre* stitch; detail right. (Private collection; photo by Kerr Photography, London, Ontario, Canada.)

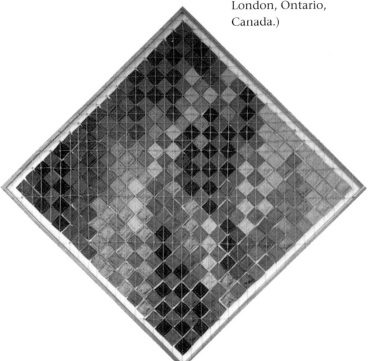

JAN KOZICKI
Inner Eye Series: City Seen #5

1988; 6 in. by 8 in.; rayon and metallic threads, muslin; machine embroidery. (Photo by Bottega: M. J. Manhoff.)

JACK D. SMITH
Spectres in the Acid Rain

1990; 42 in. by 53½ in.; black cotton canvas, lines stamp-bleached then dyed with Inkodye; machine embroidery. (Photo by Jack D. Smith.)

DOROTHY L. WOODSOME
Prairie Rain

1988; 20 in. by 22½ in.; fabric collage; embroidery. (Private collection; photo by R. A. Woodsome.)

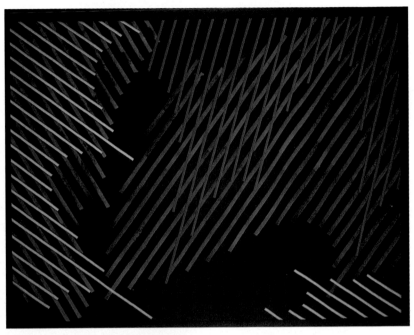

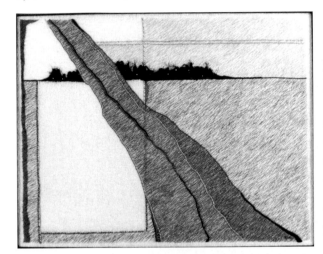

FLO DUTKA
The Way Home

1986; 20 in. by 26 in.; fabric collage, embroidery. (Collection of Mr. and Mrs. D. Humphrey, Edmonton, Alberta, Canada; photo by Joe Bally.)

Point of View

POEMS AND
PORTRAITS

RENIE BRESKIN ADAMS

Tea Time

1987; 10⅜ in. by 9⅜ in. by ¾ in.;
cotton thread on cotton fabric;
embroidery. (Photo by Barry Stark,
Art/Photo, Northern Illinois
University.)

Point of View

Overleaf: 1986; 23¾ in. by 27½ in.;
cotton thread on cotton fabric;
embroidery. (Photo by Deb Cooper.)

Hovering between the real and the imagined, a poetic mix of memory and fantasy occupies Renie Breskin Adams's embroideries. She frequently portrays herself in the work—as mistress of surreal ceremonies in *Tea Time* (shown above), as the artist observed sketching in *Point of View* (on p. 48) and as the child in the richly figured carpet in *Fear, Laughter and the Unknown* (on p. 55).

There is such a wealth of detail in Adams's work that her portrait, her point of view, may slip by almost unnoticed.

As elusive in conversation as she appears in her embroideries, Adams discusses her work with a somewhat distracted air. Yet a firm discipline emerges when she talks about design. Sometimes she works from a specific idea, sometimes not. In any case, she usually begins by relaxing. "I start by sketching—or maybe it would be better to call it doodling—and looking for shapes." These shapes may pertain to her original idea ("like something that has my husband in it or a picnic, for example..."), or the shapes themselves may suggest an idea. She describes the process for one work, *Tea Time*:

> I didn't have a representational idea when I sat down to doodle. I just started and happened to draw that funny little figure that's polka-dotted. I think she's hawking plums, and it's funny that the spots in her garment match what she's hawking. Then, I was also drawing cubes and trying to checker them, and there's no way that you can checker a cube that you see three sides of. So I split two sides and put in a gusset, and then it struck me that I'd turned it into a table or tablecloth. So there are cubes that have a gusset in the background, and in the foreground it turns into a tablecloth. Then I thought, "Well, this is a wonderful setting for our pet fly, Walter," who was flying around that fall. He's kamikaziing that watermelon. The watermelon is very scared, and the table is sympathetically scared with the watermelon.

Tea Time measures only 11 in. by 10 in., but it contains as much movement and mayhem as the Mad Hatter's tea party. What Adams does not mention in describing the work is her own self-portrait that fills the upper left corner. Waiting, a bit bemused and with politely folded hands, she appears eager to be offered a cup of tea. Could this quiet guest really have created all this chaos? You bet she could!

Adams's stream-of-consciousness approach to designing is the product of many years of analyzing what works for her and what doesn't. She has found that breaking down the design process into segments enables her to add layers of visual complexity to her work. First come the doodles, the shapes and a composition where the action is taking place. It is important to her that the shapes are well composed in addition to telling a story well. Her sketch is translated into a small cartoon where she determines the colors. She uses colored pencils to show both color and texture. From this cartoon, she sketches the basic shapes on a medium-weight artist's cotton canvas.

Now she is ready to embroider, to "invent structure." She prefers to "invent one thing...or a limited number of things at a time. At the point when I'm about to start stitching, I've already invented my subject matter, invented all the shapes, invented colors and invented, or at least suggested, textures that I can translate into thread." She aims to fill up space with as much detail as possible, increasing its complexity, and this procedure ensures just that.

The stitches are minute and form a delicate structure for her complex images. She plies strands of sewing thread to blend colors for stitching. She uses rather flat stitches—satin, detached buttonhole, needleweaving and couching (see the sidebars on p. 52 and p. 54)—relying on subtle textural and color changes for contrast. In fact, it is important to her that the work look like a blend of stitches and that no single area call attention to itself.

Although shape is her initial focus, Adams de-emphasizes it once she begins to embroider. She wants to avoid an outlined composition where, she says, "line identifies subject rather than being used to create space, atmosphere and volume. When I'm doodling, I come up with all the shapes and textures. But, when I get to the thread and think of color and texture, the shapes become subordinate to what else is happening. What becomes important to me is that I lose the contour of the shape, and that attention is really focused on either side of the contour. There are not so many lines in the final piece."

This breaking down of the outline shows up in *Tea Time*, "where structure and texture

Needleweaving

Needleweaving reproduces on fabric the over-under tabby, or plain weave, created on a loom. This tabby weave is made up of a warp, or lengthwise foundation threads, and a weft, or crosswise filling threads that lace alternately over and under the strands of the warp.

In needleweaving, long, straight stitches worked close together on a fabric ground form the warp, as shown in the drawing below. Making these long stitches with most of the thread exposed on the surface of the fabric is known in embroidery as "laying threads." These warp threads can be of even or uneven lengths, depending upon the area or shape to be covered and the effects sought in the embroidery. Next, weft threads, woven over and under the laid warp threads, create a plain weavelike texture. A blunt tapestry needle works best for the weaving process because it won't spear a thread during the weaving, although it's also possible to turn a sharp needle around and weave with the needle's eye leading the way.

Unlike working on a loom where there is no fabric ground, needleweaving on fabric can be easily worked in irregular shapes. The weft, or weaving, thread can be brought up from the back of the fabric at any spot before beginning the weaving process. This means that long sections of weft thread that extend beyond the weaving could, in turn, themselves become a new warp. Shifting the orientation of the threads is sometimes referred to as discontinuous weft. In discontinuous weaving, the threads do not need to meet at right angles as they usually do in a loom-woven structure, and the resulting shapes can be irregular or eccentric. Adams discusses weaving:

"I think my favorite structure in the whole world is a woven structure. I see warp and weft as absolutely equal, a balanced tabby. Sometimes I'm putting in weft threads, but they might extend beyond the current warp, and then the wefts become warps for putting new threads in. I do like the idea that structurally, when it's finished, there is no real warp or weft, there is no clear up or down orientation. The threads shift function. I love that about it. I wove on the loom before I ever did embroidery, and my favorite thing was tapestry weaving, which is discontinuous weft. And you can just carry that to the utter extreme absurdity with embroidery because you can have discontinuous warps and wefts. It takes a long time to needleweave, but I don't mind doing it. One of the things I love about needleweaving as a structure is that it is so simple. It's like crosshatching in drawing."

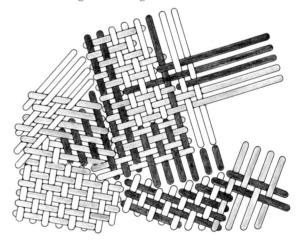

NEEDLEWEAVING

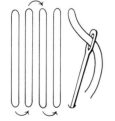

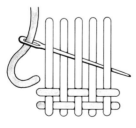

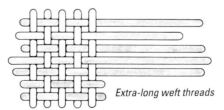
Extra-long weft threads

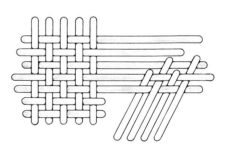

1. Laying threads with long, straight stitches are worked close together on the fabric ground to form the warp for needleweaving.

2. Filling, or weft, threads are woven over and under the warp to form an even tabby weave.

3. Weft threads can be brought up from the back of the fabric ground at any spot, making it possible to lay long threads that can be used as a new warp for more weaving.

4. Once this new warp is woven, a new weft can again be extra long and serve as yet another new warp, with the cumulative results an irregularly woven shape like that shown at top.

pass over the edges of shapes. The figures should always shift and change so that there's a lot of activity on either side of an edge." The embroidery appears to flow effortlessly across the fabric like a smoothly woven tapestry, as if there were no stops or starts in its creation.

She is in fact, well versed in tapestry techniques and still enjoys using a kindred embroidery technique, needleweaving. Its over-and-under process creates a crosshatched appearance, which contrasts with the looped texture of the detached buttonhole stitch. Couching, worked in a heavier thread, though still no larger than a fine perle cotton, is used for a stronger linear element, and satin stitch, often worked in the shape of crosses, is found mostly in the borders and frames.

Adams has made very complex borders and frames for many of her pieces, and while affirming her interest in their connection with traditional textiles, she has also used them to create a sense of distance from the work, to make the work look like "a portrait of an embroidery."

David, (shown at right) a portrait of the artist's husband, grew out of an interest in frames. "In David's portrait I had been looking at a lot of embroidered mirror and casket [a small box] surrounds. Both works had a tradition in textiles, the center image surrounded by decorative information." She enclosed the central image with small, colorful figures depicting their family and various interests. The plain "mat" is actually solidly worked detached buttonhole stitch. To achieve the appearance of mitered corners, Adams stitched from the outer, wider side of the frame toward the center, always decreasing at the same spot in each of the four corners, to form a distinct, angled line.

The frame itself is a combination of knotting and crochet, with some occasional satin stitching. She explains:

Most of the frame is plain single crochet. I make a band of double half-hitch, which is a looped knot, similar to detached buttonhole, worked over a core thread. When you double half-hitch a band, the core element turns back and forth and makes a little turn-around loop on each side of the band. I crochet right into

David

1985; 13½ in. by 12⅝ in. by ⅞ in.; cotton thread on cotton fabric; embroidery. (Photo by Barry Stark, Art/Photo, Northern Illinois University.)

the selvage edge of the half-hitch band, sticking my crochet hook through each of those turn-around loops. The embroidered fabric is stretched over quarter-round molding so that the fabric is not lying on a right-angle edge of the wood. The frame of half-hitches and crochet is then attached to the edge of the embroidered fabric.

David is not all frame and border, however. The central image contains some of the most subtle color Adams has ever obtained. She used a

Working detached buttonhole as a filling stitch

The detached buttonhole stitch, the basic structure of needle lace, is often used as filling for design motifs that are meant to be worked in relief or slightly separated from the fabric ground. The stitch is actually a looping technique that, when worked closely together, creates a slightly raised, but generally smooth texture. By increasing or decreasing the number of loops made into the row above, the embroiderer can achieve sculpted effects in the piece.

Start with a base row of chain stitch, stem stitch or back stitch, as shown in the drawing below. Bring the needle up near and just below the left side of the base row. The point at which the needle is brought through the ground determines the height of the row. Using a tapestry needle will ensure that you do not pick up any of the ground fabric as you stitch. Working from above, slide the needle behind the first base stitch.

The working thread should be behind the needle as you pull down to form the looping stitch. When you reach the right-hand side of the row, stitch down into the ground fabric and come up just a bit below the previous row, again determining by that stitch what the height of the row will be. The needle now slides from above down between the vertical loops. Again, the working thread is behind the needle as you pull down gently to form the next row of loops.

It's often easy to stitch in one direction, but not the other. It's helpful to remember that the working thread is always looped ahead of you in the direction that you are stitching. If you are working from left to right, the thread loops to form an L-shape. If you're working right to left, the loop will look more like a J. The final row can be held in place by a simple straight stitch over the base of each loop.

DETACHED BUTTONHOLE

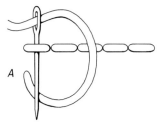

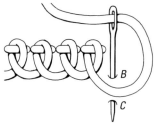

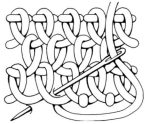

1. Stitch a base row of back stitch, then bring the needle up just below and to the left of the row (A). Slide the needle behind the first base stitch without piercing the ground fabric, and pull the working thread down gently to complete the first loop.

2. Repeat the process in all the stitches across the row. At the row's end, stitch the needle down into the fabric (B) and bring it up just below the previous row at C.

3. Slide the needle from above through each loop of the previous row and pull it down and over the working thread to form the next row of loops.

4. Continue in this fashion for the desired number of rows. Then stitch over the base of each loop in the final row to secure the embroidery to the fabric.

photograph as reference and worked with over 20 values of neutral, warm and cool grey sewing threads. Working in detached buttonhole stitch, she used three threads at a time, blending them to achieve the extremely subtle changes of dark, middle and light values she desired.

Adams's works are often autobiographical and contain portraits of family, evocative interiors and even her cat. She reveals herself through self-portraits in a number of pieces. In *Point of View* (see p. 48) she keeps her back to her audience and invites the viewers to look over her shoulder to observe what she herself sees as she sketches, the artist's-eye view. She is also sharing her living space, the worn Oriental rug, a sketch of her cat, Sylvia, and the sense of ease that comes when she is enjoying the work. "When I'm involved in this process, doing tiny passages, it's a way of forgetting myself. You really do go someplace else while you're working, and it's sort of nice."

The Oriental rug in the background in *Point of View* figures prominently in one of Adams's earlier works. She based her first and one of her finest embroideries, done in 1978, on its composition. Discovering a snapshot of herself as a child initiated the idea for the work, which looks at first glance like an embroidery of a highly patterned rug. But like a game of discovering the number of hidden objects in a picture, closer examination reveals dozens of tiny portraits of family, friends, toys, monsters and tea sets tucked within the formal framework of the design, and the child, Renie, at the center. The effect on all levels is ultimately awe inspiring and haunting, underscored by its title: *Fear, Laughter and the Unknown* (shown at right).

She has rendered a portrait of an old textile, worked within a textile tradition and transformed the textile into a portrait of childhood. Contained within the comforting symmetry of a carpet, she has stitched her point of view about childhood and family, fears and fun, a work that resonates with the child in everyone. Rather than simply decorating fabric, Renie Breskin Adams transforms it. She hides her serious and often

Fear, Laughter and the Unknown

1978; 30 in. by 24 in.; cotton thread on linen; embroidery. (Photo by Barry Stark, Art/Photo, Northern Illinois University.)

poignant observations behind wry and witty images, dancing, by way of her art, through life:

> I have thought of dancing as a metaphor for style. The only thing you can work at in life is style. People want to take control over their lives and sometimes it's hard. Circumstances frequently control you, but what you can control is your style, the way you approach dealing with all your problems. Dancing, for me, becomes a metaphor for that. Life is just one sad story that we dance around.

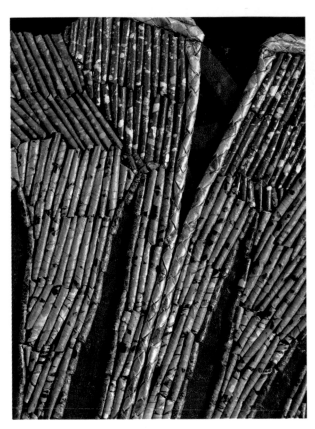

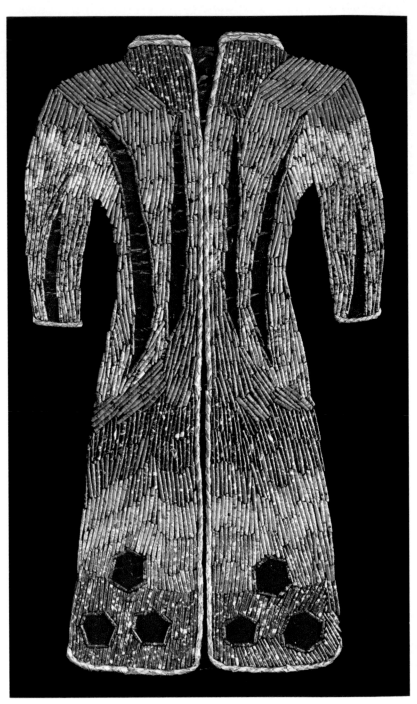

Royal Coat

1989; 43 in. by 24½ in.; painted paper, waxed linen; sewing; detail above. (Collection of Mary and Fritz Weis, Claremont, California; photos by Hudson Pate.)

Working with simple materials, the stuff of countless scout and school projects, Carolyn Prince Batchelor stitches subtle images of timeless tribal garments. These "garments," made of paper beads sewn to cloth, are not wearable, but instead are visual references to the garments of the ancient cultures that inspire her. Batchelor's reinterpretations of ordinary materials and cultural context infuse her garments with a sense, at once poignant and proud, of their imaginary wearers. She discusses her work:

> Inspiration for my beaded coats comes from tribal beaded and quilted clothing. I'm drawn to children's garments, which communicate a feeling of vulnerability and a sense of the infinite care lavished on their adornment. Also, the process I use — rolling paper beads — is a popular pastime for children.
>
> I begin to make the beads by treating large sheets of heavy paper with a process I've developed to add texture and make it more malleable. Next I cover both sides of the paper with layers of latex paint, then build up the surface on one side with additional layers of acrylic paint. Depending on the size and type of beads I want to make, I tear the painted paper into strips or triangles, which I roll one by one and secure with white glue. I use linen thread to construct dimensional coat shapes and to sew on individual beads. The finished piece is varnished with acrylic polymer medium.
>
> I enjoy using paper because it's lightweight, yet strong, and can be manipulated to look like other materials such as bone, glass or wood. In the beginning, I establish painterly color and texture, which carry through in the finished work. The dense surface is composed of thousands of individual bead elements, which remind me of counters recording the hours and thoughts that went into the fabrication of each coat. Not meant to be worn, these coats are symbolic garments.
>
> Frequent trips to the Southwest rekindle my enjoyment of Indian beaded crafts, which incorporate the old glass trade beads with sewn, embroidered or woven techniques. All my pieces are constructed with a threaded needle. Although I have thought about gluing beads to shorten the laborious application process, I continue sewing them on one by one. It is important to me to fasten the beads firmly with a continuous thread. I value this form of beaded embroidery not just for its aesthetic appearance, but for the meditative time the working process offers.
>
> Because of the exceptionally large size of *Royal Coat,* (shown on the facing page), I used long 2¼-in., intricately textured beads. The large format also provided the surface for an expansive design in pairs of complementary colors.
>
> When I began the piece, I had in mind certain 19th-century Plains Indian coats I had recently seen. These coats were made of buckskin but were cut like officers' coats. The combination of tribal and European materials (hide, ochre paint, beads, military braid) and shapes (fringed and formfitting) intrigued me because of its richness. I visualized my own ceremonial coat, stiff with green beads and gold braid, that would evoke a sense of celebration rather than preparation for war. Like elaborately decorated armor, *Royal Coat* symbolizes both protection and attractiveness. The painstaking labor involved in its embroidery testifies to the worthiness of its imaginary wearer.

MARY SNYDER BEHRENS

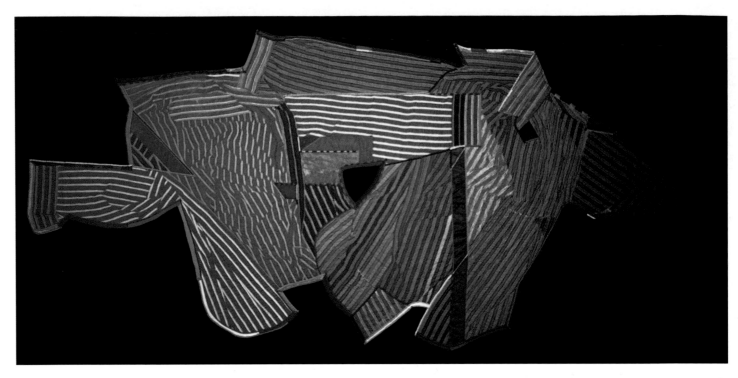

What About It

1987; 33 in. by 70 in.; two men's
shirts, ribbon, bias tape; machine
stitching. (Collection of Clyde and
Paula Brown, Cincinnati, Ohio;
photo by Mary Snyder Behrens.)

"I think I can do as much, if not more, working
with thread than I could ever do with paint."
Mary Snyder Behrens is one of many artists trained
in painting and drawing who has discovered the
limitless possibilities of thread. Using discarded
shirts as her canvas, she probes the artistic potential of fabric, appliqué and machine embroidery.

Behrens looks back on a steady progression
of questions and answers that led her from painting and drawing to her current work. Her first
step was to move away from oil painting into
gouache and watercolor. She built up layers of
color in gouache and examined the subsequent
color interactions. She was concerned with what
happened when one color was applied on top of
another or laid side by side. This layering of color
suggested possibilities in collage, and she put
painting aside for a time in order to work with
paper and found objects. Having sewn clothes
since she was quite young, she naturally had fabrics on hand to add to the collage. The urge to
stitch, then, could not be resisted.

Her paintings and collages were done in a typical rectangular format, but the fabric pieces suggested other possibilities. Behrens was interested in the wearable-art movement, but knew she did not want to make garments exclusively. The kimono shape particularly attracted her, however, since it related to the rectangular format of most paintings and collages. For a time she explored this shape but felt it did not have sufficient visual tension:

> I did a lot of figure drawing when I was an undergraduate, and the gestural shape just really intrigued me. However, my gouache paintings were still lifes, and I'd gotten so far away from the gesture that I felt I needed to get back to it somehow. A lot of beautiful, jewel-like kimonos were very far removed from anything I considered a gesturally motivated art. They never showed any conflict. Working with the shirts, getting that almost human form without the face, was important for me. You could feel the tension in it.

The gestural effect is particularly powerful in *What About It* (on the facing page), made on a base of two men's shirts. The outflung arms and overlapping shapes are accented by the rhythmic pattern of lines, checks, dots and stripes that cavort across the surface. All that is missing is a body or two inside to bring it to life.

As she moved away from paint toward embroidery and appliqué, Behrens found new ways of exploring color interaction. Working with threads, she says, allowed her to "put colors on top of one another and they didn't turn into mud." For example, a pink fabric worked with yellow stitching gives an orange effect but still retains the individual colors of pink and yellow. By altering contrasting color values and hues, Behrens transforms the flat surface of *What About It* into a sequence of shifting planes. "I can make areas of the shirt recede or come forward, or disappear, so that you don't even know it's

Edo Wan

1988; 38 in. by 45 in.; man's shirt, woman's shirt, ribbon, bias tape; appliqué, machine stitching. (Collection of Robert and Dianna Delgado-Mullen, Covington, Kentucky; photo by Mary Snyder Behrens.)

part of the shirt anymore. When I was painting I liked breaking up the picture plane, creating the illusion of having different angles. I can do that kind of breakup with ribbons and stripes now."

Edo Wan (shown above and in the sidebar on p. 60) has strong contrasts of hot and cool colors. It is constructed from a man's shirt and a woman's shirt, fused to make a harmonious form. Overlapping patterns, curving ribbons and strong, angular lines work over and around the surface, creating new shapes that activate the entire piece.

Analysis of a design

A finished piece of art rarely reveals the process by which is it made. A good work appears to have been conceived and developed all at once. In an after-the-fact analysis, Mary Snyder Behrens shares the compositional choices she made as *Edo Wan* (see the photo on p. 59) was created:

"The top drawing shows the combination of two shirts, an orange one (1) and a blue one (2). Broken symmetry was used in the sense that the arrangement of the shirts was symmetrical and yet at the same time, intentionally asymmetrical. The stripe pattern of the blue shirt was used to establish strong vertical, horizontal and diagonal axes. The two predominant colors, blue and orange, are highly similar in value and intensity, but highly distinctive as complementary hues (they are opposites on the color wheel). Note that variations of blue and orange are also used as accents (3 and 4). The axis lines were intended to be parallel to each other. There is both repetition and variance in the thickness and length of the lines used. For example, the scalloped line and the larger serpentine line are different in certain ways, and yet they both echo the movement of the bottom edge of the artwork.

"The bottom drawing is based on the the repetition of the square as a motif (5); the vertical and horizontal axes were linked in such a way that a diagonal axis is also implied. This same device was also used to blend the blue shirt and orange shirt together, confusing their boundaries and causing them to overlap visually by creating a common denominator. The flower motif (6) functions in much the same way. By moving the flowers into other areas of the work (7) where they did not occur initially, the blue and orange territories begin to be confused, in part because flower shapes and square shapes are similar enough to tend to be mistaken for one another."

Mary Snyder Behrens diagrams the design decisions that went into the making of Edo Wan.

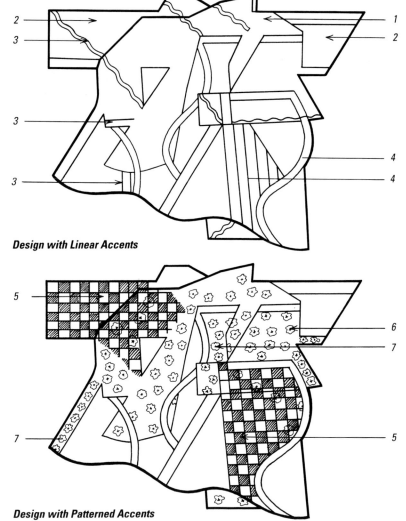

Design with Linear Accents

Design with Patterned Accents

Red Rockets

1988; 31 in. by 40 in.; fabric collage, bias tape; appliqué, machine stitching; detail at right. (Courtesy of Miriam Perlman Gallery, Chicago; photos by Mary Snyder Behrens.)

Metallic squares on a dark ground, like illuminated windows in a nighttime city, are a leitmotif in *Red Rockets* (shown above). Over this pattern float curving shapes splashed with flowers, stripes and brushlike strokes of color. Pure high-intensity hues of blue and red stab the darkness. One outflung sleeve, the suggestion of shirt fronts and a crisply cut shirttail serve as a reminder of the garment this once was.

Angles and corners dominate the work. "In painting they tell you that the hardest part is the corners. I've eliminated the four corners of the rectangle, but I've added many more." Rather than finding an easy way out of this compositional challenge, Behrens has developed it into one of the strengths of her work.

Behrens takes advantage of the irregular shapes of shirts, whether keeping them intact and unfolding them, or cutting them apart. A basic shirt shape is always symmetrical, but in her hands it is reconstructed into a composition that is invariably asymmetrical. She thoughtfully appraises this unbalancing act:

> There is a sense in which it is true that nearly all my works are more or less asymmetrical. I don't dwell on that while I'm working, but I do think about it now and then. On the one hand, I think it might be fair to say that I avoid symmetry, especially the stagnant and stifling kind that is commonly found in kaleidoscopic images, pinwheels, mandala symbols, snowflakes and wallpaper. For my purposes, it is usually too redundant, too predictable and virtually always too easy to read.
>
> On the other hand, there's a sense in which all of my artwork is strongly based on symmetry. I rarely, if ever, use centric or kaleidoscopic symmetry, but I frequently begin with bilateral symmetry, in which one side of the artwork is an echo or answer to the other side. But even

then, I always use broken symmetry in which I set up a precarious blend of continuity and disruption, of repetition and surprise.

In *What About It,* two shirts are laid out side-by-side in a relationship of bilateral symmetry, but the symmetry is never allowed to dominate the asymmetrical complexities, the features that tend to be seen as erratic, unpredictable and disturbing. There is a wonderful passage in one of E. H. Gombrich's books in which he says that beauty lies "somewhere between boredom and confusion." That's part of what I'm attempting to do. Unrelieved symmetry tends to be boring, extreme asymmetry confusing. I want a disquieting mixture of both.

From her collection of thrift-shop shirts and other materials, she begins to assemble a piece. "I throw it around and select other things that I think I might want to use with it. It snowballs for a while, and then I start eliminating things. I cut things up, arrange and rearrange them until I have a shape that I like." She builds on a base of unbleached muslin, arranging the shirt shapes. Small squares or flowers are ironed onto WonderUnder fusible interfacing, cut out and applied to the composition, again with heat. The WonderUnder prevents raveled edges and adds a slight stiffness to the fabric. At this point the work may rest for a while, because Behrens wants to be sure it is compositionally strong before the stitching takes place.

There is no going back to rip out areas once the machine stitching begins. She must work over the entire piece since she uses a lot of long, diagonal satin-stitched lines. There are many layers of fabric, already stiffened by WonderUnder and machine stitching, and the work is bulky. Using a zigzag foot on her professional model Singer 20 sewing machine to help keep the fabrics in line, Behrens sews row upon row of color.

Finishing the work so it retains its irregular edge is also quite a feat of engineering. Behrens works with many layers of stiff fabric, adding even more as she backs the work. A finished piece can be as thick as ½ in. After all the sewing on the front is completed to her satisfaction, she presses the work from the back, then fuses two layers of Pellon, a nonwoven interfacing, to begin the final steps in preparing a piece for mounting. At several strategic points within the work, she will add extra stiffening with Pellon so the work will ultimately remain flat against the wall. Bias tape sewn around the work finishes all raw edges. Next, she makes a backing. She traces the outline of the work onto muslin, which will form the base of this separate backing section. She then cuts the muslin out, leaving some extra fabric all the way around. On this muslin base, inside the lines of the finished shape, she fuses layers of heavy Pellon and organdy. The extra muslin is folded over all the raw edges of the backing and sewn in place. A strip of Velcro® sewn across the backing will mate with a Velcro®-covered bar for hanging. To sew the finished front to the backing, she uses a line of satin stitch just next to the bias tape around the edges. This satin-stitched line pierces both the work and the backing, holding front and back together.

Despite the elaborate construction involved in every finished piece, Behrens is not one to let technical complexities pose obstacles to her inventiveness. She is thinking that it may be time to apply paint to her work, but she is concerned that paint will stick to her sewing-machine needle and possibly clog the machine. Although she is biding her time on this decision, she may indeed be coming full circle. Having left paint behind to work only with fiber and fabric, she may now return to it to provide another means of transforming her ideas into challenging works of art. "But," she says, "artworks have the same compositional requirement, regardless of media. I was trained as a painter, and although I work in fiber now, my goals and my process are largely unchanged. I think that art should wake us up."

SALLY BROADWELL

Butterfly Wings

1988; 13 in. by 12 in.; fabrics, beads, other embellishments; piecing, quilting, beading. (Private collection; photo by Daryl Bunn.)

Sally Broadwell works on a refined scale to stitch portraits and settings that have a large-as-life sensibility. Her portraits predate the figures and settings, but they carry visual cues to later pieces. She discusses her richly textured works:

I've always been fascinated by elegant, decorative and often whimsical examples of historic and ethnic needlework. The delicacy of Oriental embroideries, the intricacy of Persian rugs and the opulence of European ecclesiastical vestments have all inspired my contemporary approach. They invoke an emotional response that I strive to recreate with modern materials.

The miniaturized scale in which I work helps promote a personal interaction with the piece and its complexities. It is this complexity that draws the viewer into the frame to explore and discover.

The materials I use are not precious, although they try to be—they're seductive and intriguing. I collage elements borrowed from various historic and ethnic cultures and recombine them to create my own statement.

My embroidery technique was adapted to get a pointillist effect in the portraits. I begin with a black and white photograph, which I visually transfer to graph paper in shades of grey. These blocks are then worked on an even-weave fabric in corresponding values of colored threads in a satin stitch. As each block of the fabric is filled, the pictorial illusion emerges. I use 50 to 100 different colors of thread in the solid value areas in order to create an interesting visual texture and complexity.

I'm interested in working with light. This light is either emitted from within through the manipulation of values or reflected from the surface embellishments. The inner light is implied and creates an illusion. The surface sparkle is real. It changes with movement and brings the image to life.

My work exemplifies what women have been creating throughout history. It contains the subtleties, the tedium and the pride in workmanship that is the core of women's work.

David

1984; 15 in. by 13 in.; cotton floss on cotton, embellishments; embroidery, piecing, quilting. (Photo by Daryl Bunn.)

MARY BERO

Duel: Self-Portrait

1987; 4 in. by 4 in.; cotton floss on
cotton fabric; embroidery.
(Collection of the Sadinoff Family;
photo by Jim Wildeman.)

Straight on and unblinking, Mary Bero's iconic
faces confront their viewers. They look us right
in the eye, forcing us to address their highly patterned, fragmented features. Like force fields
made up of waves of color, thousands of tiny
bright stitches work together to generate tremen-
dous energy—"crackling energy," as she calls it.

Because of the power of the image, it is easy
to think of her work as much larger than it is.
Her pieces are quite small in reality, ranging in
size from 3 in. by 3 in. to little more than 12 in.
But like a tiny baby's cry in the night, they generate an immediate gut reaction.

What is it about her work that provokes?
First, it is the high-energy color—strong, unsettling combinations, worked over and into what
we usually consider a precious commodity, the
face. The features are all there, rendered in a very
direct manner, a bit larger than life in proportion
to the size of the head. The effect is masklike.
And like some painted masks, the faces are divided
by stripes, dotted with bits of color, heavily
highlighted and full of raw energy. The lips are
either bright and sealed or parted with teeth con-
spicuously bared.

The head usually fills the center, right out
to a stitched frame, itself highly patterned and
creating its own dynamic field. In the space remaining behind the head are more patterns,
checks, stripes, pointillist dots or zigzags. There's
no place for the eye to rest, and the work pul-
sates, barely contained within the simple fabric-
covered mat and black frame. These are challenging, memorable and haunting works.

One such piece is *Duel: Self-Portrait* (at left).
Highlighted in the arresting gaze of its glowing
topaz eyes, the face is divided. Richly colored
French knots blend smoothly, defining the contours on one half, while the other is covered
with geometric patterns of lines, angled and
abrupt. Tiger-striped tufted hair echoes the color
of the eyes. Within the noisy patterns of squares,
stripes, dots and dashes, the lips are sealed, but
the eyes clearly glow.

Bero does at least one self-portrait a year,
sometimes more. In all her work, she engages
herself as well as her audience in exploring and
confronting the nature of seeing and perceiving.
"If I did something on a previous piece, I try doing something different, continually changing,
challenging myself." She calls this approach
working from a "neo-viewpoint," one in which
she makes demands on herself to see in new

Graffitti: Still Life

1988; 4⅛ in. by 4⅛ in.; cotton floss
on cotton fabric; embroidery.
(Collection of Fran Saltzer; photo
by Jim Wildeman.)

ways. She begins without a preconceived idea. There is no story to tell. But she says, "By the time I work on a certain area or a certain figure, I have a relationship, a rapport with it. It's just a growing thing. I think it's best that way; it stays fresh. You don't really control, you develop."

Bero's working processes have developed over many years, and part of her process includes improvising on new ways to begin a work. She feels her way into a new piece, often beginning with the border. As patterns and figures emerge on the border, she establishes her visual language, releasing ideas for the central portion of the work. Using the ideas generated in the border has worked well for Bero, but she is uneasy when a process becomes too comfortable. In *Graffitti: Still Life* (above right), she challenged herself to work in a different way. "It was a breakthrough for the embroidery; I jumped out of the border. I had ideas about a lot of things and instead of thinking I'd use them in some other pieces, I just used them all." The graffitti resurface, taking over the foreground in *Ideogram* (below right).

Another way Bero begins a work is by using the sewing machine to stitch a preliminary grid on the fabric. This forms a simple pattern within which to begin developing the language of the piece. The machine stitch also adds extra body to the fabric, making it a sturdier surface upon which to work. Varying her designing methods keeps the work fresh.

Working on several pieces concurrently allows Bero to maintain her intensity. Keeping a number of pieces active also enables her to achieve some space and distance from a work that may be giving her problems or one she's tentative about, not knowing where "to take it next." As she focuses on one piece, her mind explores possibilities for another. This way of working has its frustrations, however, since it seems

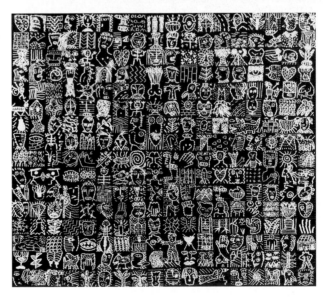

Ideogram

1988; 8 in. by 8¾ in.; cotton floss on
cotton fabric; embroidery. (Photo by
Jim Wildeman.)

Notes from an artist's journal:
A work in process

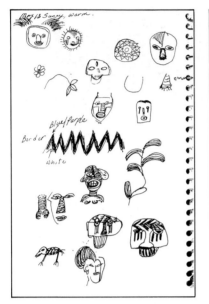

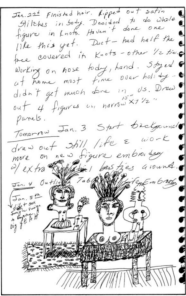

Mary Bero's notebook reveals the development of Ideogram *and sketches for* Grafitti: Still Life.

Mary Bero likens *Ideogram* (shown on p. 65) to a visual diary, worked over many weeks in 1988, wherein a few tiny segments were recorded each day. Its close to 300 images are packed within an 8-in. by 8¾-in. area. As Bero worked on this piece, she kept a journal of the designs and the process, recording what she was stitching and thinking and doing as she methodically worked out each miniature section. Some pages from her journal reveal this day-by-day process. Since it's completion, *Ideogram* has become the source for other work as she extracts a tiny motif and magnifies it. Her notebook pages reveal her mind at work and its energy transformed into art.

to her that no one piece is ever finished. "But that is part of the whole process, part of accepting the fact that that is how I'm inspired and the way I work best."

Bero is a self-taught artist. She is aware of what she has missed by not having a traditional art education and, conversely, what she has gained by discovering art on her own and "what I didn't have to unlearn." She cites a number of influences. She admires the work of the Mexican artist Frieda Kahlo, whose unflinching gaze in her many self-portraits locks with the viewer's own. Like Kahlo, who was married to the painter Diego Rivera, Bero is also married to a painter, Dennis Nechvatal, and credits him and a circle of their friends with discussions about art issues that were instrumental in challenging and enriching her learning. She studied off-loom weaving and surface design while Nechvatal was in graduate school at Indiana University, but by the time she was ready to return to school, there wasn't a program that seemed appropriate to her. She was already working at her own artistic discovery process and had begun to produce and sell her work. "I was hooked."

Bero recognizes the influence of Vincent Van Gogh, who, she notes, was also self-taught and worked outside the mainstream art world all his life. She has studied his paintings abroad. "It's encouraging that he didn't have to have that stamp of approval to make art. He approached his work with such freshness. He was direct. I've studied the way he used the paint on the surface of the canvas. It reminded me of embroidery, the way that you build up a surface on fabric."

That building up of a surface, layer upon layer, is an important element in Bero's work. Not only does she layer ideas, patterns and information, she also overlaps her tiny stitches. In some mixed-media pieces, she uses paint and thread on a textured Japanese paper. Working on the stretched paper, she paints small dabs of acrylic, frequently adding bits of thread, which adhere to the wet paint. *Head with Braids* (shown at right) is one of this series. She adds the embroidery last, handling what could be a technically difficult combination of paper, fabric, paint and stitches with apparent ease. "I don't really think about doing it or not being able to do it. It just works."

This technical proficiency is even more impressive considering the minute size of the work. Although Bero did some large quilts when she first explored art and fiber, dyeing and piecing them, she found the limitations of a small size, something that could be held in her hand, more appealing. Whether working large or small in scale, she finds the art-making process similar. "It's really the same process. If it works, it works. The one thing I try to stay away from is 'cute,' especially working with embroidery. I don't want to get near that at all."

Bero need not worry about "cute." Her work has been likened to an embroiderer's version of music video, pulsing and always in motion. But unlike most videos, Bero's work commands close attention. It draws viewers into its tiny dynamite-energy world and impels them to look both into the work and within themselves.

Head With Braids

1987; 6¼ in. by 4½ in. by ¼ in.; paper, acrylic, fabric, thread; embroidery, mixed media. (Photo by Jim Wildeman.)

KEIKO YAMAGUCHI

Figure #30 (Absence of Mind)

1989; 17¾ in. by 6¾ in.
by 4¾ in.; mixed media.
(Private collection; photo by
Kyu Sakamaki.)

Figure #37 (Dancing)

1989; 14¼ in. by 12¼in.
by 8 in.; mixed media.
(Private collection; photo by
Kyu Sakamaki.)

Keiko Yamaguchi was born in Japan, but now lives in New York City. Her exquisitely wrought dolls combine materials and embroidery that share the Oriental and Western traditions. She writes about her work:

My parents manage kimono shops, so I was always surrounded by kimonos during my childhood. My father often took me with him when he visited master kimono makers in Kyoto. I've been interested in beautiful fabrics since then.

I studied oil painting and printmaking in high school and college, while I continued to be interested in fabrics. In 1976, while still in college, I began making dolls as gifts for friends.

For the past ten years, I've been collecting old fabrics from kimonos and other clothing, and these materials have inspired my dollmaking. My work began to have more freedom after I saw several fiber sculptures at the Paris Biennial Show in 1980.

I make dolls by combining planning and improvisation. I start with a general idea of the shape and size of the image, but the textures, colors and fabrics will often change as I proceed with the making of the doll. The body is formed from cloth stuffed with various materials. The face is formed from clay, then covered by cloth and painted with watercolors. Cotton and other natural fabrics, as well as old kimono fabric, are used. The cloth is hand embroidered and quilted. The height of the dolls ranges from 2 in. to 24 in.

A lot of my images come from literature, film and music, as well as from visual art. Recently I've become interested in the art of medieval Europe. I'm interested in creating dolls that include images from both the East and the West.

DEIDRE SCHERER

Consideration

1988; 10 in. by 8½ in.; fabric, thread and paper on paper; machine embroidery. (Photo by Jeff Baird.)

The faces are furrowed, lined with living; the eyes look as much inward as outward. There is hardness and sweetness and pain in these portraits. Deidre Scherer takes a strong, unflinching look at life and the inevitability of death. Working within a culture that idolizes youth, strength and physicality, she examines age, weakness and deterioration. By journeying into taboo regions, she is able to celebrate the richness of life and reflect on its passing.

Scherer didn't set out to do portraits of the elderly. As is so often the case in a creative endeavor, she was searching for one thing and found another. In 1980 she was working on a series of wall hangings portraying symbolic images from playing cards. She felt she needed live models to pose for the queens, models who had wisdom and experience in their faces. She went to a nearby nursing home and received permission to sketch some of the residents. The drawings she translated into fabric became so important to her that she never finished the playing-card series. She has focused on portraits of the elderly ever since.

Scherer learned that she needed to focus most clearly on her own understanding of aging and dying. As a child of the Nuclear Age, she accepted death by illness, accident or catastrophe, possibly occurring at a young age. Considerations of growing old—the accumulation of years of experience, ironically offset by diminishing of physical abilities—these were harder issues to face. She recognized her fears, and, in confronting them through her work, has shared her direct and honest vision. She quotes writer Cassandra Langer: "Artists have a powerful advantage.... They can visualize fear, take it, use it, and reach some resolution that helps them affirm being alive."[2]

Scherer's directness and honesty are shared with those she draws. She sketches her models for as long as three hours at a time, with breaks for both herself and her sitters. Over time she shares the stories, songs, reminiscences and dreams of those who sit for her. She takes the gift of these moments very seriously. She listens and responds, and realizes that the communication is important, both to her and her sitter.

The most powerful piece of drawing that I experienced was over a period of a year. I made a wonderful connection and had an incredible rapport with a woman who was in her late eighties. During this year she was dying. I had a lot of guilt about going in and drawing her. Not many people were visiting her, though, and so she encouraged me. At times I felt I was truly invading her personal space and I'd say, "Should I give you space and leave?" She'd say,

"No." So I'd stay there even longer. I saw her through many changes. There were days when she was bitter; she had done the best she could, yet life had dished her up some pretty hard things. And then there were days when she was really fine, going through all kinds of forgiveness. And I could draw her in all these places. I got so much from her, but nobody could understand this. Then a nurse told me that people need a witness and a listener, and I was a listener through my drawing.

Over the years Scherer has accumulated sketches, photographs from books and magazines and pictures that friends send to her. Taking elements from these sources, she creates composite faces. She reflects that the individual face is less important than the visual experience, which reveals a greater truth. Whether it portrays a distinct individual or is a composite, each of these portraits has its own story.

Scherer is reluctant to tell these stories. She is concerned about the privacy of those she portrays, and she has discovered that those who view her work are reminded of their own stories, possessed of a beauty and intensity equal to those that actually inspired the work. The portraits, then, do indeed reflect a universality of experience.

Scherer's experiences with the aged seem to have added an urgency to her own thinking about making the most of one's time. She talks eagerly about the importance of making a space in which to work. Claiming a space, she says, goes hand in hand with claiming time to work. "It doesn't have to be much space, but it has to be a place that you don't have to clear off when dinner comes. That's pretty elemental. I've had a studio established for years, but I'll never forget what it took to actually chop it out of this house and say, 'This is it.'"

There is much to store in her studio, especially her collection of fabrics. Cloth, because of its universal appeal, is the perfect medium for her work. She recognizes that those who view her work also share the experience of cloth. We have cloth next to our bodies from the time we are born until we die. We understand it, are warmed by it and have layers of associations with it, all of which adds to our appreciation and understanding of her work. She says, "Nobody goes up to a painting and imagines themselves swathed in oil."

Scherer speaks with tenderness about cloth: "You can say just about anything in fabric. The eye is led through the fabric field that you've created. It's also exciting that it's tactile. People always want to touch the stuff, and they will if it's not behind glass. The fact is that we've had it on our bodies and we have a deep memory of fabric in us."

Cloth has its detractors in the art world. Scherer remembers beginning to work with it. "I think the bravest thing I ever went through in all this body of work was about ten years ago when I had this image in mind, and I thought, 'I don't know if that's possible.' People would say, 'What are you doing? Are you making baby quilts? That's not a real material to use as an artist.' I worked through that anyway. It's amazing to me when I look back."

There are some limitations Scherer sets when working with cloth. For ten years she has chosen not to overdye the fabrics she works with, so her color choices are sometimes constrained by what is readily available. Some colors may be hard to find if they are not currently in fashion, but because she uses both sides of the printed fabric she has two choices of color with each piece. She enjoys working within these imposed limitations and doesn't worry that she may wait a year to finish or begin a project because the right fabric isn't to be found. She feels that the limitations have helped to ground her. "It's as if you're painting yourself into a corner, and in the next instant that corner has become a door." Another door may be around the next corner, however, since she is beginning to explore combining some dyes and inks with the fabric.

Developing
Time and Place

Like the gradual effects of time in molding a face, Scherer's working method consists of adding one layer at a time. She uses fabrics and machine stitching to appliqué and embroider her portraits.

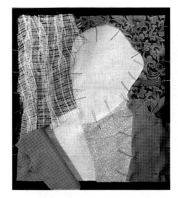

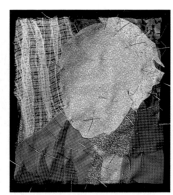

Working on a base fabric of unbleached muslin, Scherer cuts, arranges and pins the first layer of fabrics. (All photos by Diedre Scherer.)

She sews the fabrics in place with a long and wide zigzag stitch, which both positions the fabrics and prevents the edges from fraying.

A delicate print in soft pink tones is added for the face, darker fabrics for shadows and a lighter value for the hair. As these are added, the initial background fabrics begin to lose their dominance, and the face becomes prominent.

A third and fourth layer are added, with each line of stitching providing additional shading and highlighting. Dark lines are added to the curtain on the left. Scherer uses both zigzag and straight stitch to soften the features and accent or diminish edges where fabrics meet and complete Time and Place *(1989; 9½ in. by 8 in.).*

Layers of fabric form the structure for Scherer's work. On a ground of unbleached muslin she pins rough shapes and outlines them with a wide and long zigzag stitch on her Pfaff sewing machine. She uses very fine pins, finding that thicker ones cause the fabric to pucker. After much consideration ("it goes up on the wall, then down on the floor"), she overlays smaller bits of fabric to define features and add highlights and shadows. Drawing with machine stitching, she adds lines and shadows. These drawing and shading lines simultaneously secure the fabrics.

Scherer enjoys the process of cutting the fabrics in the air with scissors, delighting in creating simultaneously an edge and a shape. Working with line is very important to her. There is the line that the scissors make, cutting directly into the fabric. There is the pencil line of her sketches, which follows the push or pull of the hand. And there is the machine-stitched line that forms between her fingers. "You're moving the ground, and the point is happening between, so it's a completely different way of producing a line."

She stitches on paper for some of her work, and finds it a demanding material to use with the sewing machine. "You're really on the line with it. You can see the puncture wounds, whereas in fabric the holes fill in." *Consideration* (shown on p. 69) is a work that combines paper and fabric. The elderly woman appears to be in a harsh light. "She was in her garden, and her look is not just being in her garden, but someplace else in herself. She is definitely reaching back." The strong value contrasts her tired, inward expression.

Affirmation

1989; 9 in. by 8 in.; nonwoven fabric, dyes, thread; machine embroidery. (Photo by Jeff Baird.)

Eva's Alma Mater

1988; 28 in. by 24 in.; fabric, thread; machine embroidery. (Collection of Arnold and Stella Herzog; photo by Jeff Baird.)

The woman in *Affirmation* (at left on the facing page) peers out in a hawklike manner. She has conquered fear and, with an immense effort, has turned it into affirmation. Scherer experimented with black dye on a nonwoven, translucent material for this work, creating a strong portrait in black, white and grey.

Shifts in color value are important in Scherer's work. Her early pieces, primarily in black and white, were frustrating to her at the time, but, in looking back, she recognizes their strength and the base they gave her for her current work. She still limits her use of color, allowing for subtle shifts in values to give the work a gentle complexity. *Eva's Alma Mater* (at right on the facing page), although rendered in soft, warm tones, could easily be imagined in black and white. Scherer uses very light areas surrounded by dark to focus attention on the woman's face and hands. "You enter the portrait through the hands in her lap."

In all of Scherer's work, attention is focused on the person. The stories the pieces evoke are enhanced by visual clues that suggest a sense of place: the faded, richly patterned wallpaper; a chair; a lamp or a plant. Even when place is not revealed, Scherer evidently has one in mind, as in the harsh outdoor light in *Consideration*.

In some recent works exploring stronger color contrasts, Scherer eliminated markers that revealed a setting. In these the face takes up the entire canvas with only a minimal background. In *Converse* (above right), a portrait of Scherer's father, the colored background sets off the strong definition of his features. Sadness and solitude are reflected in this portrait:

"I thought about his inside conversation, and also my youngest child's geometry book. So the title plays with the meanings of the word *converse*. It also has a very spiritual side. To help underline the kind of conversation that was going on, I chose colors that wouldn't necessarily agree. I had an incredible attraction to Van Gogh's heads and their color, and that's where the mustard color came in. I wanted to take a challenge and see if I could bend the rules. I actually don't think that *Converse* came as close to his likeness as another that I did, but I really like it better."

Converse

1989; 10½ in. by 10 in.; fabric, thread; machine embroidery. (Photo by Jeff Baird.)

There are always decisions—about materials, style and degree of emotional involvement. In making these decisions, she says, the visual element must always come first:

Once I was inspired to build a piece around a fabric that never became part of the finished work. In this portrait there was a mirror behind the sitter that caught the back of her head. I was having a lot of trouble. I finally singled out the fabric I had started with as the problem. It was like a mirror itself—a metallic silk that cost about $50 a yard! I cut it out, put something else in that area, and the piece finally settled down and worked. No matter what level you are working at, the technique is always visual first.

Scherer firmly believes in the power of the visual. While her pieces evoke strong emotions, she notes that some may "fall apart" if she works only from an emotional component. She is first and foremost a visual artist. "It takes a lot of trust to believe that the visual will deliver you."

CAROLINE DAHL

Terror Sampler II

1987; 17¾ in. by 14 in. by ½ in.;
cotton floss on muslin;
embroidery. (Photo by Newell
Color Lab, San Francisco.)

Caroline Dahl is a visual narrative artist in the tradition of Southern women writers like Flannery O'Connor. Dahl's stories, much like O'Connor's, are short, simply told and possessed of humor that packs a deft punch. Her characters are frequently depicted in pairs, at loose ends, and almost always in conflict. They play and party, but life is far from easy for them. They may not be at their best, but they are surely real.

Characters of this sort populate Dahl's series, *The Terror Samplers,* which depict couples living on the edge—the edge of murder, mayhem and poverty. Yet they are saved from the more lurid realities of that state by Dahl's humor, albeit occasionally black.

Trixie "Baby Doll" Lamé and Serge L'Amour are going at it tooth and nail in *Terror Sampler* (at left). Around their battling figures float the embroidered axioms of their everyday lives: "lower back pain," "corn dogs," "broken dreams," and "low down dirty dog." It is as if these phrases are the truncated songs and advertisements blaring from a country-western radio station played at full volume, adding to the chaos at hand. The sampler reads, "You've made my life a living burning hell."

Dahl's animal subjects, however, seem to have more fun; she treats them with a lighter, more whimsical touch. They are infinitely more resourceful and talented, have great adventures and pursue rich fantasy lives. Skwabby, Dahl's small green Bolivian parrot ("He's an actual pet, so he's like a person") comes in for plenty of excitement. In *Four Faces of Skwabby* (on the facing page), the parrot dreams of the future. We see him dressed as Quetzalcóatl, one of the principal gods of the Aztec pantheon, honored as the inventor and patron of the arts and crafts. He appears next with cape and tights as Super Skwabby,

Four Faces of Skwabby

1988; 14¼ in. by 25½ in.; cotton floss on muslin; embroidery. (Photo by Newell Color Lab, San Francisco.)

defending against a menacing predator, the huge cat lurking behind him. Then Skwabby is robed and crowned as a king, "a beneficent monarch," and finally, he dreams of piles of money and the "Road to the Future."

Skwabby is cast as the lead of another work, which resulted from a dream Dahl had about her pet and survival. She describes the story, which is illustrated in two scenes:

> There was an evil, dark force seeping out of the room, letting me know something was wrong, so I made it a cat. I walked in the room and it was all disheveled, and I thought, "Oh my God, what's happened to Skwabby?" I heard a little noise and looked under the table and there was Skwabby. He'd been shot in the chest, had two black eyes and was seeing stars [depicted as little birds flying around his head], but I knew he was okay. He was up walking around and I knew everything was all right.

The anxiety generated by the dream is graphically communicated by the scene of destruction we see in the first segment. We move in closer to see that what was a tiny patch of green under the table is Skwabby, beaten but unbowed. He's a survivor. The work, with a nod to Goya's *The Dream of Reason* is titled *From the Sleep of Reason* (shown on p. 76).

It is easy to get involved in the stories Dahl stitches and forget that these works are embroideries. In her matter-of-fact manner, she describes getting started in embroidery:

> Embroidery is just something I started doing one day. I found some of my mother's old floss, some muslin and a hoop lying around and got going. I taught myself the stitches by looking at other stitches, on clothes mostly, and copying them. I still do embroidery because I enjoy it and it fits well in my life. It's a very portable business, requiring no heavy equipment or large areas of work space. The materials involved are pleasant to touch, and I like working with the vibrant colors of DMC floss.

1985; 14 in. by 18 in. by 2 in.;
cotton floss on muslin;
embroidery. (Private collection;
photo by Newell Color Lab,
San Francisco.)

Dahl's vocabulary of embroidery stitches includes couching, stem, satin, long and short ("sometimes longer, sometimes shorter"), chain and French knot (see the Glossary on pp. 225-227). Once an idea has struck her, she sketches the basic outlines. When she is satisfied with the spatial relations, she draws the main outlines on muslin with a pencil. She makes color decisions as she works.

Borders frame the work, repeating motifs and adding to the ambience rather like background music or sound effects on a radio drama. In *From the Sleep of Reason* the evil cat steals around a doorway and out into the border, which is littered with little squares and "Skwabby tracks." The little squares are also used, combined with a fancy rendering of Skwabby's name, around the edge of *Four Faces of Skwabby.*

The use of a frame surrounding a central motif is part of the textile tradition, and in her *Terror Sampler* series Dahl also evokes the traditional motifs of early American samplers. Her platitudes are not exactly lofty or exalted, but they come straight from the heart (or they aim for it). She may stitch rows of flowers, but they grow over a dead body, someone who is obviously "pushing up daisies." She scatters motifs within the work, but they are more likely to be skulls and crossbones than hearts and flowers. "I like the idea that samplers are some of the earlier forms of needlework, and it just seemed like a perfect opportunity to do something similar. I just wanted to fool around with it. That always seems to be my preference, to make fun, get some humor out of it."

Music and embroidery

The Will to Dress

1987; 17¼ in. by 17¼ in. by 1 in.; cotton floss and beads on muslin; embroidery. (Photo by Stone Photo, Lexington, Kentucky.)

Caroline Dahl is a pianist who has performed solo and ensemble work since 1972. She speaks of the relationship of music and embroidery:

"I'm not thinking of a specific song or even a specific style of music while I'm working that I'm aware of, but music permeates all of life. I think it's in the way we walk; certainly rhythms are in our lives, just the rhythms of the way we do our everyday things. Music is something that I had a very early attraction to and have kept it, and so all of that is working when I'm designing and embroidering, but it's on a pretty subconscious or unconscious level. The music and the embroidery seem to me to be two different things. Music is a sort of active, spontaneous, right-at-the-moment sort of thing; the needlework is a more thought-out, contemplative, quiet activity. Of course, they're both very individual processes, especially the needlework. I do play piano by myself, but more often with other people. Performance is a large part of the music in my life and is the most exciting part. I would never really say that the actual working of embroidery is very exciting. It's the planning and thinking of it that's the exciting part. I don't think making music and making art answer the same questions, although it all helps me to express whatever it is I want to express."

There is no sign of the peaceful, sweet and moral tone of early samplers in her work, but because of the visual references she makes, we recognize the connection and are let in on her joke. The works don't terrify, as the sampler titles suggest, but we laugh and wonder what prompted Trixie and Serge to try to throttle each other. Her stories set the scene; we supply the conclusions.

What is the source of these characters, these ideas? Caroline Dahl has another life as an artist. Her livelihood is derived from playing the piano with a blues band, and she is on the road with them most of the year. Quite possibly, she has met some of her characters along the way in smoke-filled bars or at parties. On the road she looks and listens "for just funny things that exist in life," her musician's ear enjoying words as well as music. "I know I heard, 'You made my life a living, burning hell,' probably somewhere in a comedy routine. Sometimes I go at a piece from a strictly humorous standpoint and create the characters and imagery around something that's funny, like a human foible."

Dahl stitches the foibles and frailties of people and household pets, treating them with understanding and tempering their troubles with a touch of wit and whimsy. Dahl stitches a comical world—edgy, often biting, earthy and energetic, detailed and full of action—to the beat of accompanying music—the insistent rhythm of rock and roll, the moan of the blues—and always with the lusty warmth of a lot of soul.

DEBORAH J. FELIX

A Bird Told Me the Answer

1988; 34 in. by 34 in.; paint, fabric,
charcoal; fabric collage, quilting.
(Collection of Elaine Ann Spence;
photo by Deborah J. Felix.)

Deborah Felix cuts through layers, quite literally, to explore relationships and individual attitudes. Much of her work has relied upon reverse appliqué, a technique primarily associated with the molas made by the Kuna Indians of Panama. Created by layering fabrics and cutting through each one to reveal colors beneath, molas characteristically feature intense color relationships and strong patterns. Felix has enlarged the scale of the classic mola for her work but often upholds tradition with her choice of bright colors and the singular patterns that she uses. Her recent pieces also include painting and drawing on the fabrics, and her subject matter has evolved from examining the relationship between two people to focusing on a single figure. She describes her work and the changes it has undergone:

> In the past few years I have concentrated on creating larger-than-life wall pieces that depict two people engaged in their daily activities. Each piece shows a specific environment: the living room, the kitchen table, a couch. While the figures were abstracted through the use of patterned fabrics, the backgrounds were intentionally created so that they could be anyone's home, anywhere.
>
> Recently, after a move to San Diego, California, there has been a noticeable shift in the subject matter and the use of fabric. Now there is one large central figure that is painted very realistically and confronts the viewer's innermost thoughts about love, death and the future. Each background is awash with a strong sense of light. Patterned fabrics are combined with painted fabrics so that the line between commercially printed and hand-painted cloth is blurred. The figures have moved out of the home and into an outdoor environment.
>
> In spite of the seriousness of of the work, there is still the attitude portrayed in each piece that one must laugh at one's failures and successes in life, and keep plodding on with blind faith in the future.

Artists who work with fabric and thread speak fondly and often passionately about their materials and tools. They appreciate the enormous palette of color, texture and pattern available. There is the added value for them of working with fabric, a material with which each viewer has both physical and emotional associations. Artists are frustrated when fabric works are often considered "less-than-fine" art, but that doesn't stop them from creating with it.

Tools may be as simple as a needle, scissors and a thimble or as complicated as a computerized sewing machine, but they are the means for producing a finely crafted object, and as such, are treated with care. Working as one with the materials and tools, the artist enjoys the sense of mastery that comes with practice and control.

ON FABRIC, THREADS AND OTHER MATERIALS

B. J. Adams: "Fabric and thread can give a variety of surfaces not possible with paint. I get seduced by beautiful materials. I've decided that's all right. Why don't I just collect beautiful materials instead of something like teacups?"

Deidre Scherer: "Fabric is soft and you can say just about anything with it. It's very accessible. People go and stand in front of a piece of my work whether they want to or not; they're just sucked right in."

Susan Wilchins: "I love cotton. It has a sturdiness that I really like, and it has flexibility. I love the way that it frays on the edge, which is very different from the way rayon or silk or linen frays. There is a connection to that material for me with the kind of images I'm trying to do. It has a life to it, but it's not like the life that silk has, for silk is a very alive fabric. Cotton has a kind of life too, but it's basic and earthy. If silk is royalty, then cotton is middle class."

Lee Malerich: "Although I'm making art, maybe the craftsperson in me allows me to see more of the process than a painter would see. We let the materials say more, do some leading. A layer of meaning is superimposed on my work, I believe, because of the materials I choose to use; fabrics, special virgin ones that come together in new ways, and old ones—discarded garments or, especially, the commercial fabrics. These are from the end of a printing run where the ink runs with great frenzy, gradating from raw fabric to grand intensity."

Joan Schulze: "I use a lot of silk because of its luxurious feel and its sheen. I get a really sensuous experience from it. I love cotton for its variety and strength; it is the foundation of the work; it holds things up. I like nylon for its transparency and tissue paper for collage. I like paint for its plastic quality, and also because the child in me long ago thought that painting was what you did as an artist. I think I can do a lot with paint that still leaves the integrity of the cloth and makes it even

more personal. I'm creating my own cloth; I don't have to search for it in stores; it's not going to be like anyone else's. It's this unique thing that I can hardly repeat myself. I like cloth a lot, and, in fact, I think I'm a constructionist. I like the cutting, and the piecing, and the building. I think that if I hadn't found cloth, I probably would have found wood and built things."

Stephen Beal: "When I was a toddler, my mother could always quiet me down by letting me play with her spools of thread. I loved being able to pick up colors and put them together. This delight has not diminished over the years. I feel real joy holding in my hands the colors I'm using. I've just gotten over a five-year crush on DMC #817 (red). Now it looks like I'm heading toward blue."

Merrill Mason: "I work in fiber because I'm drawn to its associations with the feminine and the domestic. By using fiber collage, I can mix painting, printmaking and photography with fiber in a way that allows spontaneity in the creative process."

Jan Kozicki: "Choosing embroidery as a medium of self-expression provides me with a world of sensitive material I need to fulfill my imagination. I want to use fabric and threads and make colors with stitches. I want to look at it, hold it and feel it. It begins to talk to me from the first piercing of needle and thread through fabric."

Nancy Erickson: "I think there's a big advantage to working with fabrics in that you can juxtapose colors, and you can't do that in a painting. It's kind of a technical problem to rip a painting apart."

Robert Burningham: "Stitches as such were of little interest to me — only what effect I could produce with them. I use stitches mainly to secure the threads to the base material. Direction, content and effect are most important for me. I tried everything and anything I could get hold of at electronic-surplus stores (wire, bits and pieces, flotsom and jetsam). I finally found out about beads. What a day!"

Sandra Nickeson: "While beads do not find their way into each and every one of my works, they have become an integral part of my visual vocabulary. I continue to marvel over the magic they suggest, even scattered — as they often are — over my studio floor. "

Lynn Sward: "I'm certainly not ready to pack it in. I have all this fabric to sew."

ON TOOLS

Lloyd Blanks: "It's very possible that I have the distinction of being the only needleworker in more than ten years who has never lost a needle. After five years of good and faithful service, still in its prime and showing no wear, my first tapestry needle was retired to an index card for my files.... I came across an extra-long needle, a no. 16

darner's needle, which I filed to bluntness. I am comfortable with the way it goes in and out of the canvas, and it suits the size of my hands better than a regular tapestry needle."[3]

Merrill Mason: "Using a copy machine to transfer a photograph to fabric is a liberating thing. A lot of people don't like the imposition of a machine in their process, but for me it is liberating. I can control the machine only to a certain point, and that absolves me of a certain amount of responsibility."

Beverly Moor: "I'm always watching to be sure that I'm breaking the rules concerning the capacity of the sewing machine, which takes concentration and discipline. I enjoy the holes left from the needle with no thread, so I run the machine without thread quite often."

ON EXPLORING NEW MATERIALS AND PROCESSES

Arturo Alonzo Sandoval: "How do I get acquainted with a new material? Initially, if I have something new, and if an idea does not come to me at all, it just sits there in the corner and I look at it. That is part of the listening process. There is no need for me to jump in and make a sample and a study and take valuable time away from what I'm doing at present. I can look at that and just say, 'When will that become part of my repertoire?' I try not to force anything. I don't believe in that. The word *force* is not a part of my

philosophy. *Experience,* maybe, but not *force.* And *choice, offering choice.* But in terms of new materials that come my way, I have some wonderful things that I haven't done anything with, and one of my students will need something, and I'll share it with them. I'm not madly rushing into places where angels fear to tread."

Merrill Mason: "I don't take classes on technique. I think about the effect I want to produce, and how I'm going to do it. I'm solving technical problems in the process and trying to end up with something that looks fairly spontaneous. It's difficult just to face it and work through a technical problem. The anxiety never goes away, but after you do it enough times, eventually you gain enough experience and self-confidence to know that you can solve each problem. It's surprising how often I will use some discarded process in another work. It really ends up expanding your base of knowledge, and for me, there's a real sense of pride and a feeling of mastery and self-confidence."

justine Vaughn: "Since I started to dye and paint fabric, I've not bought a commercial print. The satisfaction of being in control of color is too great."

WORKING FROM A PATTERNED FABRIC

Anne McKenzie Nickolson: "Begin with a patterned fabric. It can be a simple commercially printed fabric, a pieced fabric, a dyed, silkscreened or otherwise custom surface-designed fabric.

"Analyze that pattern. Look at what the basic skeleton or structure is, look at the color placement (if it is multicolored). Look at how different parts of the pattern sit in space. Do some parts advance and some recede? Look at the movement created by the pattern. Does it move in one straight direction? Does it stagger? Does it hop from place to place? Does it have a special rhythm to its movement?

"Think about how you can make one of these observations become real. What kinds of lines and shapes can you add to the original pattern that will change its overall impact?

"Experiment. Try your ideas out on paper first. Cut a plastic eraser to replicate your pattern on a smaller scale and print it on paper using a stamp pad for ink. (This is just like doing a potato print). Photocopy this to make several copies. Use colored pencils for your additions. Can you clarify the basic structure of the pattern? Can you add colors that will make the existing colors more vibrant, more exciting? Can you make some parts advance in space? Can you make some parts recede? Can you exaggerate the movement of the pattern? Can you change the movement of the pattern?

"Try different kinds of lines. Try laying shapes over the pattern. Try putting shapes behind the pattern. Try anything you can think of, then look at what you have done. You won't be able to do everything with any one pattern; you'll have to see a hint of what exists already and then work at bringing that out.

"Use embroidery to develop one of these experiments on your patterned fabric. Remember, don't just outline or restate what already exists. Make new lines and new shapes that will change the impact of the pattern. Don't limit your decisions to what you have done on paper. More colors are available, more kinds of lines are available. Look carefully at what you have done after each addition. Analyze it again. Continue to strengthen the new image.

DRAWING WITH YOUR NONWRITING HAND

Salley Mavor: "This will help to explore and stretch possibilities in shapes and images, to simplify drawing, to achieve work as fresh as a child's art.

"With your nonwriting hand, draw from life. For example, draw a figure, face, hand, chair or flower. Use a crayon, and go about your drawing in a slow, deliberate manner, with purpose and surety. Try to forget about what you may know about your subject or about drawing technique.

"Observe your subject. *Look,* and draw what you see. Be accurate, but not necessarily realistic. Include the important parts of your subject in your drawing, not every detail. Use as few lines as possible. Stop when you have communicated an image of your subject.

"Do several drawings of different objects or subjects. As you get used to drawing with your nonwriting hand, you may find that you speed up. Don't go too fast. Continue to look at your subject carefully.

"Now try drawing with your writing hand. See how this exercise may have changed the way you draw. You may see a fresher, free approach.

MANIPULATING STRIPES

B. J. Adams: "Use a crisp commercial fabric with either printed or woven even, alternating color stripes, to explore the following ideas:

"How many ways can you change the stripe? There are no limitations. Think three dimensional, manipulation, texture. Think two dimensional, mitering, changing the stripe, direction of the stripe. Consider spirals, circles, curves.

"Draw stripes on paper, fold, cut, connect. How can you use them in drawings? Try some of these drawings in fabric.

"Cut up strips of striped paper and make patterns, both three dimensional and two dimensional. What geometric shapes can be developed using stripes to an advantage?

"Consider stripes in other art and fiber techniques."

GALLERY

THEODORA ELSTON
Artist at Work
(detail)

1986; 2½ in. by 4 in.; silk, painted, paper beads, paint brushes; embroidery, knotting with nylon. (Private collection; photo by Theodora Elston.)

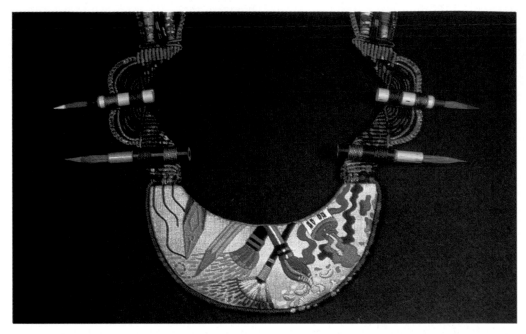

SUSAN SHIE
The Lost and Found

1988; 96 in. by 96 in.; fabric, paint, beads, shells, glasses frames, purses, wooden camel; hand sewn with floss; applied three-dimensional figures of stuffed and sewn fabric. (Photo by Stark and Hansen.)

"This was the first quilt I made during a six-month residency at PS # 1 International Studios Program, in New York City, which was sponsored by the Ohio Arts Council. It deals with homesickness (lost) and becoming acclimated (found); also about searching the local 'lost and founds' for the prescription sunglasses I lost my first week there!"

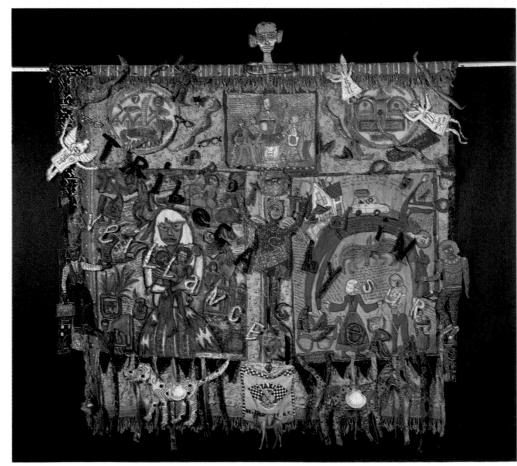

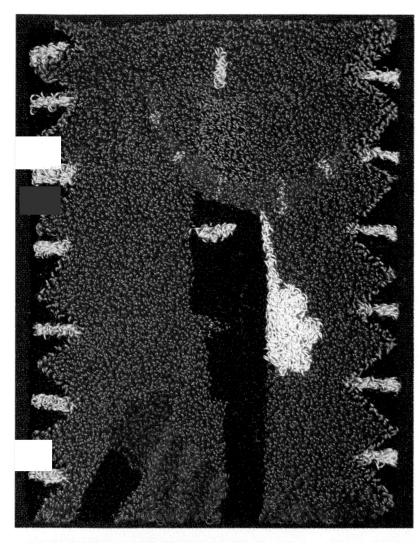

CONNIE LEHMAN
black sarah

1988; 5 in. by 4 in. by ½ in.;
various fibers; igolochkoy
(miniature punch needle) on silk.
(Photo by Connie Lehman.)

"To work the igolochkoy, silk
noil is tightly stretched in an
embroidery hoop. A drawing is put
on the silk, and using silk, cotton
and metallic thread, the
embroidery is worked from the
back with a special punch needle, a
smaller version of that which is
used for hooking rugs."

THEODORA ELSTON
Southwest

1989; frame (not shown): 17 in. by
15 in., embroidery: 6 in. by 4 in.;
silk and cotton embroidery;
padding; acrylic paint on canvas;
painted wooden frame; detail at
near left. (Collection of Mr. and
Mrs. Lawrence B. Rehag; photo by
Theodora Elston.)

"This is one of a series entitled
'Having Fun, Wish You were Here!',
my version of travel postcards. The
postcard-size embroidery grew out
of many car trips taken through the
desert and Indian country when I
was a child. At different ages, many
impressions began to collect in my
head, and a desire to re-experience
the land and cultures of this area
grew. *Southwest* is a release of some
of those impressions."

MARGARET CUSACK
Celebrity Stockings

1984; 16 in. by 23 in.; hand-painted portraits; dyed fabric, glue; collage, machine embroidery. (Photo by Ron Breland.)

JEAN MORROW
On the Beach

1988; 19½ in. by 31¼ in.; assorted fabric snippets, pleated, twisted, overlaid; hand stitched, allowing raw edges and stitches to be exposed. (Collection of Mr. and Mrs. J. B. Fritsche, Eden Prairie, Minnesota; photo by Potter's Photography, Rochester, Minnesota.)

SYBIL RAMPEN
Angel

1988; approximately 4 in. by 4 in.;
milkweed, fabric fragments, thread; machine
sewn between fused layers of plastic wrap,
plastic wrap removed by ironing onto paper;
at left. (Photo by Sybil Rampen.)

GINGER CARTER
Wendy

1984; 7 in. by 9 in.; cotton, silk,
polyester/cotton threads; laid and
stitched on linen; above. (Collection
of Mrs. O. Richards; photo by
Ginger Carter.)

HOLLY HUGHES
Asian Elephant

1989; 48 in. by 60 in. by 24 in.;
chicken wire and canvas frame
covered with grey fabrics;
stitching and appliqué; detail
above. (Photo by Lynn Lown.)

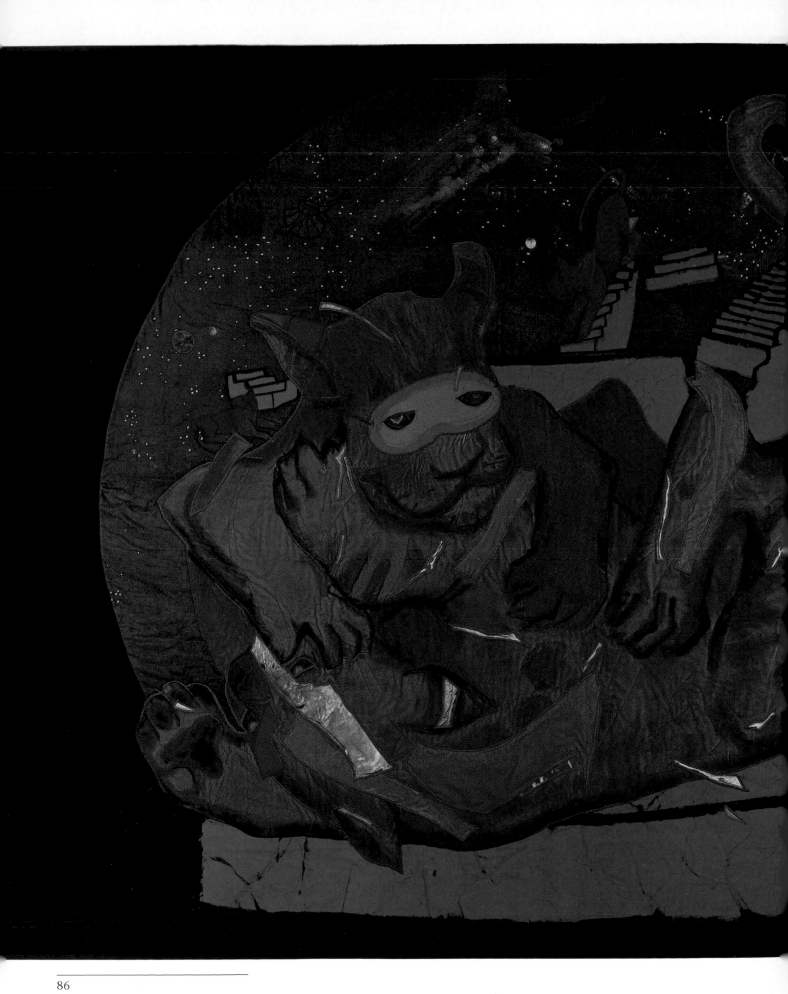

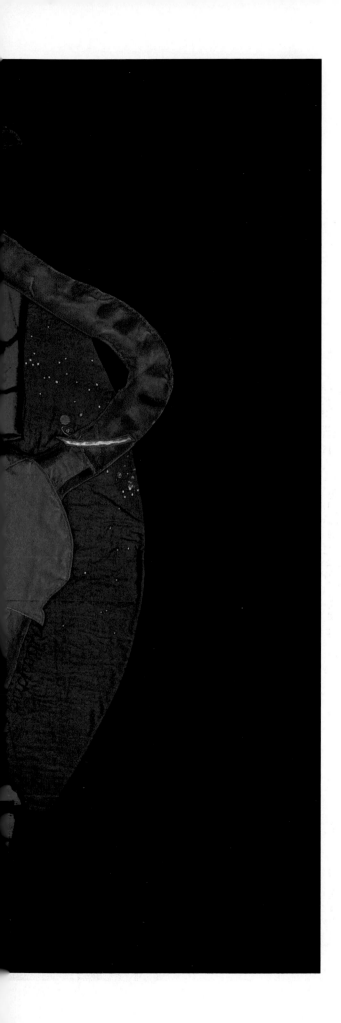

MYSTERIOUS MESSAGES

NANCY N. ERICKSON

The Clear and Present Danger

1987; 86 in. by 77 in.; painted and sewn fabrics. (Photo by Nancy N. Erickson.)

The Forever Wrestlers of Triton

Overleaf: 1989; 69 in. by 73 in.; painted and sewn fabrics. (Photo by Nancy N. Erickson.)

Nancy N. Erickson sees the world as it is and presents it as it might become. Her artwork considers the problems of our planet and forecasts a cataclysmic conclusion. In this end, however, Erickson imagines a new and hopeful beginning. Her world of the future is one built on possibilities, where humans and animals coexist on a nonhierarchical plane, at peace and at play upon the ravaged landscape.

Erickson is well trained to articulate her concerns eloquently, with degrees in zoology, nutrition and fine art. The landscape that is so central to her art has always been a driving force in her life. She grew up on a ranch in Montana, and she and her husband live in a canyon area near Missoula. Her large wall quilts depict a woman at ease in the outdoors, one who finds companionship with large cats, lions, cheetahs and the unusual capybaras. Capybaras, native to Central and South America, are large rodents that can grow to 160 lb. Despite a reputation for intelligence and docility, they are seldom the subject of myth or other preconceived notions that cultures attach to most animals. This makes the capybara welcome material for Erickson's narrative works, as are her own household cats, which serve as her unsuspecting models. Erickson draws them in various poses and angles, projecting the personalities of the domestic creatures onto their wild counterparts.

Many of Erickson's pieces depict a postnuclear holocaust. As survivors, the lone woman and the animals coexist on an equal basis, companions in the midst of the destruction. The old order of cat and mouse, hunter and prey, magnified here to lion and capybara, has been replaced by a new order of cooperation.

The detritus of civilization surrounds them; remnants of dwellings and stairs, as if uncovered at an archeological site, provide for the cohabitants a sort of shelter and structure. Signs of tech-

Vesuvius Revisited: Model and Capybara

1988; 97 in. by 91 in.; painted and sewn fabrics. (Photo by Nancy N. Erickson.)

nology—a light bulb, a television set—are left over in the landscape that is occasionally lit by tongues of fire, man's first technological discovery.

Fire was one of the first elements central to Erickson's work. In the late 1960s much of her work was made in response to the burning in Vietnam. She says, "There is an out-of-controlness about fire. Humans all feel helpless in the presence of fire, whether it's an erupting volcano or a forest fire. I was dealing with the primitive force of fire and alluding to the unnatural part that we had created; how little control we have over nuclear energy, for instance." But fire is both a destructive and a cleansing force, and Erickson sees it both ways. Her fears for humanity are continually balanced by her hopes for change.

The light bulb and television appear in outdoor settings in a number of her works. "I've tried to use other symbols, but they don't work. I don't know if it's the light bulb as an archetype, or whether it's technology itself. If things get too sweet and lovely, I like to do something that's ugly, like a bare light bulb. And I don't even like to draw television sets, but they keep reappearing." She ponders the role of the computer in our society and where it will lead us. Computer, light bulb, television: technology's modern-day light sources, full of potential for use and misuse by the humans on whom the choice depends.

Many of these elements appear in *The Clear and Present Danger* (shown on the facing page), which depicts a woman in an exaggerated pose and cats watching television. Erickson explains:

> I think the background and all the mannerisms are akin to painting; it's all exaggerated. The animals are showing surprise, and she's showing shock and horror. They're all kind of funny, actually, because, after all, it's a community of animals sand a naked woman watching television, whatever is happening on the evening news. The flames are indicating trouble, and also a cleansing.

In *Vesuvius Revisited: Model and Capybara* (above), all hell is breaking loose around the woman who sits, posed and poised, utterly oblivious to the erupting world:

> *Vesuvius* is a comical situation where this self-absorbed late '80s model is totally unaware of anything going on around her. She's having her little event. I loved the capybaras, because they seemed humorous, just because of their size. I made them much larger than they are, more like hippos. The one on the right could be defensive or angry, but I think he's yawning. It's total boredom for him. The one on the left is sort of keeping his eye on things, knowing something is happening behind them. She's egotistically involved in her own thing, the "perfect woman," unaware that the world is going to explode at any moment.

A working process

Nancy N. Erickson's large works start with small sketches, usually no larger than 6 in. by 6 in. Working on a light table, she makes 10 to 20 drawings, "correcting them over and over," while deciding on the juxtaposition of the various elements. An old, enclosed handball court on her property is a convenient setting for the next steps in the process. The court can be easily darkened, which facilitates the use of an Artograph Super AG 100 projector to project one of her drawings onto butcher paper or clear plastic taped to the wall. With the room darkened, she traces the projected and enlarged outline onto the paper or plastic using paints or felt pens. Next, she cuts out the shapes, places them on the appropriate fabric and traces around them with paint. Once she cuts out the fabric shapes, she lightly glues them to the Thermolam background fabric and sews them in place with a straight machine stitch. When all the pieces are sewn in place, she embellishes the work with satin stitch, more bars of fabric and straight stitches, which now become quilting lines. After the piece is finished, she backs it with cotton or velvet, gluing and tacking it by hand, back stitching every 14 in. to 16 in. to stabilize it. She turns under the edge and sews it in place using bias strips as needed, then attaches 2-in. wide Velcro® for hanging.

1. Working on a light table, Erickson develops a small drawing. (Photos by Nancy N. Erickson and Ron Erickson.)

2. In a darkened room she projects the drawing on butcher paper and paints the outlines.

3. Using the paper as a pattern, she paints the outlines on fabric and cuts out the shapes.

Erickson and one of her models, The Frieda, rest for a moment in front of the big cats, which have been glued to the backing.

Sewn, painted, embroidered and quilted, Triton's Serengeti is finished (1989; 57 in. by 60 in.).

There she sits, lipstick just so, lost in a little cloud, while the volcano behind her comes apart at the seams. The visual energy of the scene is reinforced by the irregular edges of the work and the cutout section to the right, which contrast with the motionless model on her lavender-draped base.

Erickson's ideas, her powerful drawing and the sheer physicality of the work itself are confronting. These are very large pieces, often 8 ft. or 9 ft. across. Large works, she says, "move you out of the ordinary. I love to be surrounded by someone's huge painting or huge environment. I like to merge with it." Her drawing is vigorous and appears spontaneous, but she practices continually, working with five other women once a week drawing from a live model.

Trained in drawing and painting, Erickson chose to work in textiles. "The reason I don't use canvas and paint is that the textures of the fabrics (satin, cotton, velvet) combined with the visual narrative seem more versatile than oil and canvas for me. I can easily do the shaped pieces, as well as pursue various ways to deal with edges and images more expressively." Erickson refuses to put a frame around her works or glass over them to make them seem more like paintings. "I feel that it is possible to work in a humble medium and be taken seriously." But she occasionally despairs at the unwillingness of the art world to consider work in fabric and threads as worthy of notice. "Twenty-five years is a long time, and I don't feel I've seen much progress."

Erickson doesn't dwell on difficulties, however, since she delights in the versatility of the medium. Her finished work has an urgent quality, with wrinkles, threads left hanging, paint splashes on the fabric and bars of energetic color punctuating the surface. The spontaneous effect is the result of a well-considered designing and working process.

She works and reworks her original sketches, some of which she may have drawn on her computer. Then, she experiments with paint on the fabrics, sometimes throwing it on and allowing it to drip, so the painted outline will smear. During the tracing process the pattern is destroyed. "It stays crude, in that I have a lot of creative work to do when I get the pattern done. If I

solve all the problems early on, then the rest gets boring." This process allows her to work freely, painting each of the elements before the final work is assembled. Each section is then stitched with a simple machine straight stitch onto Thermolam, a thin battinglike material. There are still many adjustments to be made at this point and many decisions.

"I do have favorite parts of the process. I love the part where I'm working in the colors and where I'm actually working on the piece and cutting it. I love destroying! I love cutting up and breaking up those edges." Breaking up the edges is very important in her designing process, and through this and the addition of bars of color she aims to reconcile the background and foreground areas. She mentions Monet's use of color bars as an influence on her ideas. She will either cut out the top layer of fabric, revealing an under layer of color for a bar, or will add the color on where needed by painting or applying strips of fabric.

Once the work is tacked together (first with a glue stick, then followed by a simple machined straight stitch), the bars laid and major areas finished, then color choices are made for the wide machine satin stitch that surrounds each area. Since the strong satin-stitch line emphasizes both direction and shape, choosing the right color for the line is of primary importance.

Erickson's colors are bold and pure, rarely muddy, interacting at full volume. Color is endlessly fascinating to her and helps to generate a work. Her initial ideas involve hues and textures that appeal or challenge her at the moment. It was a love of working with color and understanding how it works that first drew her to study art. "More than anything else, there was that desire to work with colors and to get them to really work individually and yet be with others." She works intuitively now, only going back to color theory when some color relationship is not working. "If you put some colors together you know they will vibrate at the edge."

Erickson challenges herself to use colors she doesn't like at all. In *The Forever Wrestlers of Triton* (see p. 86), she chose to use a very bold orange. "That orange is a totally obnoxious color, and that's one reason I got a whole bolt of it. I thought, 'things are just getting too sweet.' I tried some other backgrounds, and ended up with a tried and true one." The strong blue background of the sky is a great foil for the masked lion cubs who are "forever wrestling." The inspiration for this work came from a note in Kafka's *Diary*. Erickson says:

I read it a long time ago, but the idea was hanging around in my consciousness. It had to do with an entry he made about a man living in a hotel room who gets a tap on the door, and into the room comes another man. They wrestle without uttering a word. After one hour, the man leaves and closes the door. I thought of these lions wrestling forever somewhere. I wanted to add more context, so I put the sky in, and Triton seemed a logical place for them, because at the time I was working on it, we were watching Voyager 2 go out past Neptune.

The masked cub is a bit of a mystery even to Erickson. She comments on animals having their own persona and perhaps the need to pretend or hide. She has done drawings of masked animals in the past, even timid animals with predatory masks. However, the determination to add the lavender over the orange was a very basic color decision; the mask provided the right spot.

The spherical sky behind the lion cubs suggests the night sky and fits within a series Erickson is exploring. Living away from city lights, she enjoys the feeling of being totally surrounded by the night sky, a feeling of "falling off the world." Erickson says, "It's a glorious experience. You can see how early people lived looking at the night, and how all these constellations they watched had such meaning, and how closely they watched them. We've gotten so far away from it, because we can't even see them. We don't live outside any more."

Erickson puzzled over how to make the stars, then realized that a machine satin stitch would work well. The satin stitch and metallic paints, brushed on lightly at first, then more heavily if needed, worked splendidly for the Milky Way.

These night scenes, inspired by star maps, have a serenity about them. There is plenty to wonder at in the darkness, but nothing to fear in most of them. The half-round dome inspired one

friend to call them her "firmament pieces." She muses on "a probable change going through here."

The expanse of the star-filled night sky and the stairway form a backdrop of possibilities for the woman and the lion in *After Midnight* (shown on the facing page). These are separate elements working together. "There's an inwardness in the person." When asked why she depicts women and no men, Erickson replies simply, "I have never felt the need, actually." Her "Everywoman" in *After Midnight* is naked, strong and serene, with the lion a fitting companion. There is power in their movement.

The stairs offer several meanings for Erickson. First, she sees them as elements found in archeological excavations. Since she often views her work as taking place in the future, the stairs provide an element of time, something that rises out of the past. She also uses them as a strong visual element in a curvaceous kind of composition, a kind of sharp edge, angled, repetitive and geometric. As a universal symbol they suggest possibilities for new interpretations, perhaps a connection with Mesopotamian ziggurats or Aztec civilizations.

In the past few years she has had to stop work for periods of time. "Even then the mind doesn't stop," she says. "The dreams don't stop. They keep on formulating their own solutions in the back of my mind." She keeps on working, continually fascinated by the challenge each new piece presents, more concerned with the work and the message it conveys than with her material success. Erickson's willingness to tackle important themes, her desire to use homely materials to fashion monumental works reveal a strength of purpose and determination to speak plainly through her art.

After Midnight

1989; 78 in. by 69 in.; painted and sewn fabrics. (Photo by Nancy N. Erickson.)

D. R. WAGNER

The Poets Dream

1986; 8 in. by 19½ in.; cotton and
metallic threads on canvas; needlepoint.
(Courtesy of D. R. Wagner and The
Allrich Gallery, San Francisco; collection
of The Redding Museum of Art, Redding,
California; photo by Robert Hollis.)

"Hardening of the categories leads to art disease."
—Kenneth Snelson, sculptor

THE TICKET TO RETURN

those not admitted
will be required to have
a non-admittance ticket
in their possession or
they will be admitted.[4]
—*D. R. Wagner*

There have been occasions when Wagner started planning an embroidery around a title, only to discover that as the title lengthened to a page, he had begun a poem instead. Sometimes he must decide if an idea should be read, viewed or heard, or possibly be a combination of all three. In performance works, slides of his embroideries may be projected on stage as Wagner and his collaborators read poetry and perform their musical compositions.

It was music that first led Wagner to embroidery. In the early 1970s he was on tour with his rock band, Runcible Spoon, and was sailing near the Bahamas. Inspired by a beautiful sight and finding no painting or drawing materials on board, he settled for some embroidery floss. He discovered that he could actually draw color through his fingers and direct its motion, a powerful moment for him. Here was another medium through which to direct his considerable energies. His fascination with embroidery led him to study historic works, experiment with various techniques and materials and to settle on fine needlepoint canvas stitched in tent stitch with cotton floss.

While color was the first element of needlepoint to intrigue Wagner, he soon became aware of its potential for depicting narrative. Wagner had been telling himself stories for years, and now these stories began to inspire the embroidery. He discusses one of his favorite works, *The Poets Dream* (above left):

> That piece is thrilling to me. For a long time I wanted to do a big ship. I'd written a poem called "The Body of Dream in Autopsy," which is about a kid waking up from a dream and the dream being caught inside the house, and it gets killed. An autopsy is done, and when they open up the dream, one of the things that comes out is one of these huge ships of memory. The doctors still talk about how these ships

Just as the idea in D. R. Wagner's poem feeds on itself, so the many ways he expresses himself nourish one another. Wagner tells stories and writes poems, embroiders miniature needlepoint tapestries and paints, composes and performs music, collaborates with other artists in performance works and, as if all that were not enough, teaches. This multitalented individual doesn't concern himself with the confusion and limitations set up by those who insist on classifications in art. Instead, he delights in the ability that allows his ideas to find expression in so many ways.

came right through them and the walls and everything. They never did find out why the dream died.

I searched for months for the image of the ship, and then I worked and worked on it. One night, after I got all of the lights on the ship stitched in, I went to bed. It was finished. It was quite late at night, and I could hear the orchestra playing on board the ship, so I had to get up and work on it some more.

Multiple images that at first seem unrelated resonate with one another in this complex work. A young boy, the "little puppeteer" seen behind his puppet screen, is an image to which Wagner admits a personal connection. "I love puppets. This one is sending messages to the universe." Wagner reuses some favorite elements, and the little puppeteer reappears in other works, on one occasion performing for an electrical storm.

The jungle, another favorite Wagnerian image, figures prominently here in both the meticulously detailed plants and the elaborately painted "native." Wagner based his watchful native on photographs he had taken of a friend who had painted her face. Lions prowl out of the jungle and along the waterfront, yet they pose no menace. Wagner's interest in historic and contemporary art is evidenced by the inclusion of these "repoussoir" figures, which are seen in silhouette, surrounded by light. This method of highlighting a figure has been used by a number of the Imagist painters, many of whom share a Chicago background. Wagner has taught with and associated with some of these painters, and he especially notes the influence of Roger Brown, whose works frequently feature dark figures surrounded by light against a dark ground.

The equally idiosyncratic images of the emblematic hand-held torch and the cartoon hero Flash Gordon balance one another in each of the upper corners. Poised and alert, Flash Gordon looks down on the display from the upper right side of the work. Wagner says, "He's up there looking over the whole thing. There's a feeling that it's being cared for."

Great pink stars light up the midnight blue sky over a tweedy blue-green sea and a tile-patterned blue-green quay. One image after another, each with its own set of associations, creates layers of meaning, allusive and elusive, poetry made visible. Wagner explains:

I don't think I could sit down and tell you a story about this boat or about this kid, but I'm trying to set up something that will be consistent with itself all the way through and at the same time do something to the viewer. It's like when you go to the movies and they have a picture from the movie on the outside, and when you leave the movie and look at the picture again, you say, "That wasn't in there." It's part of the movie; it's part of that same scene, but it's different. I like that aspect of it. It is not a twice-told tale. You get to see it only once. You only get to see it here. It's like watching a fire. A fire is always changing.

The process where an image and story come together can be extraordinarily delicate, according to Wagner. *Don't Hit the Artist* (on the facing page) is an expression of the vulnerability of the work and the artist during the process of creation:

I was thinking about how often, when we're creating something, before we have an idea solidified, people come up and point to an area that's not done and say, "What's going to go there?" I just want to grab their face and say, "Stop that! I don't know what's going to go there, and it's okay! I'll know what's going to go there when it's done." They'll ask, "How will you know when it's done?" and I'll say, "When the spot is filled up."

To me that kind of thing is like getting whacked. Whacked hard! I put this artist on the edge of a cliff over this beautiful sea, and he is getting whacked by this very authoritarian-looking guy. The painting he is doing has nothing to do with the seascape. It's all reds and blues and yellows swirled on there, like 'how am I going to get to this picture?' Well, it struck me (pardon the pun) that it was about that kind of confusion. People are coming in and saying, "Well, what are you doing? What is the picture about?"

I just said, "Don't hit me. I'm not ready to be hit. When it's done—go ahead."

Wagner refers to his designing process as straightforward. ("That's why I don't do workshops on process. It's boring.") He is a great collector of images that engage his vital imagination. "I believe that most artists are image junkies." He appropriates images from newspapers, magazines, comic books, his own drawings, text—anything can spark a new idea or fit with one he's had earlier. He works and reworks these ideas, drawing them on tracing paper, from which he composes the works. He uses a fine graph paper (10 x 10 squares to the centimeter), which is not to scale with the needlepoint canvas. "I think if it were one to one it would get boring. I approach the work as a painter, so with the slight change in scale I'm always surprising myself the whole time I'm working."

Color choices are next. Sometimes Wagner can put the colors together in advance. Other times he begins with a grey scale of the design, or he picks just the light and dark colors, working the dark areas first. He doesn't make color choices easy for himself, since he uses a palette of over 600 colors. He seldom gets stuck, but when he does, he admits it is with color. "Sometimes I realize I have gotten myself in some real deep yogurt by putting some color combinations, some color relationships, together. I have to ask myself, 'Now what happens in between, Mr. Wagner?'"

Don't Hit the Artist

1987; 4¾ in. by 4½ in.; cotton/Lurex on cotton; needlepoint. (Courtesy of D. R. Wagner and The Allrich Gallery, San Francisco; collection of Mary Nolan, San Francisco, California; photo by Robert Hollis.)

The Artist as Poet

In this poem D. R. Wagner comments upon the artist's magic:

PAUL KLEE ALONE

Paul Klee would
often wake up
with small deposits
of color collected
on the ends of his
fingers.

He knew he had washed
before retiring, that his
hands were as clean as
his vision.

Carefully, he would rise,
scrape these ghosts
of color from his
hands and mix them
with water.

He painted.

Klee suspected the
colors were the remains
of dreams; the blossom
end of sleep, collected
as bees do pollen
from the unnamed rooms
of his sleep.

No one has ever
reported this
phenomenon before.[5]

Wagner works on a 25-gauge canvas that has had the edges taped, but is unstretched. "I like to scrunch it all up and move it around." He marks the centers and edges of the canvas, but does not draw out any of the images ahead, preferring to rely on the out-of-sync chart. He feels free to change and alter the design as he is working. "I start in just as though I were painting, working all over the canvas. If I see that there has to be a particular element in one part, or it has to be a particular color, I do that. I use four strands of cotton embroidery floss and take them apart and reblend them. I found out you can take them apart even further if you want to get really nutty." He will overstitch the tent stitches when he needs to delineate features or outline an element.

When the work is finished, Wagner washes it in Ivory Liquid, blocks it and wraps it around an acid-free board. He uses a process similar to dry-mounting photographs to secure the work for framing. He cuts ⅜-in. strips of Fotoflat and lays them on the back of the board. He wraps the canvas around the board and uses a dry-mount tacking iron to apply heat to the edge of the canvas for about 30 seconds. This softens the canvas so he can manipulate the edges and straighten the corners. The process is heat reversible, so he can reheat and remanipulate if the edges are not straight the first time around. Finding black the most dramatic background for his work, he positions the work on a black 100%-rag board and finishes it with a metal frame. When a work is to travel, he uses Plexiglas to protect its face.

Wagner's work has traveled all over the world. In 1987 he won the Traditional Technique Award of the prestigious Kyoto International Textile Competition. Technique is all that is traditional about Wagner's work, however. His layering of images, each stitched to fit the square of the canvas, has led reviewers to comment that his work is similar in impact to video art. Certainly the pixel approach bears this out, but there is much more than the flickering and fleeting image of video behind these complex works.

Wagner sees his art as being closer to music than to video. It is not possible to hold in one's head all the sounds of a musical score from beginning to end. Rather, a phrase is revealed by the phrases on either side of it, and the effect of the whole accumulates within the listener:

It's like my writing. When I talk about stories, I think of my poetry as lyrical and narrative too. But they're not point A to point B. I think you're dealing with emotions when you make pictures. That emotion or emotional state isn't defined by just one thing, like "I'm mad," but by a whole series of things that surround it. The emotion is sort of like a void, and all these feelings and associations surround the void and give it its shape. That shape is the emotion, and those feelings and/or events also shape the composition for me.

Wagner is articulate in explaining his work, and he enjoys teaching about the power of words and images. He worked for a month in Reno, Nevada, with 572 third through eighth graders in an artist-in-residence program. He tells about the creation of one of his works during this time:

My favorite area is between the visual arts and literature. How do they influence each other? What happens when you say something in your mind? What kind of image do you get? Even on "Sesame Street" they show someone saying something and thinking it at the same time. I was just finishing a piece called *Poets Exchanging Images,* and we were talking—kids of all grade levels and I—about how hard it is to show something like that. You just can't see someone give another person an image of snow or something.

Wagner agreed to try to do something with this idea for the students to see. Stars have been an important image for him, and in Reno ("not in the middle of Nowhere, but from there you can see the middle of Nowhere"), the stars appear vast and close, "about two feet away." Wagner had also been looking at Mexican folk paintings, which cast their spell upon the work he did

La Noche de las que Brillan

1986; 7⅛ in. by 14 in.; cotton on cotton canvas; needlepoint. (Courtesy of D. R. Wagner and The Allrich Gallery, San Francisco; collection of Bruce and Jacqueline Whitelam, Sacramento, California; photo by Robert Hollis.)

during that month with the students (see the photo above). He explains:

> The figure is sort of a self-portrait reaching up from a kind of idealized Alhambra to the night sky. Through that gesture, and the suggestion that the lights may be imagined or really that bright, I wanted to get the sense of mystery, the stars flying through the sky and the changing colors. The kids got it. They knew what I was talking about. I was saying, "Is this how you create the stars? Are they more beautiful if you think about them?"

A small hill is introduced in the background of the piece that resembled the hill near the school as closely as Wagner could make it. "I said, 'I didn't imagine it, but this got in the picture. Some of this must be my imagination.' The students could imagine too. In their homes there are real things and imagined things." The piece is titled, *La Noche de las que Brillan* (The Night of the Things That Shine).

With a mind that contains so many images, ideas and plans, it isn't easy for Wagner to unwind, but he says that gardening, growing vegetables and being with his young twins provide him with a change of pace. He also enjoys travel, collecting more images as he goes. But, for the most part, he wants to create. "I most strongly feel that if you can, you must. So many people can't. Whether it's making music, doing dance or making pictures, if you have a gift or an ability you must exercise it. It's the stuff that keeps us going. I seem to be gifted in that it keeps bubbling up. I keep going at it. It's just a matter of finding a form for it. I'm never bored with what I'm going to do next."

DARREL C. MORRIS

Darrel C. Morris uses sewing thread, packing stitches of seductive, jewel-like colors into compact, sardonic narratives. *One More Little Shove* (shown at left) chronicles a cat's revenge on his unsuspecting owner. *Baby Race* (below) skewers society's fostering of competitive childrearing. Morris manipulates his images so skillfully that he always hits square on his mark. Morris comments on his work:

> The attitudes that have developed in my work have their origins in storytelling, Appalachian arts and crafts, lawn art, explicit religious art and technical drawing. As a young child I wanted to be a cartoonist. I wanted to create my own world. I feel now that as an artist I have become more of a satiric reporter of sorts, reporting on events from my personal and public life. I report on things I have witnessed or experienced, using techniques and materials that come from and integrate into my daily life. The majority of my work reflects how people present themselves to the world and how they interact with other people.

One More Little Shove

1986; 7½ in. by 6¾ in.; sewing thread, found fabric; embroidery, patchwork. (Private collection; photo by Lewis Toby.)

Baby Race

1988; 10 in. by 11 in.; sewing thread, fabric; embroidery. (Photo by Lewis Toby.)

ROBERT TROTTMANN

Surrender

1988; 23 in. by 35 in.; cotton, silk, metallic threads, rayon and wool fabric; embroidery; detail below right. (Private collection; photo by Kathy Hollis-Cooper.)

Robert Trottmann's message is indeed mysterious—a glimpse of a ritual, possibly painful, a secret seen at night; figures widely separated, but all part of a whole. He uses cotton, silk and metallic threads for his embroideries, which contrast densely stitched areas with delicate pinpoints of stitches and fine traceries of lines.

Trottmann has selected words and phrases from his sketchbooks to "demonstrate the mysterious forces" that empower his work:

> Embroidery promotes the power and mystery of touch and affirms the larger forces that created the hand. Cloth and threads are familiar to everyone, and the communicative potential of them is stupendous. My work just taps into this potential.... In a world of mind-boggling, expanding dependence on technology, the tools of embroidery remain technically simple and proportionate to the construction requirements of my visions.

> My embroideries can also be thought of as the following: Elegant hostilities. Storage vaults. Puzzles with some parts missing. Directives. Marks of repair. Peep shows, phantoms and afterimages. What I saw. What I see approaching. Glimpses. Sensations of mappings, markers and signs. Chordings and refrains. Tears during dreams. Occurrences that twinkle, disappear, then recur. Dioramas. Parts of the painful. Seeing from faraway. Positions, spots, localities and situations. How it feels when you are only able to peer at something and the distortions when you stare. Reverberations, echoes, replies, retorts and answerings. Tangible light, tangible sparks or flashes of light. Lying on my back in water. Being outside. Things at first sight. Only aspects of the source are needed. Selections, prunings and trimmings. They are hideouts, places of escape.

> My embroideries perform the same psychic function as flowers at a funeral. They are prayers with the skin peeled off.

Tom Lundberg

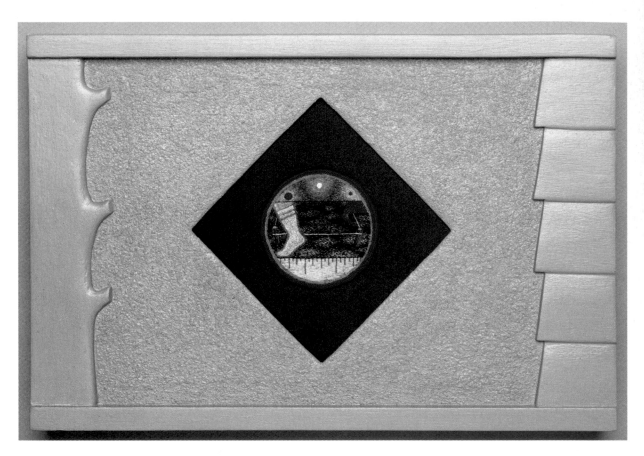

Another Planting

1989; frame: 12 in. by 18 in. by 2¼ in., embroidery: 3½ in. in diameter; cotton, silk and metallic embroidery on wool; painted wood frame; detail at right. (Private collection; photo by Colorado State University Photographic Services.)

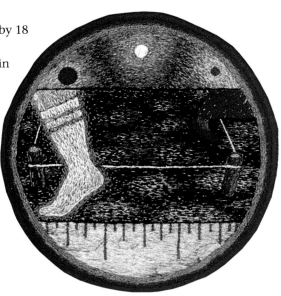

Tom Lundberg's embroideries capture moments and record the fleeting glimpses of experiences, thoughts, dreams and desires. He calls them "time markers, grounded in particular locations and momentary light conditions." Each work is composed of Lundberg's personal vocabulary of images, yet each speaks poignantly of heartfelt truths and the beauty of the familiar. "English teachers," he says, "were among the few people I knew who discussed and analyzed creative communication, and their standard dictum to 'start in your own backyard' has never lost its ring of truth. Some part of me still expects those childhood mentors to appear at an exhibition of my work, checking to see how often I've used specific details from my everyday surroundings." [6]

Lundberg is the chronicler of a still moment in a season's changing cycle or a day's solitary rituals. He listens intently to the rhythms of rural America. If it were possible to hear these embroideries, they would sound more like the contemplative *Appalachian Spring* of Aaron Copland than Leonard Bernstein's insistent *West Side Story*.

Lundberg uses recognizable elements from the external world to illuminate the experiences of his inner world. There are details of Lundberg's home and companions: Jet, his old black Labrador, often seen in profile, or a glimpse of a another dog, a boxer, who always seems to be running ahead, out of the picture frame, leaving only his hindquarters in sight. Comfortable socks, a curtained window, all speak of home and private moments, of settling in a familiar place to watch time pass.

The seasons change in Lundberg's work. It is almost possible to smell the spring soil in both *Planting* (see p. 106) and *Another Planting* (on the facing page). "They were done a year apart, but they were from the same impulse. I was thinking about the seasons. They're very straightforward in my mind, about seasonal activity, agricultural activity." There is evidence of marking and measuring: the size of the garden plot, the distance between the seeds, the length of the rows, the wood needing to be stacked, even the length of the days are noted in these two works. Time passes, seasons change and the glowing color of *Running* (on p. 104), with its darkened leaf in the foreground, suggests the coming of fall. The path is one which the man and dog walk together in a daily ritual.

While Lundberg's work has a tranquil quality to it, it is not without a certain edge. Nature is not always gentle or generous, and the maxims that parents pass on to their children seem at home in Lundberg's works: "Look both ways before you cross the street." "Don't let the dog off the leash." "Never swim alone, especially at night." Caution notwithstanding, the world beckons, and the risk taker is rewarded by moments of quiet magic.

Lundberg connects his fascination for seasons with both his rural Iowa heritage and his admiration of ecclesiastical textiles. Just as the changing leaves alter the appearance of trees, the seasonal changing of the textiles in the church transforms the sanctuary, adding color, light and mystery. Lundberg recalls the impression made on him when he was a child by the use of vestments and altar frontals in his own church:

My family and I were members of a small Presbyterian church in a town of 500 people. The minister at that time brought the idea of vestments into the congregation. It had been a very "low church" environment before that, and then he introduced the idea of seasonal altar cloths. I was in the sixth grade, so the discussions went over my head, but I could see how the vestments changed everything. I really liked peeking into the Lutheran church in town or the Catholic church in other towns, because they looked terrific. Their spaces were so much more mystical. My mother was on the altar committee, so we had all these catalogs of hangings and crosses and crowns. My brother and I would go through the catalog and pick out our favorite copes. Dad built the chest that the cloths were kept in. It all made a very big impression on me.

The experience for Lundberg generated a deep interest in ecclesiastical textiles, which has informed his work ever since. In graduate school at Indiana University, his formal focus was ecclesiastical art from the Middle Ages and the Renaissance. He also remembers the impact of "Raiments for the Lord's Service," a monumental exhibition of historic and contemporary ecclesiastical pieces at the Art Institute of Chicago, which he saw just before starting graduate

Evening Serving Tray

1987; 25 in. by 16 in. by 2½ in.;
painted wood, fabric; embroidery.
(Private collection; photo by
Colorado State University
Photographic Services.)

Running
(detail)

1989; frame (not shown): 12 in. by
18 in. by 2¼ in., embroidery: 3½ in.
in diameter; cotton, silk and metallic
embroidery on wool; painted wood
frame. (Private collection; photo by
Colorado State University Photographic
Services.)

school. He studied ecclesiastical textiles in their own settings on trips to Europe, observing the way the textiles and the architecture influenced and echoed one another. He noted the carvings in stone and wood that reproduced the drape of a curtain. His first reaction to these early textiles was a "heart response." He has noted a change in his reaction over time. "They are as beautiful as I remember them, but I enjoy them for reasons other than just visual now. I appreciate the way that they participated in a bigger picture, part of a composition that was church and faith and Mass. Maybe that's where travel helps, because you see them tucked away in the dusty treasury and not the centerpiece of a big book." The works he has studied as well as the context with

in which they exist contain the seeds of ideas he is still exploring.

Many of Lundberg's embroideries resemble badges, emblems of rank, office or membership. Some are patterned literally after badges, round embroideries set in diamond shapes. While acknowledging this interest, he can't always specify why a piece took on its final form. "I understand where they came from, but when I look at them, I couldn't have predicted that they would look that way."

Vestments, carpets, scarves, molas—textiles of the past and of other cultures—are cherished frequently for their particular beauty, while the uses for which they were intended are somehow considered separate and distinct. Lundberg, however, sees himself working firmly within the utilitarian textile tradition and is somewhat uneasy with the "fine-art" side of embroidery:

> If all of the artists with the most commitment to embroidery are doing pieces that are not "functional," that don't participate in the physical lives of people, are we cheating or are we moving the medium in a way that it can't have the same kind of spiritual connection that it would have had if it were a tablecloth for a special occasion? Would I really invest the time to make a tablecloth that is as complete as I want my "art" to be? Can this medium of embroidery ever be as meaningful if we don't touch it?

Then, again, Lundberg wonders if perhaps "the ritual of art viewing" may be close to a contemporary spiritual experience. Never free of questions, he ponders the idea that looking backward to tradition and ancestry can blind the artist to the future.

Lundberg's concern with making nonfunctional craft, coupled with his interest in the way wood and stone were carved to represent cloth, has led to his unique methods of framing many of his embroideries. These frames of carved and applied wood, gesso and paint started with some trays he made for an exhibition of his work. Like *Evening Serving Tray* (on the facing page), these shallow trays with their own painted napkins and plates could be displayed on the wall. But they were also equipped with a cloth tacked to the top of each that could work either as a towel or food cozy over the contents. When hung on the wall, the cloth was gathered at the top of the tray, "like a curtain or a bunting that would lower over a painting."

Lundberg developed the idea of the trays, altering the function to frames that could "serve" the work to the viewer. The frames are made like a shallow box with a diamond cut out in the center. Commercial moldings add a lip or shelf to the bottom of the frame. Perlite, a sand-finish aggregate that Lundberg purchases at a lumber yard, is added to the gesso to give a stuccolike texture before the frames are painted. He carves Masonite for the additional elements of applied trim, which resonate with the ideas within the embroidery.

These elements transform the frame from merely a large mat for the work to a hard-edged echo of the softly stitched scene, enlarging and containing it simultaneously. He brings in other visual imagery that reinforces the stitched narrative, leaf shapes for gardens, the edges of siding on his house, the jagged line of a fence. The stylized corner of the house and a suggestion of a pruned tree run along the sides of the frame in *Another Planting*:

> I first used the siding motif in 1982, during a time when I was preoccupied with another backyard image, the wooden fence. Within small rectangular embroideries, the fence top was a sharp, agitated line amidst softer shrubs and shadows. Its zigzag reminded me of patterns in traditional textiles, and gradually I realized that I was looking for other abstract patterns in my neighborhood. At the corners of the house, where the slats of siding converged, I noticed a vertical variation on this zigzag. Like the fence, this slightly angular edge was part of the man-made world, punctuating the view of branches and houses. But where the fence top spoke of barriers and distance, this siding edge suggested the rhythms of a domestic life sheltered within. This corner line, with a minimum of detail, was able to convey the interdependent realms of outside and inside.[7]

Making the frames appeals to Lundberg. After the quiet, restricted motion of embroidery, he enjoys the physical pleasure of working with wood. "I know that when I teach embroidery, I praise the pace of another era and talk about how the needle and thread pace is just as important and valid as the computer pace that everyone else is embracing. And now I use a buzz saw, a very 20th-century tool!"

Like a page from a Book of Hours, Lundberg's precise, contained embroideries can be viewed by one person at a time at very close range. If removed from the large frames, many of his works would fit in the palm of the hand. These are not works to wrap around oneself; rather they are thought sized and accessible. One glance is not enough, however. These are compelling works, which invite lingering and reflection. "When I think about doing larger work, I think about doing more moments or more small things put together. The pieces I make are almost all I can think of, the periphery of my ability to focus on one thing at a time. They're not like a

Communicating through color

Planting
(detail)

1988; embroidery: 3½ in. in diameter, frame (not shown): 12 in. by 18 in. by 2¼ in.; embroidery on wool; painted wood frame. (Private collection; photo by Colorado State University Photographic Services.)

Tom Lundberg speaks of the role of color in communicating the rhythms of changing seasons, in the rituals of ecclesiastical garments and in the relationships of traditional textiles to the cultures in which they are made. Each has had an influence on the expressive use of color in Lundberg's own work:

"Where I live in Colorado, the enormous sky dramatizes our daily rotation through light and darkness. Within the rhythms of night and day, color is always shifting, always becoming something new. My own use of color is inspired by this succession of fleeting hues and by the slower movement of the seasons, in which colors come to fullness and then eventually fade.

"As the church layered its liturgical calendar onto European cycles of planting and harvest, color was used to heighten a variety of moods throughout its yearly sequence of rituals. Vestments changed with the seasons and with feast days, appealing to the senses in order to enter the invisible world of the spirit. In the small town in Iowa where I grew up, the church designed its vestments with economy, making them reversible, two colors and seasons per cloth. I think that I've been influenced by those glimpses of contrasting colors on the undersides of altar cloths.

"Cultures all over the world have selected intriguing colors to express their important ideas and feelings. Textiles traditionally have been worked with colors that convey identity and social relationships. While the symbolic meanings of colors may vary, the desire to communicate through color seems universal, springing from the biological impulses at work in foliage and plumage."

meditation, but more like a daydream, just looking, staring at one thing."

Lundberg notes that his mind is continually filled with ideas, and that he must break into all this activity by "focusing on something that I could actually make with my hands." He reflects on the designing process:

Let's say I'm looking at the top of the fence outside my window and at my neighbor's hedge, and I might be struck for some reason at that moment that that's the right thing to work on. There are a million billion things that stimulate or inspire you, and you think you might use them, but somehow you just can't do them all. Life's too short, and maybe that's where my own limitations come in, too. So, when I sit down to work with the pencils and the thread and the cloth, that's when the choice is really made. That's really what has to be, because maybe you can do nothing else.

Another way that Lundberg focuses his thoughts is with a camera. He takes hundreds of photographs, "a filing nightmare," but about the "closest thing I have to a diary." He will use up the end of a roll of film shooting "close-ups of some garden changes, of rocks and household objects placed on the rocks; a kind of diary entry. It's done with the hope that maybe that snapshot will be pinned on my bulletin board and be a source for a drawing." A sketchbook and an occasional record of dreams and photographs work together to provide the images and settings he uses.

Most of these embroidered images are small enough to be worked in a plastic hoop. Lundberg has wrapped a cloth strip around the inner ring of the hoop to help grip the fabric without damaging it. Using two to three strands of cotton embroidery floss, he starts by laying in solid shapes with long and short stitch and satin stitch, moving freely between the two as needed. This is followed by couching and small directional stitches that he uses to refine or modulate a color. By the time he is satisfied with the result, the stitching may be six layers thick, a richly dense surface.

The works enveloped by the off-white frames glow with color and light. These solidly worked strokes of color blend to subtle gradated harmonies, then surprisingly react with and bounce off a neighboring color. Lundberg uses sharp contrasts of light and dark, and despite their inviting and intimate quality, the embroideries are amazingly strong when viewed at a distance. "I think I have a tendency to get a lot of color into a small space. I think that's part of the pleasure. It's funny, because when I look at the textiles I most admire, the colors are really selected very judiciously for very specific reasons. What happens if color can be limited further?" Each piece raises such questions and contradictions, which he aims to answer in the next piece.

The red diamond shape within the white frame reminds him of a flag, or the proportions of a flag. This may also reflect his interest in *punto rosso* work, historic textiles he saw at London's Victoria and Albert Museum in which the background is solidly worked in cross stitch (generally in red), leaving the white foreground figures unworked. Stories, such as those found in the Book of Genesis, are stitched in horizontal bands. "I have postcards showing these works on my bulletin board. They aren't the main spark for my use of red and white, but they exemplify my interest in getting to pure essences, pure symbolic colors, like the red and white stripes used in Shiva temples."

Lundberg doesn't just make passing reference to traditional and historic textiles. His knowledge of them is broad, and he has a strong intellectual connection with the work, the techniques, patterns and images, as well as the cultural and historical context. But there is a deeper connection, one in which the honor of working within this distinct tradition is shared. He is moved by majestic ecclesiastical works and the way they fit the medieval buildings and ceremonies. He is equally moved by the urge to decorate a homely fabric to make a tablecloth for important family occasions.

Lundberg aims to generate appreciation for the artistry of traditional textiles in his students at Colorado State University. Students learn both techniques and patterns through a series of samplers, and develop textiles transforming what they have learned with their own personal imagery. "For embroidery to be viable, it has to relate to people's lives. When it is preoccupied only with technique, only other embroiderers may be interested, and then for only a short time."[8]

Lundberg sees the classroom, where he is in the company of other investigators, as a larger laboratory than his studio:

> You can look into other people's processes; maybe it's a form of company, because we need to work by ourselves when we're making our own thing. But we also need to have periods where we're with other people who are striving for the same goals. I know that every syllabus I write is a letter to myself. It made me feel more confident as a teacher when I realized that maybe the only thing I could do was to offer to other people the problems that I think about myself. In a way that's more like teaching who you are than what the medium is, but so be it.

Lundberg shares "who he is" as a teacher and as an artist. His works, based on an ardent embracing of the traditions of embroidery, quote from moments he marks in the present, "the life that is being lived."

MARY E. PRESTON

*Hathor Gals Won't You
Come Out Tonight*

1989; 46½ in. by 59½ in.; Lumière
fabric paint, cotton floss, brushed
cotton denim twill; stenciling and
embroidery; detail below. (Photo by
Steve Meltzer.)

There is a ritualistic presence to the garments Mary E. Preston sews. Each garment narrates its own story, whether of Preston's creation or a myth retold. She has lived in many countries and traveled extensively, collecting the images and experiences that inspire and authenticate her work along the way. Most of her garments picture the distinctive stylized stenciled animals for which Preston has a particular affinity (see the sidebar on pp. 110-111). She embroiders the garments with cotton floss in simple running stitches and knots, thereby adding a linear element suggesting direction and completing the energetic crispness of her compositions.

Preston writes about her personal connection with the work and tells the story of one of her magical garments:

I'm aware that my life is a process—a way, not a goal. My work, therefore, is a real adventure, with each piece a journey to some new part of my psyche. Illustrating a myth not only entertains me, but, I hope, enables those who view my work to appreciate the wisdom of the myth. People have often remarked that many of the pieces seem "priestlike" or ritualistic in nature. They are always made in praise of and respect for the mystery of life, so this perhaps explains the response.

For me, animals represent one of the keys of life's mystery. They are true gifts that connect us to the beauty of the Creating Power's imagination. They are natural in the truest sense; I respect them and give them voice in my work.

Hathor Gals Won't You Come Out Tonight [shown on the facing page] reaches back into part of my childhood. When my friends were reading Nancy Drew mysteries, I was absorbed in Edith Hamilton's *Mythology* and reading stories about ancient Egyptian civilization. When I was about ten years old I desperately wanted to be an archaeologist and go to Egypt. (When I did finally make it to the Nile in 1982, I realized how claustrophobic, literally, this work would have been. Romantic visions are so much better than reality!)

Thanks to one of Bill Moyers's interviews for his public-television series, "World of Ideas," with religion professor and author Elaine Pagels, I was reminded of my attraction to Egypt. Pagels mentioned her encounter in the museum in Cairo with Hathor, a beautiful serene cow who forms the pedestals and arms of a chair. I knew immediately what she was talking about, for I had had a similar experience looking at this piece. I knew I would have to sing the praises of this goddess who appears in the form of a cow.

One of my favorite books on mythology is Buffie Johnson's *Lady of the Beasts* (Harper & Row, 1988). In it I read, "Hathor is the face of the sky, the deep, and the deity who dwells in a grove at the end of the world. One of her names was Lady of the Sycamore, and the tree was considered her living body. Hathor's fruit provided the seeds of renewal. Beyond the grave as a cow, she suckled the newly dead. 'Seek the Cow Mother' is the legend written on the walls of the tomb of the early kings.... As far as we know, Hathor is the first divinity depicted in Egyptian art...."

At this point I had all the information I needed to begin a piece. I had some special beads I had set out to be used "sometime." (I put out buttons or beads near my worktable to energize my thoughts, but also to remind me to use them in something special.) These were large discs with zigzags of blue and rust, which suggested the colors for the coat. It seemed appropriate to give Hathor a night sky to play in, so stars, shooting and otherwise, were a must. Finally, the title of the piece fell into place. Humor always plays into my work in one way or another. I remembered the title of a song, "Buffalo Gals Won't You Come Out Tonight" while I was working on the coat. The rest, as they say, is history.

Stenciling a pattern on fabric

Kit and the Mystery of Life

1988; 23½ in. by 58½ in.; Euro-tex and Lumière fabric paints, beads, plastic, buttons, rayon yarn, cotton floss, cotton twill fabric; stenciling, appliqué, embroidery. (Photo by Monika Young.)

For this and other work, Preston stencils her images before adding fabric appliqués and decorative stitching, beads, yarn and buttons.

Mary E. Preston illustrates her stories on garments with a combination of stenciling, embroidering and sewing on beads, buttons and other small objects. Her stenciled shapes, though simple and direct, are the result of a process that involves meticulous preparation.

First Preston washes or dry-cleans the background fabric to remove any nonpermanent finish. Next, she makes test samples of fabric and paint and has them dry-cleaned to determine if the paint will adhere well. She notes that some fabrics have a coating that paints cannot penetrate, and it is wise to find this out in advance. From her drawings, she makes copies at a copy shop, enlarging and reducing them until she has from ten to twelve sizes of each shape so she has a variety of sizes with which to work. Preston traces the design onto .003-in. thick Mylar (available in art-supply stores). The transluscent Mylar has a matte side and a glossy side; the design is traced on the glossy side. If she wants to use a mirror image of the shape, she flips the first Mylar drawing over and traces the reverse of the image onto another piece of Mylar of the same size.

Preston cuts out the stencil with a Grifold No. 7B blade knife (see drawing 1 on the facing page), then applies a spray adhesive to the dull side of the stencil. The adhesive temporarily holds the stencil in place on the fabric and does not leave a residue. The stencil can be cleaned with rubbing alcohol after each layer of paint is applied, and the adhesive will last through a number of cleanings. She must clean the paint from the stencil each time to ensure a crisp edge when she stencils the next image.

Preston makes a dauber for applying the paint through the stencil, using a method she learned from a videotape demonstration by surface-design artist Lenore Davis. First, she cuts two pieces of ¼-in. thick foam rubber into approximately 4-in. squares. She folds one into a smaller square and inserts it into the other, and secures both with a rubber band. The result is a very simple and inexpensive dauber that lasts through several cleanings (see drawing 2).

If Preston's design calls for stencils to line up, she makes registration marks on the Mylar, never on the fabric, and uses this as her guide for repeats. Next, she applies the paint. She uses either Lumière or Euro-tex fabric paints. She pours the paint onto a plate or plastic lid and picks up just enough to daub the first thin layer of paint (see drawing 3). If too much paint is on the dauber, it will run under the stencil despite the adhesive backing. Preston applies paint several times until an even coat has been achieved. Then she carefully lifts the stencil off the fabric, making sure not to let the stencil drag over the painted area (see drawing 4). Once the paint is dry, other markings can be stenciled over the first shape, if desired, and additional smaller designs can be painted on by brush.

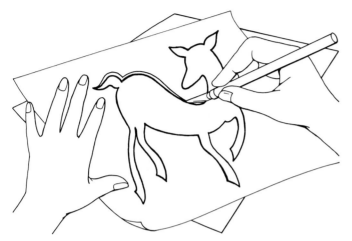

1. With a piece of cardboard as a cutting surface, Preston carefully cuts out the drawing, leaving the Mylar stencil.

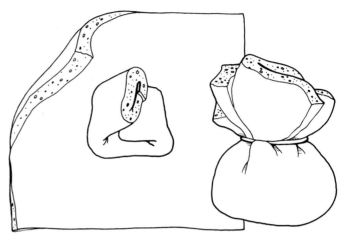

2. To make a dauber, she folds one of two 4-in. squares of ¼-in. thick foam rubber into thirds and then folds both ends over to make a tiny folded square. She fits the small folded square inside the larger one and secures the 'package' with a rubber band.

3. She places a small amount of paint on a plastic plate and daubs thin layers onto the fabric through the stencil.

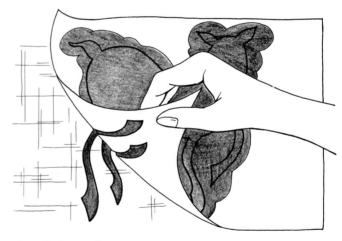

4. Once she has applies an even coating of paint, Preston carefully lifts the stencil from the fabric, revealing the painted image.

LOUISE JAMET

Totem III: Wolfe

1988; 21 in. by 18 in.; fabric dyeing *(shibori)*, photocopy transfer, thread, fabric, dyes, bamboo, color photocopy, cardboard; sewing, hand embroidery, wrapping; full piece above right. (Photo by Robert Vaillant.)

Totem VI: Kingfisher

1989; 25 in. by 17 in.; fabric dyeing *(shibori)*, photocopy transfer, fabric, dyes, paint, colored pencils, color photocopy, bamboo, thread; sewing, hand embroidery, machine embroidery, painting on sticks and fabric, drawing on sticks. (Photo by Robert Vaillant.)

Louise Jamet believes that art is closely connected to the artist's life and is a "tangible imprint" of that life. She describes herself as a city person who has chosen to live in the hilly countryside of the Eastern Townships in Quebec. Her early work had strong feminist underpinnings and explored what being a woman artist means. She used cloth, thread, lace and other domestic materials to create small shrinelike collages dedicated to the materials themselves, referring to women's work of the past and present. The collages also included imagery of these same materials, which had been photocopied and heat-transferred to fabric. She continues to use these basic materials, but now they describe her new environment and the feelings it evokes in her. Her city-oriented vision is enchanted by the black and white patterns of Holstein cows, the tracks of animals in the snow and the geometric patterns cast by the shadows of reeds in a pond. She elaborates:

> The recent *Totem* series describes personal states of mind or key elements in my new country environment. These little flags or banners are personal emblems, and the subject of each one represents an essential aspect of my life with meaning reaching far beyond the obvious formal shapes. Initially inspired by early medieval banners, they combine several techniques such as sewing, embroidery, photocopy transfer, wrapping, fabric dyeing and painting.

WILCKE SMITH

Small Star Shrine

1988; 14 in. by 11 in.; pieces of
native copper, quartz crystals, wool
fabric; machine embroidery.
(Private collection; photo by
Joe Foster.)

Richly colored and well-defined shapes, meticulously constructed from a variety of fibers and found materials, serve the fanciful imagery of Wilcke Smith. "I suspect my designs subconsciously search for an element of secrecy and 'other-worldness.'" The mood she creates may be whimsical or menacing and unsettling. "I'm actually pleased when peers have disliked a work, calling it 'too frightening'...surely that's more interesting than its being merely pleasing."

Small Star Shrine (above) both illustrates hidden elements and reveals Smith's whimsical imagination, where a cave becomes a secret, secure spot. It is quite possible that, while on a teaching tour in 1988, a visit to the Waikato glowworm caves in New Zealand inspired this work. She remembers being enchanted by the tiny glowing pinpoints of light in the limestone caverns and thinking of the glowworms as stars. She imagined a birthing chamber, a nursery for baby stars. She incorporated natural elements with the threads: "The crystals and copper in the work are very earthy kinds of things that work in the cave."

Smith often draws inspiration from art and artifacts of other cultures and earlier times. Prehistoric graphics and folk art serve as visual references for her work. She has an extensive collection of folk art objects, many connected with the ritual life of their particular cultures.

Smith reads and researches. "Books and words are as important to my designs and to my methods of working as the visual images are. Even my sketchbooks contain as many verbal notations as drawings." She keeps note of phrases, titles that come from disparate sources, a scrap of conversation overheard, impressions of readings, a phrase in a letter from a friend. "They give me a nudge and I immediately see an image. I think most of us see words as well as hear them."

Words and image converge in Smith's titles. "I think that having a title to work with gives me a very specific direction, and it enhances and supports my imagery. I seem better able to unify my thoughts toward a single statement."

While titles help her define an image, the places she creates are usually full of the spirit of the Southwest, her home for many years. She has traveled extensively through the Southwest, Mexico and South America. "I'd like to think these trips as a whole provide me with a wider philosophical view of the world that helps make my microcosm richer, but frankly I don't think that's the case. I'm more influenced by sights along the way, like visiting the Gold Museum in Lima, Peru, where I saw thousands of incredible pieces of gold modeled into enchanting figures and vessels. They're so close to what I've been trying to do for years."

Just as makers of ritual objects from other cultures combine materials freely, so Smith, without hesitation, uses a variety of materials in her work. She incorporates painted or fiber-wrapped twigs, Mexican amate paper handmade from the inner bark of the wild fig tree (often used as a background), small votive charms, bits of copper, crystals, beads, feathers and, recently, figures she sculpts from Polyform.

Like *Small Star Shrine,* many of her works contain small niches. Sometimes these niches become secret hiding places for a fetish; other times they form an enclosure or an entry for an heroic figure, a spirit, a wraith. She constructs these niches meticulously, embroidering the top layer and carefully cutting and turning back the opening, which is glued and/or stitched in place. The embroidery is planned so that it appears to curve around the edge of the opening. In *Spirit Hand* (facing page, top), the niche is a more formal setting, enhanced by richly regal colors. An arch frames the hand, its simple lines contrasting with the complex figure.

The construction of *Spirit Hand* reveals Smith's technical finesse. The work is mounted in a Plexiglas shadow box. Starting from the back of the box, burgundy Thai silk is wrapped on $\frac{3}{16}$-in. thick FoamCore board. The hand is sculpted from polyform (either Fimo or Sculpey III), which Smith hardens in her oven. She adds black volcanic sand to the surface before firing it in order to dull the finish, and gold leaf is added after firing for highlights. The hand is secured with stitching to the FoamCore. FoamCore is fragile, so to prevent a hole from forming in it and to secure the thread, Smith stitches around brass washers that she has glued to its back. The red coils are plastic-coated telephone wire wrapped with fine perle cotton. There are seven rows of these coils, each separated by a strip of painted balsa wood. The outer layer of the construction is made of a lightweight wool, and, as in *Small Star Shrine,* is solidly covered with machined whip stitch made on Smith's Bernina 830 sewing machine.

In contrast, *The Dominator* (facing page, bottom) actually leans forward from the work, a menacing figure looming in the foreground. This work was Smith's response to Riane Eisler's book *The Chalice and the Blade* (Harper & Row, 1987), which presents two models of society. One is typical of a patriarchy or matriarchy where rank is of supreme importance. The other is a partnership where all members work together, diversity is welcome and linking rather than ranking is the norm. The major figure in *The Dominator* is made of polyform with volcanic sand embedded in the body. Smaller figures, seen by Smith as good forces, are of smooth textured polyform with soft, wrapped adornments. The sun shape, with massed areas of machine whip stitch, is gathered and stretched over slightly padded cardboard. The horsehair strands emanating from the sun were looped through the gathering stitches before the shape was appliquéd to the background. The strong, dark, vertical shape against the central disc is balanced by the smaller, lighter horizontal figures. Smith comments on the balance of darkness and light in the world: "It's a fact of life."

Smith's ability to generate strong images that combine unusual materials with embroidery is masterful and technically elegant. Smith is a student of embroidery whose work is built upon, but not bound by, a knowledge of the history of the medium. She employs hand-embroidery and machine-embroidery techniques; detached stitches based on weaving, netting and lacemaking; and wrapping and knotting in her work (see the sidebar on p. 116-117). Her approach is flexible and experimental, yet she honors the tradition of samplers in her own working process. These samplers are not intended as decorative objects, but as practice pieces for study and reference. They reveal to her how a stitch will look in varying fibers, how thread colors will interact with one another and with the background, and how variations on stitches or techniques from other sources will work.

An ongoing series of samplers is worked only with the machine whip stitch, a distinct raised line that is made by loosening the bobbin tension and allowing the bobbin thread to "whip" around the top thread (see the sidebar on pp 38-40). Smith uses Natesh, a fine rayon thread, in the bobbin and a regular sewing-weight thread on top. Because of the sheen of the Natesh, it is difficult to imagine how it looks when stitched. Thus, she makes small samples of every one of its several hundred colors for reference. She does a few at a time, using any new colors she has chosen for a project and adding a few more selected at random, until the fabric stretched in her hoop is filled with small samples. These are cut apart, the edges of the fab-

Spirit Hand

1988; 14 in. by 11 in.; polyform hand, wool and Thai silk fabrics; machine embroidery, wrapping. (Photo by Bill Atkins.)

The Dominator

1989; 14 in. by 11 in.; polyform figures, wood, Prismacolor, Aquarelle, horsehair, dyed cotton percale; machine embroidery, wrapping. (Photo by Joe Foster.)

ric are stabilized with Fray-Check, and they are sorted by color into envelopes.

Color is of consummate importance to her: Through sheer personal curiosity, plus the requirements of teaching the subject, I have collected, analyzed and compared so much data on color that now I automatically combine the academics of color theory with what I feel is most expressive. So-called harmonies have never seemed that important to me. Chroma, the purity or dullness of color, one just knows. But a careful selection of an overall range of just how light and how dark and especially where to place a dominance, is very important. The choices I make can be intuitive, but it is easier, more logical, to make some deliberations, to make intellectual decisions based upon color theory, especially in the area of value. I use hue intuitively, and I work with value in a more time-consuming manner, combining theory with whim.

The wide variety of materials, techniques and textures Smith uses requires a keen eye and sensibility to keep the color and design under control. "I know that I'm going to use a lot of textures, a lot of value contrasts and very likely will have materials other than fiber. I know that I will need very strong, basic shapes and contrasts in size. I may break them up, but I need those shapes to contrast with the intricate areas."

Connecting weaving techniques and embroidery

Silent Conversation
(detail)

1986; 12 in. by 9 in.; Amate paper, weaving stitches. (Private collection; photo by Wilcke Smith.)

Wilcke Smith uses a number of weaving techniques, adapting them for embroidery. Each of these "stitches" is worked on a base of long stitches laid on the surface of the fabric like a warp. The distance between the laid threads and between the rows of raised stitches will determine whether the stitch looks open and lacy or firm and solid. The appearance of the stitch also varies with the size and type of thread or yarn used on warp and weft. Smith's stitches generally have a solid, textured appearance, as illustrated in her work *Silent Conversation* (shown at left).

Smith comments on her favorite stitches, shown on the facing page:

"Once these weaving techniques are used as embroidery stitches, they may change names. *Raised stem band* is familiar to embroiderers and just as common to weavers who call it "soumak." There's also a variation of this stitch in which rows of *detached buttonhole* are worked over rows of raised stem stitch. *Detached coral knot* is sometimes used in multiple rows to space and secure the warps at the beginning of a weaving. In a heavy perle cotton it makes a beautiful texture. *Ceylon stitch,* or *cross looping,* is an ancient form of netting and may actually predate weaving. Its finished appearance looks like stockinette stitch in knitting. Working it over laid threads makes it firmer.

Here, her ability as a technician is matched by her discipline as a designer:

Long ago I designed things for other media, and I had a physical pleasure in the very feel of making a fluid line. But apparently when I moved to the Southwest my lines got stronger. I saw vital lines in rocks and earth shaped by the elements. Most of my pieces are vertical, with a dominance in vertical edges. I'm wary of angled lines. I know they're very dynamic, but I feel the need for stability of sorts. Often I run two or three of the edges off the work asymmetrically. Maybe in a subtle way it's connecting things to other times and places.

Smith combines intellect and imagination, the result of years of study, thought and practice. Schooled in literature and journalism, followed by work as a graphic designer, then as a mosaicist before she came to embroidery, Smith brings a rich background and a blending of the mind and hands to her work. She continues to research her craft, adapting from other media and techniques and recording these adaptations as references for herself and her students. The work itself inspires her. She travels to study, absorb and teach, but she always leaves a half-finished piece in her studio, waiting to welcome her home.

RAISED STEM BAND, OR SOUMAK

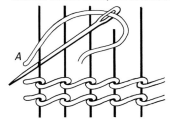

Stitch variations

Lay in warp threads. Bring the thread up at A, and keeping it above the line of work, cross over and slide the needle behind the first warp thread, being careful not to pierce the ground fabric. Repeat the process with the second warp thread and continue working from left to right.

For variation A, work the basic stitch, alternating rows and skipping every other thread. For variation B, work the basic stitch over two threads at a time.

DETACHED BUTTONHOLE OVER RAISED STEM STITCH

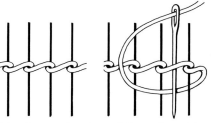
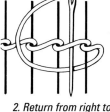

1. Lay in warp threads and work one row of raised stem band, from left to right.

2. Return from right to left, sliding the needle behind the warp thread and working a row of detached buttonhole stitches.

3. One or more detached buttonhole stitches can be worked over each stem stitch (three are shown here). Slip the needle behind the warp thread and continue working as shown.

DETACHED CORAL KNOT

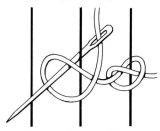

Lay the warp threads. Work a coral knot (see the glossary of stitches on p. 216-221) over each warp thread from right to left by sliding the needle from upper right to lower left behind the warp thread and passing the

working thread over the needle and under its point to make a loop as shown. Slide the needle through and pull the knot snugly around the thread (placing the thumb lightly over the loop helps to position the knot. Continue working to the end of the row, and sink the needle into the fabric to anchor the row.

If the next row is to be worked from left to right, loop the thread in a left-to-right direction and angle the needle from upper left to lower right.

CEYLON STITCH, OR CROSS-LOOPING

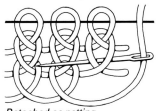

Detached as netting

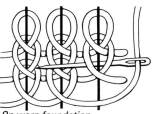

On warp foundation

This stitch can be worked detached to form netting (above) or over an anchored warp of laid threads (above right). The latter gives a firmer, denser In either case, work continuously from

left to right to achieve the effect of knitted stockinette stitch.

ARTURO ALONZO SANDOVAL

Are You Watching? Are You Listening? No. 4

1988; 32 in. by 38 in., framed; color photographs, transparent acetates, paint, thread, veiling, fabric; stitching on rag paper. (Collection of Lynn Sweet; photo by Mary S. Rezny.)

It is easy to be seduced by the surface and structure of Arturo Alonzo Sandoval's large works. They are brilliant, shiny, orderly, colorful and made from an intriguing mix of materials. Beneath the surface, however, lies a powerful, sobering message that addresses the devastating problems and debilitating fears of life in the late 20th century. The message is conveyed through printed images of weapons, nuclear blasts, acts of terrorism and pornography, which forewarn ex-

ploitation, destruction and death. Yet his works bear the conviction that hope and humanity are not antique notions. Sandoval's message is ultimately plain and passionate: be aware, be thoughtful, be hopeful.

The compositions that carry this message are direct, balanced and basic. Sandoval often uses a circle or a circle within a circle, with wedge shapes moving out from the center in a formal, almost symmetrical balance. A circle suggests wholeness, contemplation; it is a shape that is trustworthy. Superimposed on this traditional symbolic content is the contemporary intention of the circle as ground zero, the target seen from the air just prior to destruction. The wedges radiate; nuclear force releases murderous energy:

> For me, part of removing fear is placing myself inside or surrounding myself with the threat and seeing that it's not that threatening. This image, this form that I'm trying to bring to the public is, I hope, a softening of what may or may not be inevitable, but also an understanding that it is a part of us. We have created it; our technology has. We have to accept it, because we have no other way of dealing with it as a taxpayer. I have put myself in the position where I can create imagery that talks about color, form, the nature and intensity of the problem, but in a manner that is more abstract. There is a target, and there is a title that draws the spectator into the work. I hope there is, maybe, a conscious effort once someone reads the title or discovers the message, that they will question its meaning for themselves, and its relation to them personally.

The Nuclear Age is also the Industrial Age, and Sandoval uses its products—film and tape, Mylar, Lurex and plastics—to construct his emphatic commentaries. Their colors are lush, glittering with reflected light, and beguiling, momentarily distracting attention from the depth of the messages that lie beneath the surfaces.

There is a certain irony in the fact that these materials, meant for industrial purposes, are often brittle and fragile, and must be treated with care. These industrial products are not meant for the ages. Even considering the archival qualities of works that deal with the ultimate destruction is perhaps anachronistic. Yet Sandoval is concerned with longevity and uses various materials and techniques to help conserve the fragile films and tapes, attempting to build in his works at least 30 years of survival time.

Sandoval's ideas take form from printed images on an assortment of background materials (sheets of acetate, film or a combination of microfilm and paper) and through several printing techniques on these materials (acetate transfers, lithography and experimental photographic processes). He begins his simultaneous construction/conservation method by interlacing or weaving his chosen materials together. These newly constructed "fabrics" are the foundation of what will be a layering and stitching process. He adds a layer of veiling to hold these materials in place, using a wide zigzag machine stitch. Once enough machine stitching is done to secure the work, he glues a layer of Pellon on the back using AC 64 glue. This adds additional body to the work so that each time he adds another layer of stitching he is building a stronger fabric. A large machine needle with a leather point makes clean holes in the materials. "The materials do pierce and can tear, so the leather needle and the zigzag stitch have allowed me to get structure without destroying the surface."

The sewing machine is essential to the construction process, and it adds line and texture to the design. For Sandoval it has also become an expressive vehicle:

> What excites me about using the machine is that it's like drawing with a pencil. I have taught drawing for years, and I have finally begun to bring to my studio some of the philosophy that I have been sharing with my students about loosening up and making the surfaces more expressive. When I'm really energized and working on a surface, you'd never be able to look and find a road that leads to anywhere, even though the sections are pieced together very much like a quilt. Every row of stitches is added on top of another to get this quality, this layering of values. The machine has finally allowed me to stop and take a look and analyze what I've done. I study it as I would add glazes

with oil paint. The veiling helps hold these fragile materials in place, like a thin skin. But the surface, the main quality and texture, the main gesture is the line work on the sewing machine.

Sandoval is amazed that he can accomplish all that he does on an old Singer machine. He looks forward to new possibilities when he buys an industrial machine with a rheostat speed control, but for the moment, "the old machine has taught me certain things; some form of patience that I might not have otherwise."

Embedded in the materials are the provocative images essential to Sandoval's work. Although he does much of the printing himself, many of his works depend on film footage or processes created by others. One such series, entitled *Are You Watching? Are You Listening?,* employs an experimental process developed by photographer Mary Jo Toles. Sandoval has combined these X-raylike photographs with photocopies on acetate, and additions of paint, fabric, thread and veiling stitched to rag paper. In *Are You Watching? Are You Listening? No. 4,* (on p. 118) a photographic image of dignitaries seated to watch a nuclear test, their eyes shielded, serves as a reminder of how little we knew once and how little we comprehend still of the energy we have unleashed. A blood-red mushroom cloud appears as if over the watchers' heads. Bomblike shapes mix with the familiar words "Top Secret" and "Confidential." A quartered circle set askew within a quartered rectangle lends a disturbing break to the otherwise well-orchestrated symmetry. Sandoval explains:

> All of the information that has surrounded nuclear energy and nuclear history has been under this cloak of "You don't need to know—top secret" for so long. It is all a part of the essence of our government's handling of the situation. I have selected to work in this manner, using the imagery more directly, because first, I see it as a healing, and second, I see it as an antinuclear kind of statement. I grew up and was around right after the bomb was dropped, and every time there was a new test, it was going to be ten times greater than Hiroshima. I kept wondering what was going to be next. We lived with this fear of nuclear holocaust.

In the materials he uses and the techniques he developed, Sandoval has found a voice for his profound concerns. He was introduced to the materials at the Cranbrook Academy of Art, where he learned to weave. He notes that he felt no kinship with the loom until he could control it and use it for his own personal statements. Since Cranbrook is close to Detroit, America's motor-manufacturing center, high-tech materials were readily available. He experimented with them, weaving and trying ancient techniques like interlacing. His imagery began to take on forms influenced by the character of the Mylar and tapes. "Prior to the work I'm doing now, my work was nonobjective, abstract and textile oriented; it was just linear and patterned, very minimal or gridlike." He explored the sky, and ideas about light. The reflective quality of the materials led him to work a series of abstracted "Cityscapes."

Sandoval's work began to change direction, and he wanted to involve his audience in it. He began to add words so the spectator would come and read. It was the music of singer Billy Joel in his album, "Nylon Curtain," that motivated him to use, first, the American flag as a symbol. The target came next:

> It just happened in the studio when I was fooling around with forms. I realized, because of my drawings, I was seeing things in a more aerial perspective. That element crept into my work, and the formal aspects of it, I think, came from my attempts to make forms that interact to create perspective, to create dynamism and some form of axis that immediately draws the spectator towards what I'm after, and then moves him away from that point.

Ground Zero No. 8—Target Babylon III (facing page, at top) is one of this series of target images seen from the air. Within the work are flickering images of terrorists, each image only partially visible, like motionless figures on movie film, waiting for a projector to give them life. The lurid hot pinks, acid yellows and dirty oranges of the central target area, Babylon ("New York is our Babylon"), are completely surrounded with blacks and greys, like the charred remains of fires. In Sandoval's targets the lines do "draw

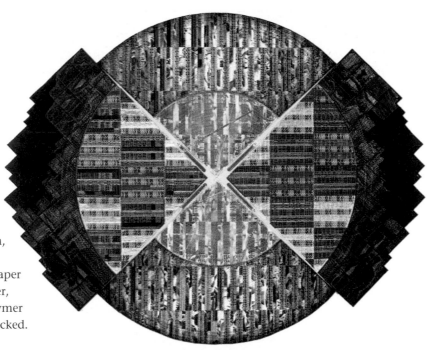

Ground Zero No. 8 —
Target Babylon III

1988; 50 in. by 63 in.;
mixed-media construction,
stitched, pieced and
interlaced 16mm microfilm,
70mm leader film, veiling,
Mylar, photocopy on rag paper
and acetate, magazine paper,
colored threads, paint, polymer
medium, eyelets, canvas backed.
(Photo by Mary S. Rezny.)

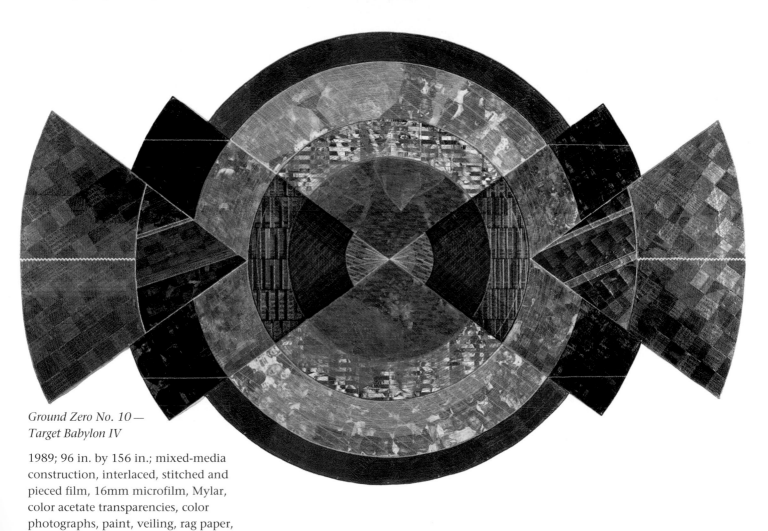

Ground Zero No. 10 —
Target Babylon IV

1989; 96 in. by 156 in.; mixed-media
construction, interlaced, stitched and
pieced film, 16mm microfilm, Mylar,
color acetate transparencies, color
photographs, paint, veiling, rag paper,
colored threads, braid, polymer
medium, roplex, eyelets, canvas backed.
(Photo by Mary S. Rezny.)

the spectator in and move him away," but so do the color and image, which both attract and repel.

Sometimes the images take over and control the work in process. When that happens, Sandoval stops and "listens" to the work before he can proceed to its finish. He defines listening as "really just using patience and not being in a rush to make another object, but trying to create something that has meaning. That listening time, for me, is really just a time to be sensitive to what is coming off those forms." He also listens to what nonartists who come to his studio have to say about his works in progress.

In one instance, it took a technique developed for one piece to solve the problems in another. In order to capture the Babylon theme more graphically, Sandoval chose to use a pornographic image in *Ground Zero No. 9*. When the work was not progressing to his satisfaction, he decided to solicit the reaction of nonartists to this work and found that each immediately responded to the pornographic image. That was not his goal for the work, so he chose to wait and listen and not act until he had found a resolution that would invite the viewer to see the entire work, not just one image or two. He allowed this work to sit for a bit while he finished the next one in the series, *Ground Zero No. 10 — Target Babylon IV* (at bottom, p. 121). The solution lay in a technique he used on the tenth piece. Rather than applying net veiling in a single layer, as he had been doing, he folded it before stitching it in place:

> I bend the netting, and then I stitch, and bend and stitch. It's more like working the veiling as a glaze. Every time it falls and goes back on itself, it adds another subtle transparency. The imagery behind is still there, but I will be able to shadow it, layer it. It's not going to take over and be just what it is. It becomes something more enriched by layering. It will still be there for the investigation without its stepping on your toes.

In discussing *Ground Zero No. 9*, its predecessor (No. 8) and the next one in the series (No. 10), Sandoval reflects on the problem of copying one's own work: "The initial structure is very much like another *Ground Zero,* and I have to divorce myself from this idea of repetition, this idea of having the image materialize in the same manner as the others have. I don't want that. I really like, from one piece to the next, to show some sign of growth. Not so much that it has to be different, but it has to be better, to grow." *Ground Zero No. 10* grew well on its own and has been exhibited in both the prestigious Lausanne Biannale and the International Textile Fair Competition in 1989.

Since 1974, Sandoval has balanced his studio time with teaching at the University of Kentucky. He attributes the influence of his students and the nature of the teaching process to his own continuing education:

> I was teaching what I thought I wanted my students to do, and my students would go and do the opposite. When I discovered that I could try this too, then the work was magical. Another thing that helps me teach is taking a risk with my own work. Teaching has helped me not be so dependent on success from the past, but to jump right into something new. Because I do have the experience of the teaching, I do see results, and I can distill that.

Sandoval listens to his own advice, and he listens to his work. "I wasn't always in tune. Younger, faster, impatient; doing things with bold strokes instead of realizing that bold strokes can be done at a pace more in keeping with the idea." There is always excitement in the next work for this man who speaks to all people of unspeakable issues. "Every piece is so new that other than basting, I never know where I'm going next on that surface."

Creating an artwork for the community

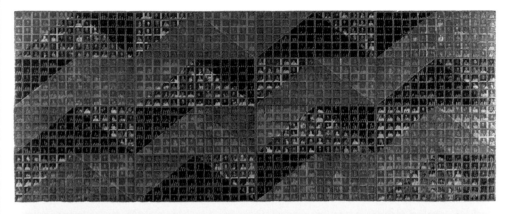

Heritage Festival Faces: Windows of Creativity

1989; 88 in. by 224 in.; mixed-media construction, machine stitched, pieced and layered Mylar, transparent acetates, veiling, paint, monofilament thread, Pellon, roplex, canvas backed, Velcro®; full photo at top, detail above. (Photo by Mary S. Rezny.)

In 1989 Arturo Alonzo Sandoval created a major public artwork, *Heritage Festival Faces: Windows of Creativity* (funded in part, by the Lexington Fund for the Arts Community Arts Development Program). This mixed-media construction measures 88 in. by 224 in. and incorporates over 300 photos of people who attended a Lexington, Kentucky, arts festival and volunteered to pose for Sandoval's camera. He describes his ideas, the working process, and the pleasures and frustrations of creating a public project:

"For the Lexington project it was my intention to utilize a public event that would attract a general audience. 'Heritage Festival Week' consisted of a week-long series of art-related events. Several artists, including myself, were invited to demonstrate their art/craft processes in Central Park, next to the new Public Library. The city had coordinated its second successful Fund for the Arts campaign and had invited artists to submit ideas for public-impact art works. My first submission was rejected, but my follow-up, *Heritage Festival Faces* concept, was awarded funding, although not the full amount I requested. The frustrating aspect of this grant was soon realized when I was informed that the actual monies funded would not be assigned until after the idea was completed and exhibited. Using personal funds to finance this artwork was a hardship, because the amount funded did not fully cover the expense of materials.

"On Saturday, May 20, 1989, at 10:00 a.m., I set up my color Polaroid camera on a tripod and began taking pictures. First it was of the artists who were there to demonstrate, then slowly, as news spread through the festival, others allowed me to photograph them. Each child was encouraged to spread the word around about the 'free' color pictures. A flyer had been posted during the week so that the public could participate in this event. Another flyer described the artwork to be designed and the imagery to be included, which would be familiar to the region. All the participants signed a photo release when they agreed to participate, and I asked for their age, address (so I could send them the picture) and their occupation. Not everyone gave me their age. Some pictures came out better than others, but I was able to use all the photographs. In all, 330 participants were used for the dominant design imagery.

"Once I gathered the pictures and began the project I had to hire some help in order to keep to my timetable. I intended to show the final piece in November 1989. My first design step was to lay out the pictures by the number assigned to each photo (first to last as photographed). Six images fit nicely onto an 8½-in. by 11-in. sheet, and this format became the module I used. The final module system required 336 images, and I had to repeat the first six images as the last module.

"I chose to use transparent acetates as the main material and made copies of the Polaroids in red, blue, black and in four-color process. These colors are typical to the copy-machine process, and the acetate transparency would allow me to use more high-tech materials behind each copied image. Colored Mylars and films were used as the backing and silver/red, gold/blue, rainbow/black and opalescent/four-color became the final color combinations. Although each color copy reproduced each image as a 'real' image, the color combinations would give an abstract distortion through light reflections and the kinetic movement of the spectators in the area where it would be placed for viewing. Painted nettings in the same colors as the color copies were stitched over the acetate surfaces to add subtle texture and solid structure. Transparent monofilament thread was used throughout.

"The completed design uses a descending twill pattern, but the four panels composing the design can be arranged in various ways. I wanted the spectator to view the four-color imagery as the primary design color and to descend in the order each picture was taken (using the logic that in Western reading habits we read from the top then to the right in a descending order).

"Each panel measures 88 in. by 56 in. and is finished off with canvas and 3M Lockfast loop-and-hook fabric adhesive (similar to Velcro®). Wood armatures have the male portion of the Lockfast material and are designed to be nailed to the wall for installation. Each panel then floats away from the wall. The

four panels are rolled separately face down for shipping and packing and can be transported in a sturdy tube. I documented the work with 4-in. by 5-in. transparancies and slides, and a color postcard was printed.

"*Heritage Festival Faces* was exhibited in the gallery of the Lexington Public Library from November 1989 to January 1990. The exhibition time was extended because of the severe winter conditions that December and because of the popularity of the work.

"There is a poem by the Appalachian poet Allen Eaton stitched on the surface of each panel that says: 'He who is creative, whether he live in a palace or a hut, has in his house a window, through which he may view some of life's finest scenes.'

"I felt that this poem typified the mood that I intended to convey to the Lexington community and to those who participated in this city arts project. It is my hope that the community will appreciate the representation and abstraction as it was stitched into a form traditional to the Southeast, the quilt."

The stitch is often compared to a brush stroke, a dab of color applied with the aid of a needle. As each stitch connects to the next, it is also a way to create line and add texture. There is a deliberation about the stitch made by hand as the artist considers where and how the needle should pierce the fabric. Or there is the latitude granted by the machine-made stitch. The machine needle acts as a drawing tool, making marks and creating the line as the fabric is guided beneath. Each stitch adds body to the fabric, and each stitch is capable of securing materials together. It is simultaneously ornament and structure. The stitch is treated in individual ways, and thus becomes the signature or style of the artist.

LINE AND COLOR AND THE STITCH

Maria Theresa Fernandes: "I really like stitchery as a form of drawing."

Susan Wilchins: "For me, it's always a drawn line. Even if it's the same color as the fabric, it becomes an object, an outline, an edge, a shadow."

Arturo Alonzo Sandoval: "The stitched line is a malleable thing. You can run it, straighten it, stretch it, reduce it. At the same time you are playing with the machine; you can reverse it, you can go forward."

Risë Nagin: "Line and physical structure are integrated. You can't have a stitched line that doesn't somehow hold the whole piece together, so it becomes part of the construction. Every single mark that you make with a needle and thread

is like a brush stroke or a pencil mark in a drawing. I see it as another way of drawing."

Kimberly Izenman: "Using compilations of seed stitch has got to be one of the most laborious methods of laying color, but it also achieves some of the greatest complexity in small works like mine. With the large number of colored threads available, it's all too easy to reach for the nearest approximate hue without exploring other ways to achieve the color. By layering and blending different colored threads, it's possible for me to obtain greater tonal ranges as well as depicting movement and dimension with stitch direction. I have more control over my medium and over the mood I wish to convey."

THE STITCH AS A SIGNATURE OF THE ARTIST

Sandra Nickeson: "My works are about rhythms, relationships, connections, continuity with the past and future, with the stuff beneath the skin of life. They are celebrational, intended as places to center and gather strength, and often, to recapture humor. As stitch builds upon stitch, I follow the path of author Anäis Nin, whose signposts read, 'Create against Destruction.' "

B. J. Adams: "The stitch is a primary, simple and familiar technique. Most people are more comfortable with a stitch than a brush stroke. Maybe that's why it hasn't, in most instances, been recognized as a 'fine-art' technique in the same way the painted brush

stroke has. However, I see the stitch as another technique along with the brush stroke. It's what is done with it that determines its place in life.

"The role of the stitch has changed for me over the years. In hand embroidery, stitches were often the whole design; sometimes they were drawing, sometimes painting to give an unusual texture. In my manipulated fabric pieces they were to pull things together and to give an accent, such as a pencil line, a ribbon or a slash of color. In the new pieces, the stitches are like wide pens or lines of paint applied with brushes or markers. The stitches are now the medium to draw/paint the designs. The whole piece is stitches, stitches, stitches, to the point where they may be disregarded, except for their texture."

Joan Schulze: "The stitches are so important! It's an affirmation of how I finally got into being an artist. I'm always celebrating the fact that embroidery got me to where I wanted to be, so I always put stitches in the work. I don't feel that the 'quilting stitch' is a quilting stitch. I think of it always as a running stitch. I get a lot of static from people who tell me that my stitches are uneven. I say, 'No, you miss the point. I'm very capable of making very, very even stitches, but I'm putting rhythm into my work. If you look at it you'll see I'm leading you like music—an ebb and flow, an up and down, the crescendo and diminuendo.' All of that is the function of the stitch. I learned that in embroidery."

WORKING FROM A HISTORIC TEXTILE

Tom Lundberg: "First, study a historic textile. Research how this textile expresses the identity of the people for whom it was intended. How is it used? How does it express ideas about place and time? Does it fit into larger patterns or cycles? Is the textile part of a larger set that rotates? Is it for use exclusively during a specific occasion or period of time, or for a general season?

"Next, make drawings from your observations of the textile. Or analyze the composition of the textile, looking at how it has organized shapes, color, line and texture.

"Then create a textile that is a descendent of the piece you have researched. How can you develop your personal imagery within the spirit of the historic piece? How can you work in response to traditional sources without superficial mimicry? Is there a difference between quoting a historic piece and plagiarizing it?"

SAMPLING THE EXPRESSIVE QUALITY OF STITCHES

Wilcke Smith: Make a small design on paper and indicate at least five to seven values (light, middle, dark). You need more than three values to indicate what you're going to do. Do a series of samplers of varying stitches with this design to see how each will translate into a particular shape. Work on color, using different threads. Look at what you've done. What's the effect of each stitch (shiny, dull, rough, flat)? Write out a short scenario. What are you trying to say in the work? What are you expressing? Then everything you do, every stitch you select, every value and color should push this point."

EXPLORING SPONTANEOUS STITCHING AND STREAM OF CONSCIOUSNESS

Maribeth Baloga: "For materials you'll need six pieces, approximately 10 in. by 10 in., of unbleached linen, muslin or any natural material that will accept paint; a small piece of organdy approximately 4 in. by 4 in.; fabric paint in a muted color; and one medium-size paint brush.

"Take each piece of linen and paint a light wash with diluted fabric paint within an area approximately 3 in. by 3 in. Use the brush freely to create a raw edge and texture. Let the first layer dry and paint on a second wash, leaving some areas open and again using the brush freely. Place the piece of organdy on top of the painted square and brush on a layer of undiluted fabric paint, letting it bleed through to the linen randomly. Remove the organdy and paint directly onto the linen with undiluted paint to create some areas of deep color. Let dry. Repeat this process for the other pieces of linen.

"Then sit back and look at each sample, and let your imagination pull forth images. Choose one and begin to stitch into it responding to the images created by the paint and your imagination. Your goal is not necessarily to create a representational image, but rather to explore spontaneous stitching and stream of consciousness. If the final product is not to your liking, turn your piece over and try to respond freely to the threads and knots on the back and the images they evoke. Remember, the image need not be representational."

GALLERY

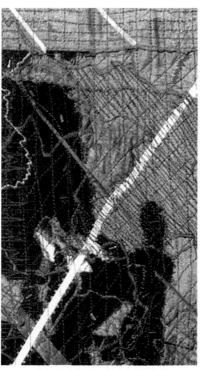

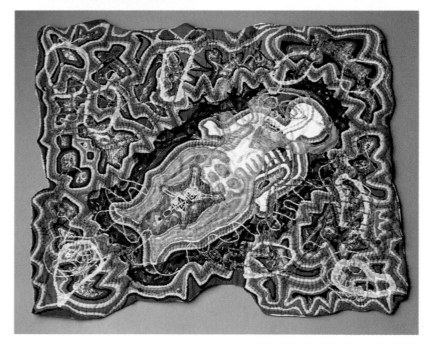

GERRY CRAIG
Journey Relic #19

1986; 39 in. by 56 in.; linen
tablecloth, ribbons; silkscreen,
stitching; detail above right. (Photo
by Gerry Craig.)

JOYCE J. SCOTT
Happy Holocaust 4

1987; 12 in. by 16 in.; fabric, beads;
reverse appliqué. (Photo by John
Dean.)

dj BENNETT
Black and Tan

1987; 20 in. by 28 in.;
India ink applied to wet
burlap; appliqué, machine
embroidery. (Photo by
dj Bennett.)

JANE DAMS
Cloak for a Recording Angel

1984; semicircular, 144 in. from nape
of neck to end of train; silk, silk
organza, velvet, brocade, gold leather
and other fabrics on silk/polyester
doupioni; screenprinting with
sublimation dyes and metallic
powders, appliqué, hand
embroidery, machine embroidery,
gold couching, beadwork; detail
below. (Photo by Judy Rumak,
detail photo by Jane Dams.)

"The basic theme was all the
important occasions in a person's
life: birth, marriage, old age and
death."

SALLY CUMMING
Out of the Blue

1989; 10 in. by 10 in.; cotton
embroidery on cotton canvas.
(Photo by Sally Cumming.)

SANDRA NICKESON
Big, Dumb Gun Speak

1990; 26 in. by 18 in. by 1 in.; fiber-reactive dyes painted on cotton fabric, quilted with silk, rayon, cotton and gilt threads, sequins, found objects (plastic guns and rubber lips); crocheted cotton and rayon border. (Photo by Red Elf, Inc.)

"International terrorism, anonymous driveby and freeway shootings and intrafamilial violence are all part of life on planet Earth in the late 20th century. Somehow, someway, we must get beyond big, dumb gun 'diplomacy' as a way of settling disputes, and on all levels pledge to 'study war no more.' This work was conceived as a sort of visual cue or memory aid to the insight that each one must find in her or his own way; that the chain of violence which begets violence which begets violence is shameful and results only in squandered beauty and lost opportunities for love."

ERICA LICEA-KANE
Veil

1988; 40 in. by 60 in.; *Shibori*-dyed cotton fabric cut into strips and adhered to a heavy canvas backing; multilayered with machine stitching, stamp printing, acrylic pigment and acrylic medium; detail at right. (Photo by Gorden Bernstein.)

WITHIN AND WITHOUT

LLOYD WALTON BLANKS

Lowland Fruit Trees, III

1988; 18¾ in. by 16½ in.; wool on canvas; needlepoint. (Photo by Susan Kahn.)

North Door and Window, I

Overleaf: 1988; 16½ in. by 18¾ in.; wool on canvas; needlepoint. (Photo by Susan Kahn.)

The still, spare needlepoint canvases of Lloyd Walton Blanks make it possible to feel the scorching heat of the Texas Panhandle, to scan the flat expanse of fields stretching into a limitless horizon. With a masterful blending of color and line, he evokes the land he remembers from childhood.

Blanks grew up in a west Texas farm community during the Great Depression, the Dust Bowl and the ten-year drought. From 1922 until 1941 Blanks lived on the family farm in the town of Caps, so named by his Grandfather Blanks, who, upon arrival, tossed his hat into the air, and said, "For want of a better name, let's call it Caps!" Near Abilene, Caps was never any larger than a schoolhouse, a blacksmith shop, a grocery store and two Protestant churches. Blanks remained in the area for a time after finishing college, teaching painting and design at nearby McMurry College, then moved on to New York City to study at the New School for Social Research. He has lived in Manhattan since 1952, but the powerful stimulus of memory still keeps the west Texas images alive in his mind's eye and on his canvases:

A large porch curved across the north and east of the Blanks house, and my grandmother called it "the front gallery." From her rocking chair at the north window, we looked across the front gallery, up the north road to the horizon for any indications of weather change, for some sign of rain, hoping the evening sun would go down behind a cloud bank in the northwest. From the front gallery, we saw the land under all atmospheric conditions at every time of day.... Disconsolate winds played their music through the house and, at the outside corners, ate the dirt away.... Blistering winds reduced every green thing to brown, and when the spring rains did not come, the topsoil of Oklahoma and the Panhandle was whipped into the sky to settle as fine dust on Caps, the southernmost rim of the Dust Bowl. In the darkness of noon the cows came up for milking, the chickens went to roost and we slept uneasily at night with wet cloths across our faces.

Like empty boxcars in endless freight trains, dry weather clouds wheeled across that summer sky on their trackless course from the northwest toward the coast, each cut to size, not one much smaller than the rest, never colliding nor passing, roiling within and rainless, promising nothing to the parched land but swift moving shadows I never could run fast enough to keep up with....

The yard, hard and bare, where not a green thing grew, absorbed the summer heat all day and gave it back at night when we had gone to bed. The red land was the last to be claimed by settlers and made a part of the community, for it resisted cultivation as it resisted sudden downpours, which ran off red and angry into branches and creeks, leaving the soil under the hot sun to bake as hard as pottery. Some sheep and goats were brought in for the meager grazing, and in time they took on its color and could hardly be seen crossing the red land.[9]

Blanks has been working on a series titled "The Front Gallery" since 1979. In almost all of these works the spindly porch pillars suggest a vantage point and reveal a view seen from within the shelter of the house or outside on the "front gallery." Light sources suggest different times of day, and subject matter may suggest a season, such as the proper time for planting seedlings. In each work, however, the main theme is always the stark beauty of the hot, dry, uncompromising land.

Blanks feels a connection to the land in the rhythmic working of the canvas. "From the time I was ten years old until I was eighteen, I chopped cotton. Chopping one row is a little bit like accomplishing a row on the canvas. The field on the canvas is the field in my mind quite often." Blanks's manner is deliberate and methodical: "I'm the opposite of spontaneous." He paces along a row of stitches, conserving energy, much as he must have paced himself for farm tasks.

Blanks was never completely at ease with the rhythm of painting or sculpting wood. He became disenchanted with painting, finding that just when he was really involved with the work, it would have to be set aside to dry. Sculpting was a problem because the noise of hammer on chisel annoyed the neighbors, and seasoned wood was difficult to obtain in New York City. When he accidentally came upon needlepoint at the home of a friend, he knew he had found the right media for his ideas and his pace. He taught himself what he needed to know by patient trial and error. Some things, he admits, a teacher could have taught him in two minutes, but he preferred to work his way in and out of problems to be solved. He rigged an unusual but thoroughly serviceable rack for positioning the stretched canvas for ease of working:

I made my own rack from found objects—a large flat board, some sloping moldings and a heavy cast-iron lid left over from the repaving of First Avenue, which became a weight to keep the rack from tilting into my lap. Some discarded barrels offered up angled pieces of wood.... Pushpins held my canvas in place, so I had both hands free to work through the 17-in. by 15-in. frame. I attached the soft pine moldings with screws so that when they became riddled with pushpin holes, I could replace them easily. I adjusted my rolling secretary's chair to the proper height and for back support to ensure long and comfortable hours of work.[10]

Life in New York City is light years away from west Texas, and Blanks wonders if he will ever be tempted to depict its urban atmosphere, noting wryly that it probably would be only if he returned to Texas. His apartment contains his studio, and he keeps long, regular hours at his work, beginning around 11:00 in the morning and continuing, with a stop for dinner, until 9:00 at night. "Needlepoint is such a terribly slow medium that if I don't put in a lot of hours, it just doesn't move very much. One of the satisfactions that I get from doing needlepoint is looking at what I've just done, and seeing what remains to be done." He delights in the technique:

> There is, in this most deliberate and regimented medium, the satisfaction that comes from watching work accumulate slowly, stitch by stitch.... There are long times when I feel suspended between beginning and end, hung on the pleasure of irregular rhythms and repetitive motion, the soft whir and the feel of friction between canvas and drawn yarn. There are many little beginnings and endings, starting new areas, and filling them, working toward certain points and going beyond.[11]

His is a minimalist approach, "eliminating unnecessary things" to capture the essence of the moment. The work, in Blanks's terms, is "basic," uncomplicated in appearance, but clearly carefully thought out. He knows what he wants to communicate through the work, and he knows how to achieve it. "There's a certain amount of my work that's intellectual as opposed to emotional. And, generally, I can always figure out what I'm going to do."

Blanks is well aware of what every line in his work will do for the composition. "For years Mondrian was my absolute god, and I preferred to work with horizontal lines and vertical lines in my needlepoint." The stillness noted in much of his work draws on his use of straight horizontals. "The psychology involved in line bears that out. The horizontal line suggests peace and repose as well as death." *Lowland Fruit Trees, III* (shown on p. 132) makes deft use of subtly shaded diagonals, with similar color values playing behind the row of trees. "I use that technique to lead the viewer where I want him to go, where I want the eye to go."

Blanks says he has been most influenced by the Bauhaus philosophy and aesthetic. "There's that tendency to work in flat areas. Although I have used a lot of circles, I find in needlepoint that circles are very difficult. I think that actually they are not in character with the medium." He has used circles or curves in tree forms in his work. They are often highly stylized, however, such as in the leaflike shapes of *Young Transplants Acclimatizing, I* (on the facing page) "I did that because they are transplants. They are not natural to the landscape, and they are simplified, almost geometric, indicating that they are not a natural growth on the land."

Just as Blanks questions imposing circles on the grid of the canvas, so he eschews texture. Indeed, he notes that the land he captures on canvas was once devoid of much texture, but he also questions using texture as a design element. "I'm not convinced that texture is a legitimate part of design. I know it is for most people, but I have a strong tendency toward purism. People have complained that I have no texture, but that's my choice. It's not natural to me."

As Blanks works, he is continually thinking about color relationships. He usually starts with an area of bright, intense color, finishing it completely before he begins an adjoining section. "I make certain that my second area establishes something vital with the first area. I proceed that way; in my third area I try to get, again, a color and a value and an intensity that will work with the other two areas. I move forward very slowly, very carefully that way. If I get three areas working, if I establish some kind of dynamic quality between these areas with color, then the fourth area has to contribute to what I'm doing."

The way the colors relate is vital. "You must keep some dynamic relationships between your colors at all costs or they can be so insipid, so weak and meaningless. If there's anything I try to avoid in my pieces it's colors working with other colors that just don't *do* anything."

His colors are not solid, but are blended of three strands of Paternayan Persian wool, which he works on 40-in. wide, 10-gauge mono canvas. "My blending is done with a pattern so that the stitches on the back are all going in the same direction. The back, in fact, looks almost like the front. That can be accomplished only by laying in patterns of stitches. I blend the colors vertically and horizontally, and now I even have a diagonal method, but it's very complicated. (See the sidebar on p. 136.)

Blanks likes the color palette of Paternayan Persian wools, but wishes there were better blues, a typical complaint from those embroiderers who use one brand of material exclusively. Blending helps solve this problem. Blues and violets are favorite colors, and the red-violets he often uses reflect the color of the west Texas earth, the dust in the sky of his landscapes.

Blanks is careful about controlling the light source in each of his works. In *Lowland Fruit Trees, III,* the trees appear to float right off the land. He notes that this effect is achieved by having the light source at the bottom of the trees, instead of the natural way that light would come from above. He connects this piece with pointillism, and especially Georges Seurat, noting that he didn't have Seurat's work in mind when he did this piece, but was reminded of it when he was finished. Each stitch is a point on Blanks's canvas, colors blending both in the needle and through the patterns to yield a subtle glow. He tries to avoid having the work look stitched. "With needle blending and stitch blending I try to get away from that 'needlepoint' look."

Blanks works slowly through each piece, listening to what it suggests for the next one. "I'm not overjoyed that I'm finishing a piece. I hesitate to put that last stitch in. But maybe I'll think how to improve it, and that will send me forward into the next piece."

Young Transplants Acclimatizing, I

1988; 18¾ in. by 16½ in.; wool on canvas; needlepoint. (Photo by Susan Kahn.)

The artist is in tune with his work, moving forward at a deliberate pace, but looking back to the land that is luminous in his recollections:

I saw the first haze in the fall preceding the first blue norther, and I watched the clouds gathering in the northwest to come up after dark as a storm, which sent us racing to the cellar, hopeful for rain, fearful of hail and a twister. We waited out the storms while they raged and tore above our heads. When the southeast rumbled and reported back and quiet had returned to the land, we laid back the cellar door and came out to nights of stars.[12]

Blending colors

To achieve the distinctive blend of colors in his needlepoint canvases, Lloyd Walton Blanks mixes plies of colors in the needle and works an intricate pattern of stitches on the surface. He begins by plying three different colors in the needle and stitching a vertical half-cross stitch, skipping every other hole. Using this "skip stitch," he lays in the first strand of three colors, repeating the process and filling in the remaining holes with a strand of three other colors. Thus he has opportunity to blend up to six colors in a given area.

He may choose to alter only one ply of color, which produces very subtle changes. Too much contrast in the second set of yarns, he has discovered, may yield a strong and possibly disturbing diagonal pattern.

Where he begins and ends an area depends on the number of horizontal threads on the canvas to be covered. For an odd number, he begins at the top left corner, skipping the first horizontal line, and places the first half-cross stitch to cover the second horizontal line. At the bottom of the first row, he moves down one horizontal line to make the first stitch of the next, this time ascending, row. He continues in this manner until the first application is completed. To fill in the skipped stitches, he begins at the lower left corner, using three colors differing from the first combination.

If an area has an even number of horizontal threads in the canvas, Blanks works as just described, except he leaves the bottom line for last. He completes this line horizontally, skipping stitches left to right, then right to left.

To work larger areas, he has developed a "3-2-2-1 skip stitch," which permits dovetailing the colors and avoids strong dividing lines. The numbers 3-2-2-1 refer to three skipped stitches in the first row, two in the second, two in the third, and one in the fourth. He uses this method for establishing subtle color changes, creating color movement and thus changes in mood.

The colors blend vertically across horizontal bands, establishing tonal shifts as the eye is led both across and up and down the composition. There is little distortion to the canvas, and the front and back of the work look almost alike.

VERTICAL HALF-CROSS SKIP STITCH

Start first yarn here. Work down the first row, skipping every other stitch.

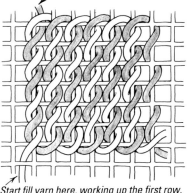

Start fill yarn here, working up the first row, down the next, and so on.

BASIC 3-2-2-1 SKIP STITCH

Work left to right

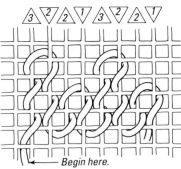

Begin here.

DOVETAILING 3-2-2-1- SKIP STITCHES FOR COLOR BLENDING

Begin second color here.

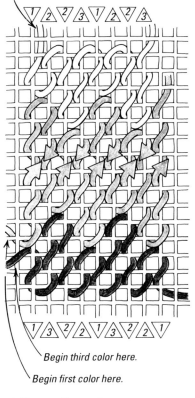

Begin third color here.

Begin first color here.

A fill yarn will cover the canvas.

Completing a Canvas

Lloyd Walton Blanks has developed a system for mounting, framing and storing his work that shows the same concern for detail that is evident in each of his pieces. He writes about his methods:

"In working out my system for mounting and stretching my work, I have relied on information from textile conservators at leading museums, especially Mary W. Ballard, senior textile conservator at the Conservation Analytical Laboratory at the Smithsonian Institution in Washington, D.C. It was pointed out to me that canvas that is stretched too tight will one day break somewhere. I came to the conclusion that the canvas must be pulled tight enough to eliminate sloppy sags,

This detail of Lowland Fruit Trees, III *shows Blanks's methods for shading and preparing the work for framing. (Photo by Susan Kahn.)*

but no more. It was also suggested that perhaps pieces should *not* be mounted and stretched as a permanent condition, in consideration of future dismantling for cleaning or other reasons we can't foresee. Certainly the fewer staples used, the more easily a canvas may be unstretched and removed, and the less likelihood there is of breakage and damage at the borders. My eye has now become accustomed to the idea and no longer requires that extremely taut look.

"Here is my method: My mounting boards are ¼-in. white Philippine mahogany plywood, cut to size. Mahogany is lightweight, low in acid content and not prone to warping. Birch is a good substitute. I sand the edges of the boards before applying a first coat of polyurethane to one side and the edges. The following day I turn the boards to coat the other side and the edges. I suspend the boards with pushpins and short strings from a rope stretched near the ceiling. When a month is up, I apply a second coat and rehang for another month to ensure that the boards are completely dry and that harmful fumes have evaporated.

"As an extra precaution, I place a piece of acid-free (nonligneous) tissue paper on the sealed and seasoned board. I fold it around to the back to cover about 3 in. on all sides, holding it for the moment with adhesive tape. Over the paper I lay a piece of unbleached muslin, again folding about 3 in. to the back. As I square the corners and pull to stretch the muslin across the face of the board, I use a staple gun on the back. I set in only enough staples to hold the muslin firmly

over the paper. Monel metal staples are a must, as they will not rust or corrode. This provides a rigid mounting base for stapling and holding the needlepoint in its display position, while keeping the cotton canvas out of contact with the acidic wood.

"On top of the prepared mounting base I place the piece of finished needlepoint, which I have lightly pressed on the reverse side with a steam iron and allowed to dry. The borders are about 1⁄16 in. smaller than the mounting board so that there will be no puckering when the frame is attached later. I position the corners first and then work out toward the middle of the edges. I strive for a consistent 5⁄8-in. border from the edge of the board to the first row of yarn. I staple, checking constantly with a ruler and an L-square. Nothing is more irritating to me than seeing a line of stitches disappear off the edge and under the frame.

"My frames have a wide lip to cover the 5⁄8-in. border. The face is 1¼ in. wide, flat, painted white and unadorned. I repeat the polyurethane treatment on the raw wood that is not painted white. I screw a stretcher to the back of the frame to hold the mounting board securely in place, but it can be removed easily.

"Pieces that may be exhibited once or twice a year spend most of their time in storage, stacked flat in unbleached muslin slipcovers in a well-ventilated room. Between the large pieces I have placed sheets of nonligneous tissue paper. Over the different stacks are thin covers, as additional protection from light and dust. I let no more than four months elapse before rearranging, airing and inspecting."[13]

CAROL SHINN

Speedworm Layers

1989; 21 in. by 30 in.;
machine stitching on
canvas. (Collection
of Herbert and
Diane Cummings,
Scottsdale, Arizona;
photo by
Carol Shinn.)

Rear View Mirror

1989; 15 in. by 19 in.; machine
stitching on canvas. (Collection of
Mr. and Mrs. Chester Luby; photo
by Carol Shinn.)

Carol Shinn explores the space between reality and fantasy. Her heightened-color works deal with permanence and change, with a species of life of her own creation and the effect of people on the environment. In addition to her machine-embroidered works, she weaves tapestries and also works in collage. The ideas she develops find their way into each of these media. She writes about her work and the subject of many of her pieces, *Veloxvermis* (speedworms):

I celebrate fantasy with my work. Metaphoric use of fantasy helps me understand and order the physical world. My images make the unreal real and become proof for the existence of whatever I choose.

Some of my work is about an imaginary genus *Veloxvermis*. This simply shaped creature sometimes operates in two-dimensional patterns and sometimes as an illusionary three-dimensional image. This duality plays upon two textile traditions: that of elaborating the surface and the physical presence of the textile, and that of negating the surface through pictorial representation.

I create with tapestries and machine-stitched canvases. My work is done out of love for the involvement with thread and yarn. The physical element, the yarn, the thread, becomes the structure as well as the image. This creates a unity between the tangible presence of the textile and the imagery depicted on it.

I draw inspiration from many different styles and media of artistic expression. The production of art in turn becomes the catalyst for understanding the joy and complexity of human existence.

Flight Layers

1989; 29½ in. by 44 in.; machine stitching on canvas; made in four parts and pieced, joined areas hidden under stitching. (Private collection; photo by Arizona State University Media Center.)

MERRILL MASON

Hurricane Gilbert IV

1989; 44 in. by 56 in.; textile pigment on cotton fabric and polyester organza, Canon laser copy heat-transferred to cotton gauze, gold foil, linen, metallic thread; hand embroidery, machine embroidery; detail at left. (Photo by Erik Landsberg.)

With fiber and fabric, paint and print, Merrill Mason confronts nature's most destructive forces. Her principal images are the hurricane's eye and the tornado's funnel; her primary materials are delicate gauzes, cottons and silks.

There is a willful approach to reconciling opposites in her work, a sometimes quirky connecting of unlike elements. They are complex pieces in the making, but, when completed, they convey a quiet sense of order. The combination of such frankly feminine materials and soft, ethereal colors in depicting such violently powerful forces seems at first incongruous, but Mason has a mindful, reasoned explanation for her choices:

> I don't think that a feminine point of view is always going to be something soft and pretty. I think that a lot of women fear the loss of their home and the loss of any kind of structure in their lives; and I think that being a woman involves a lot of living with violence and fear. Using these materials with this imagery leads to their strengthening one another. There's a spectrum in our unconscious life that involves the full scale of happy, warm, domestic things and violent, angry, destructive things. That's much more feminine than just something clichéd and pretty.

Each of Mason's works is made from multiple layers of fabrics and multiple processes to alter the materials. At the core of each piece is the image of either a tornado or the eye of a particular hurricane. The sources for the imagery vary from her own photography and drawings to news and magazine photographs. Through the National Oceanographic Aeronautic Administration she has obtained satellite photographs of hurricanes, mostly those of Hurricane Gilbert taken on September 15, 1988.

She works the disturbing imagery within a balanced structure. Her works are symmetrically composed, most with a strong central image. Allusions to quilts are frequent in her work, and in fact, she has made quilts that employ the tornado image. She sees no problem in combining the stuff of nightmares with objects intended to provide protection and warmth. She does only nonfunctional pieces now, but still retains some of the quilt attributes, layers and patches and combinations of materials.

Mason does not aim for perfectly clear images. By using photocopies of photographs and heat-transferring them to textured materials, she knows that the resulting print will be blurred, indistinct and perhaps, distorted. She aims to have the images look a bit worn and used, and as her layering process develops, the images become even more diffused.

Just as the hurricanes and tornadoes she depicts change the land, so Mason alters each piece of fabric she uses in her multilayered works. On some fabrics she prints an image; on others she uses Createx metallic textile pigments, painting dots and dashes resembling raindrops and adds Createx metallic foils, which adhere to fabric with heat. She chooses both colored and white fabrics, but has a special preference for a green/gold iridescent that has something of the color of the sky during a storm and contrasts with the colors painted on it, giving them an eerie glow.

The source of the small bits of color that transform the fabrics is in an earlier work. "I had used little elements that just floated on the borders in one of my large pieces, and then I began to bring them into the center. The little embroidered lines and painted elements are like things that float on the surface of a pond, weightless."

Having prepared the painted and printed fabrics, she is ready to construct the work. She began *Hurricane Gilbert IV* (on the facing page) by laminating painted cotton fabric to a heavy linen canvas. The painting in this case is a loosely worked map of the Caribbean, which was further

Hurricane Gilbert V

1989; 26 in. by 26 in.; layered, pieced and sewn cotton and polyester fabrics hand-painted with textile pigments, Canon laser copy heat-transferred to cotton gauze, metallic thread; hand embroidery, machine embroidery. (Photo by Erik Landsberg.)

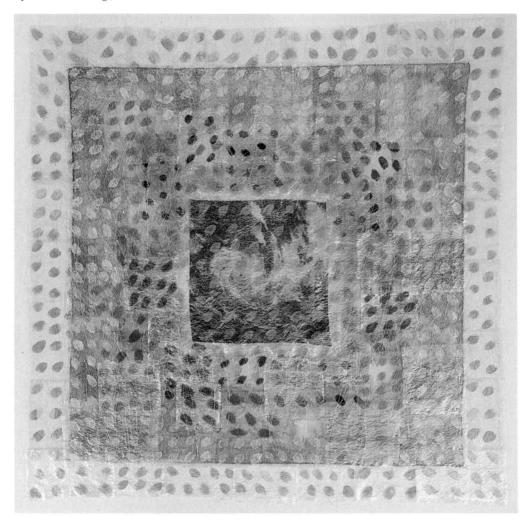

altered by scratching into the wet paint. In the center of the next layer is the photographic image of the eye of Hurricane Gilbert transferred to cotton gauze. She sewed this layer to the painted layer with fine metallic thread. The final layer is of painted iridescent fabric, which is tacked only at the top with monofilament. This layer moves slightly with wind currents in the room or if someone walks by. There are hand-embroidered and machine-embroidered areas in fine and medium-weight metallic threads, the delicate stitches like lines of repair. Gold foil is added, re-

vealing itself beneath the edges of the top layer. The embroidery acts to add a third dimension to the work as well as to secure the multiple layers.

Hurricane Gilbert V (shown above) has no laminated areas and no heavy backing. Mason painted on iridescent fabric, then cut it into squares and began to patch them together to make the multicolored fabric. The image of Gilbert is again printed on cotton gauze. In this piece, the gold metallic threads both secure the layers and add spots of color in the built-up dots of solid satin stitch, worked on her Bernina

Transferring a color copy to fabric

Merrill Mason is fascinated with printing. While experienced in various techniques of printing on paper and fabric, she has chosen a heat-transfer printing process to affix a photograph or drawing on fabric. The process is labor-intensive but is actually completed quickly.

She purchases time on a Canon laser color copier at a local copy shop and, working with the aid of one of their technicians, makes multiple copies of the images on a special heat-transfer paper, available at art-supply stores, or through Quick-Way Color Copies (see Sources of Supply on p. 222). The technician aids in manipulating the image, shrinking, enlarging or cropping it, as well as altering, adding or removing color. Since the cost of using the machine and the price of heat-transfer paper are fairly high, Mason is careful to do test runs on regular copy paper first, and to fit as many small images onto one sheet as possible, cutting them apart later for transferring onto fabric.

The largest sheet of transfer paper she uses is approximately 11 in. by 14 in., which determines, to some extent, the largest size image she will use in a finished piece. With careful planning, she can obtain images for close to a year's work with one or two trips to the copy shop.

After collecting a number of images on transfer paper, she cuts out each image, avoiding any inadvertent borders of transfer paper that would transfer as a creamy texture onto the fabric.

She prints on a variety of materials, including handmade paper. Mason has used cottons with no surface finish intended for fabric printing (available from Test Fabrics, see Sources of Supply on p. 222), polyester/cotton blends, gauzes, silk organza and a recent favorite, a translucent iridescent polyester organza.

Her procedure of printing is as follows: pad a piece of plywood with folded sheets of unprinted newsprint and place it on an ironing board or the floor. Lay the well-pressed fabric face up on top of this surface. The heat-transfer paper is positioned face down on the fabric and another sheet of newsprint is placed on top of the pile. Press hard for six seconds with a dry iron set at the hottest linen setting and with the full flat face of the iron over the image. Lift the iron and press again until the image has been completely covered. Then press firmly with a circular motion, keeping the iron moving so the fabric won't burn, although not sliding the iron around so much that the image smears. This part of the process takes practice, and a few mistakes before getting the right "feel" for transferring the image. Practice with small pictures, and transfer the image with different levels of pressure and heat while varying the ways of moving the iron until satisfactory results are obtained. Some fuming takes place, and when that subsides, the transfer is compete. The process takes only a few minutes.

Contrary to the instructions that come with the transfer paper, which suggest waiting for the fabric to cool before removing the paper, Mason has found it essential to remove the paper while the materials are still hot. This is easy for small images, but more difficult with larger works. She picks up the materials, and working as quickly as possible, peels them apart starting in one corner. If an area cools, she reheats it slightly with the iron before peeling away the paper. The printed fabric cannot be ironed directly again once the print is transferred. If the image has distorted somewhat, warm the ironing board and lay the fabric on it, which will heat it sufficiently to manipulate it back into shape

The process takes longer to describe than to do. "I'm doing something that's fast. There's this moment of revelation that's very exciting when it's all done."

sewing machine. She left the ends of the threads on the surface to form what she describes as a gold fur or scrim. "The dots that happen act almost like beads, since they're built up dimensionally. The embroidery integrates all the painterly images in a way. It's not just functional, for there's an expressive need filled here that makes the piece work."

Mason confesses to a fascination with process and technique, claiming that if she didn't need to create work, she'd probably be a dilettante and collect techniques. She feels that she was genetically disposed to enjoy mechanical and technical problems. Her grandfather and great-grandfather were well-known makers of decoys, and her father, an amateur woodworker, made most of the furniture in her home. She recalls happy Saturdays as a child spent in hardware stores and helping him with projects.

Mason studied printmaking in college and was in the first undergraduate class at Yale to which women were admitted. At that time, the art department discouraged anything connected with "feminine" fabric, fibers or imagery. She continued to make prints until allergies to the materials involved forced her away from those processes. The centralized focus of her work, however, is directly connected with her training in printmaking. "I've always been interested in the frame around a work. It's part of the printmaking format of an image or a rectangle floated inside a larger frame, the paper."

As a child she was also fascinated with fabrics, playing with a collection of her mother's handkerchiefs, and enjoying the fabrics that "were always around the house." But she didn't take the artistic possibilities of fiber and fabric seriously until she worked with the exhibition "The Art Fabric: Mainstream," curated by Jack Lenor Larson and Mildred Constantine. It was Mason's responsibility to provide installation instructions for each art work to the museums that displayed the exhibition, and to work with the packing company that crated the work. Traveling with the exhibition and helping at each venue with uncrating and installing the pieces, she considered herself "a traffic controller for art." The lengthy and intimate contact with these works confirmed for her that she needed to "get out of organizing other people's exhibitions." She said, "I wanted to get back to my own work full time and the 'Art Fabric' exhibit, in particular, was closely related to what I wanted to do."

With a background that has exposed her to many techniques, materials and ideas, and with her predisposition for research and experimentation, Mason knows she must set limitations for herself. She aims to simplify, to get to the heart of the work, rather than allowing the work to become overly decorated. She has discovered that she works in six-month segments, and she evaluates where the work is headed about twice a year. "My intention has been to push myself away from ornamentation, to drop some of the add-ons that are easy for me. I want to keep narrowing even more."

In getting to the essence of her ideas Mason aims to maintain a sense of spontaneity, "to keep some sense of passion and immediacy with what I'm doing. I don't want to end up with something too distanced from the feeling that conceived it. I don't want it to look too designed. I've worked hard to develop a technique that allows me to try things out and then pull back and evaluate. I try to keep things flexible."

Like most artists, Mason's sketchbook is full of drawings, sources for supplies, notes of ideas to try, postcards and memorable quotes. Two of the quotes recorded on those pages aptly describe the impetus underlying Mason's multilayered ideas and images. One that is unattributed states: "Chaos is the law of nature; order is the dream of man." The other is from Orson Welles: "The enemy of art is the absence of limitations."

RICHARD DAEHNERT

Richard Daehnert uses an unusual combination of processes and materials to present his contemporary pastoral visions. Like stage sets made of one material to resemble another, his works combine a unique variety of processes: photocopy-machine imagery, painting, drawing, dye-transfer printing, free machine embroidery and stenciling—whatever techniques he needs to create the lustrous other-worldly landscapes over which graze his uncommon cows.

Daehnert, an expert in surface-design techniques, discusses his works:

My fabric works are rooted in my personal experiences with, and relation to, the natural environment. Since childhood, my response to the world in general has been influenced by the moods, forms, spaces and surfaces of the natural world. Transformed within the work, they represent landscape not as a documentation of specific time, place and space, but as a metaphor for encounter and journey through Life itself.

For me, the cow is, in part, a symbolic connection to the rural landscapes of my native Wisconsin. The cow as a nurturing, peaceful, contented, free-moving, pastoral creature animates the landscape in which it exists. A herd animal, it's seldom seen alone as in these works, where I have placed it within an ambiguous, nonpastoral, landscape space. Here, landscape is an invented transparent geometry.

I have used heat transfer, collage, drawing, painting and machine stitching on these works. The machine stitching is used like drawing with colored marks, excessively layered; as such, it tends to reduce the identification of landscape details.

Spatial Emergence I

Top: 1988; 12 in. by 14 in. by 1¼ in.; transfer dye, thread, dye marker, polyester fabric, canvas; heat transfer, collage, machine stitching, drawing, painting. (Photo by Susan Kahn.)

Pastoral Trilogy

Above: 1988; 15 in. by 21 in. by 1¼ in.; transfer dye, thread, dye marker, polyester fabric, canvas; heat transfer, collage, machine stitching, drawing, painting. (Photo by Susan Kahn.)

SALLEY MAVOR

Noah's Ark

1985; 30 in. by 26 in. by 1 in.; dyed
velveteen, beads, embroidery floss, wire;
fabric relief; detail on the facing page.
(Collection of Judy-Sue Goodwin-Sturges
and Philemon Sturges; photo by Susan Kahn.)

Salley Mavor's art is simple, honest, warm and very human. The life she depicts proceeds from a sense of order: spring follows winter, crops ripen on the vine, the sun comes out after rain. The world reveals itself in all its bountiful goodness.

There is a childlike directness about Mavor's work. She deals in basics. There's no room for adult-ridden cynicism, grey areas or clouds of worry. It is not surprising that she is currently involved in creating a series of fabric reliefs to illustrate a children's book.

In all of Mavor's pieces, the figures, worked in low relief, appear to float, as if they had been pinned to the backing. There is no artistic hierarchy of space or objects, no deep space, no perspective. There is just lots of activity and delightful doings to discover.

Mr. and Mrs. Noah watch benignly over their menagerie in *Noah's Ark* (on the facing page and at right). Giraffes chomp on the trees, a bull with a contented expression surveys the scene and a turtle crawls over the edge of the bordering frame. The rainbow is hinted at in the warm colors that form the border. There's plenty of reassurance that things are under control and life will be all right.

Mavor's technical procedure is as fresh and inventive as her designs. She starts with an idea that has had plenty of time to simmer before she begins to sketch. Her sketches are very basic, just enough to get the composition settled, although she may sketch again later, after the background is made and some of the figures formed.

The work evolves, beginning with the background. "I either dye fabric and piece it together or I use an existing piece and appliqué different pieces next to one another." Making the borders delights her. "This is fun, because you get the immediate results by throwing different pieces of fabric against one another." Occasionally, during the final stages of a piece, Mason will add yet an-

other whimsical touch by extending some of the embroidery into the border. She uses upholstery-weight fabrics for most of her backgrounds, preferring to stay with wools and linens, finding silk too fancy for her style. Many of her fabrics are recycled. "A lot of it comes from people's attics, grandmothers' old pieces, a real mishmash." She colors fabrics with procion dyes, spattering or spraying it with a mister. Since she often uses old fabrics of varied colors, each dyeing session has an experimental flavor.

The three-dimensional figures are constructed separately, made in relief upon a flat back of cardboard. A piece of wool fabric is in turn glued to the back of the cardboard, which provides a surface for the needle to pierce as Mavor constructs the front of the figure. She usually starts with a basic body part, the trunk or the head. The body sections are made separately and then sewn together, giving her more flexibility when she is finally ready to place the figures in their environment.

She glues or holds in place a small amount of polyester fiberfill on the front of the cardboard shape and then begins to dress the body. There is a charm in creating these details akin to that of making miniatures or doll houses. If clothing is to be embellished, that is worked separately, then the figure is dressed. She will sew back into a figure, however, to add more details. All the work on the figure is secured in the back, which ends up a wild crisscross of thread.

The backgrounds are embellished before the figures are added and the work is stretched. Mavor finds it easier to embroider without a frame before the figures are sewn to the background because the embroidery thread would catch on an attached figure. She works on the background and the figures at the same time since she needs both the size and position of the figures to know where to embroider the background. Conversely, she needs to keep the background in mind when she is forming the figures.

Once the figures and ground are finished, the background is stretched "taut enough so it won't sag," and she sews around the edges of the figures, "just enough so they stay in place." Mavor's husband constructs wood shadow-box frames with glass fronts.

Mavor has extensive formal training in art, which, she says, she has worked hard to unlearn over the years. She was encouraged as a child to explore all sorts of art media. Her mother, an artist who trained at the Rhode Island School of Design (RISD)—as did Mavor years later—worked in silkscreen, calligraphy, batik and watercolor. "My mother taught art classes. My grandmother sewed everything. We were free to make messes. I never thought of art as just painting and drawing. Craft has a different element, a humanity in it, something warm and wonderful." Mavor's sister is also an artist who works in mixed media and performance art.

Mavor knew early that she wanted to be an artist. "I remember learning script in the third grade, and although this was not technically art, I felt really moved by this form of writing. My

later impression of art classes was of how basic and dismal they were. There was never enough time or materials." She felt unchallenged by two years of printmaking at a state university, so she transferred to RISD to major in illustration, a department where all media were welcomed. "I could have the freedom I needed. The only restriction was that I needed to communicate clearly."

It was slow going to find the folklike style that has become her own. "My family was very folk oriented. There was a lot of music and dance and art." But the attitude at the state university had discouraged this early learning. She explains:

> When I was moving into fabric at RISD, one of my instructors very perceptively knew that I was having trouble. She knew that I needed to try something new and learn that art was fun. She suggested that I do something that I did as a child; make something like a doll or do a big painting with poster paint. I got back to the joy of making art that I used to have. I would try to draw like a child and use my left hand to try to loosen up that way and use color freely. Really, I was trying to get back to that state of being a child. I can draw very well realistically, but I just don't find any satisfaction in doing that. I like to know I can do it and then move on.

Mavor's naïve style is hard earned, well informed and honestly achieved. She loves the process she has developed but has the sense to know when to stop. Her work has a certain clarity, which contrasts well with all the intricate details. She says:

> I suppose I could keep embroidering forever. I think what stops me is I just know that it doesn't need any more, I've spent enough time on this one and it's time to move on. I like having a clear design and if you put a lot of embellishment in, it sometimes makes the design less clear. I want the work to stand out from a distance; I want to be able to appreciate the design, and then be drawn close and see the details.

Her life is full of her young sons and family at present, a happily chaotic time for her. By sharing time with another young mother, she clears two hours each day for uninterrupted work. There is no time for the luxury of getting stuck. "I work so slowly and so infrequently that I don't do enough to overdo or get bogged down. When

Picking Peas

1986; 20 in. by 27 in. by 1 in.; glass
beads, spun wool, embroidery floss,
twigs, wire; fabric relief. (Collection
of Mr. and Mrs. Winslow Carlton;
photo by Susan Kahn.)

I do get to my work, it's like coming home again.
I just have to work from the moment I sit down.
I can't sit there and wonder what I'm going to be
doing." She sometimes fears that her ideas will
vanish before she has time to execute them.

She appreciated the encouragement she
received from her artist-mother, and she is repeating this pattern with her own children. Part
of that cycle is reflected in *Picking Peas* (above), a
simple scene of shared work. Carefully holding
the basket, the wide-eyed boy mimics his mother's
stance and shares her expression of serene glad-
ness. "None of my art is as important as being a
mother. I have grown as a person, and my work
has gotten stronger as a result. I have more of a
conviction to communicate. I have to express
the best. As long as I can work, the rest of my life
can be more chaotic. Seeing life happening fuels
my creativity, the everyday occurrences, the sim-
pler the better."

Stump work

Stump-work cabinet, ca. 1650, covered with white satin, embroidered in petit-point and stump work and embellished with seed pearls and coral. (Courtesy of The Metropolitan Museum of Art, Rogers Fund, 1929 [29.23.1].)

S alley Mavor's fabric relief works are reminiscent of stump work. Both reflect a love for detail, a placement of figures on the space rather than in it, and sometimes even a design incorporating Old Testament stories and characters. There is also a recognizable delight in invention, a spontaneity and a use of a variety of available materials. While unpopular with the Victorians who thought it vulgar, stump work is again appreciated in the 20th century for its charm, and perhaps as well for its connection with contemporary collage and assemblage.

In the middle of the 17th century in England, a needlework fad, later dubbed "stump work," developed. It was popular with well-to-do girls and young women who had achieved a certain expertise in embroidery. Stump work combined a naïve and childlike placement of figures with a lack of concern for proportion, and a sophisticated eye for dressing figures in the fashion of the day.

These sculptural works usually depicted a landscape with sun, rainbow and clouds, a mansion or two (occasionally with windows of attached mica) and central royal figures often set within an attached tent or canopy. Even when scenes depicted stories from the Old Testament, the Apocrypha or mythology, the figures were dressed in the current fashion and usually represented royalty.

While popular for only a brief part of the century, many of the works were preserved as family heirlooms and are available for study in museums and private collections. One such work at The Metropolitan Museum of Art, from the middle of the 17th century, illustrates many of the characteristics of stump work. It is a cabinet, or box, embroidered on all the visible sides with figures depicting the five senses.

The top of the cabinet, pictured here, shows a central figure illustrating hearing. Her costume is of tent stitch, a half-cross stitch worked on fine canvas, probably linen, with needle lace and detached-buttonhole stitch collar and cuffs.

These are applied to a creamy white satin ground. The building in the upper left corner is worked in applied needle lace; the building in the upper right corner is worked in couched silk floss of softly shaded pastels. Many techniques and stitches were used in each piece of stump work, and the work pictured includes French knots, split stitch, satin stitch and crochet.

The term "stump work" was given to these pieces long after their popularity had waned. It probably derives from the frequent use of wood or papier-mâché molds, which were used to pad faces and, occasionally, hands. These molds, referred to as "stamps" or "stumps," were only one way of raising the embroidery. Other ways of building a low relief were achieved by padding appliqué areas with horsehair, tow (unspun linen) or fabric scraps; by working needle-lace stitches over wire; or by using high,ly textured stitches and materials like French knots, purl (a springlike metal thread) or beads. The light-reflecting, animated richness for which the metallic threads were originally intended has been tarnished over time.

Professional embroiderers of the time were also doing raised embroidery, which employed seed beads and padded metallics. These were used to add to the lustre and endurance of the embroidered objects for church and state. But stump work was a completely domestic activity, and as such, retained the charm inherent in doing work for its own pleasure.

LAURA VENTRESCA MONTGOMERY

Hand To Heart

1988; 4⅛ in. by 5⅛ in. by ¼ in.;
acrylic paint on silk, cotton, silk,
metallic threads; painting,
embroidery. (Collection of Jennifer
McNerney and Hugh Morgan;
photo by Laura Ventresca
Montgomery.)

Laura Ventresca Montgomery inserts embroidery
in a painting, or she may paint the embroidery.
In some works she actually paints over and under the embroidery. Whatever process she uses,
each work is a mysterious blending of materials
and techniques; of figures in ambiguous spaces.
She comments on her work:

> I use a combination of embroidery and acrylic
> paint to build up my images. In *Hand To Heart*
> (above), a layer of paint is applied first, then
> embroidery is done on top. Often I choose
> either a book box or shadowbox to contain my

images. These two formats are important to me
because of their metaphoric references.

My work deals with what is seen and un-
seen. It is about two worlds—the known and
the unknown.

151

ANDREA DEIMEL

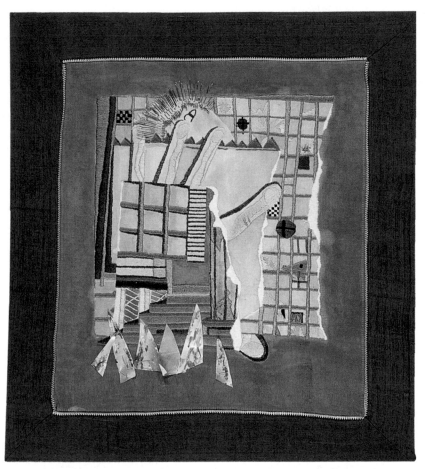

Andrea Deimel ponders how to make words visible and patiently applies stitch on stitch until the whole appears. She combines dissimilar materials—zippers, clay, foil—all of which add a jarring note to the meticulously stitched embroideries. She writes:

Someplace We Were (shown at left) is a visual representation from literature, which evolved as a means to connect my love of literature to embroidery. It's a way to portray fictional emotions and my own. I've included images of architecture—the windows that allow visions of what's inside—and have set the warmth, quiet and calm associated with "home" against images of rebellion, pushing out, screaming—the hard edges of metal piercing the piece. It speaks to the pulling challenges of home, the stability and then the fights, the trapped feelings behind windows of glass, the metal jabbing the calm, and the wish to escape.

This piece is one of a series of experiments in enlarging my work; opening it up to a looser, more picturesque style using a variety of techniques; an evolution from previous tighter, graphic designs.

Someplace We Were

1989; 16½ in. by 15½ in.; dye, paint, metal, fabric; embroidery; detail at left. (Photo by Lee Rexrode.)

LEE MALERICH

Check Mating

1989; 26 in. by 26 in.; embroidery
on painted silks and other fabrics.
(Photo by George Fulton.)

Intense and introspective, Lee Malerich looks
within and grapples with her position as a woman
and an artist in the world. She admits to being
unable to distance herself from her work, and
claims a high degree of narcissism, which both
helps and hinders her as she works. "It's like having mirrors all over your house—you can't es-

ROSITA JOHANSON

The Bike Race

1989; 9½ in. by 7½ in.; cotton thread, cotton fabrics; machine embroidery, hand embroidery. (Private collection; photo by Lenscape Inc., Toronto.)

The Story Teller

1989; 6½ in. by 4¾ in.; watch parts, photograph, metallic and cotton thread, cotton and silk fabrics; hand embroidery, machine embroidery. (Private collection; photo by Ron Elmy, Toronto.)

1987; 4 in. by 4 in.; watch parts, metallic thread, cotton thread, gold chain, cotton fabric; hand embroidery, machine embroidery. (Private collection; photo by Ron Elmy, Toronto.)

Simultaneous layers of stitches and fabrics as well as personal, cultural and religious narrative compose the intimate embroideries of Rosita Johanson. They appear fresh and bright, but there is also a feeling of the "old world" about them.

Reminiscent of a folktale, abounding in detail, they manifest a very basic message that is optimistic, expressing a sense of wonder and faith in humanity. Johanson lovingly crafts scenes from her childhood, a bike race by a lake or a day at the beach. She looks at her past, and dedicates her work to her parents and even includes a photograph of her late father in *The Story Teller* (on the facing page). A homily on time is fashioned in a 4-in. by 4-in. square in *Where Does It All End?* (shown at right).

Johanson's manner is artless as she describes making just one detail of one of her pieces: "To do the bike, I sketch first. I turn the sewing machine wheel slowly by hand and stitch four times around the bike wheels, one stitch at a time. I finish the rest of the bike with a small straight stitch, and stitch the bike spokes in by hand."

Born on the German-French border, Johanson was sixteen years old when she moved to Canada with her family. She writes:

My father was a tailor, so I learned early in life how to handle materials. I also did a lot of sketching during my childhood. I'm a self-taught artist who prefers to work with fiber. I experimented with this media for five years before participating in my first exhibition. I was awarded first prize in my category, and this encouraged me to continue further.

Some of my pieces are only 3 in. by 4 in., never bigger than 7¾ in. by 10 in. My sewing machine is a ten-year-old Singer, which has a presser-foot pressure dial. Increasing and decreasing the pressure on the foot is very impor-

tant in my work because my pieces have up to five layers of fabric.

My tools are three pair of scissors, eyelet pliers for making the wheels on the cars, a magnifying glass, a big needle, a tweezer for finding and pulling out fine threads in case of a mistake, fabric glue, a razor blade, several bobbin cases, a fine soft-lead pencil, size 9 and size 11 ball-point needles and fine cotton embroidery threads from Hungary. I prefer cotton materials. I can pull, stretch and mold cotton better than synthetics.

All my ideas are memories from my childhood or just pure imagination. I think of my miniature fiber art as a marriage of fiber and embroidery.

SUELLEN GLASHAUSSER

Fontainebleau II

1987; 4 in. by 6 in. by 1 in.; paper, thread, silk, pencil; drawing, embroidery; cover at right, interior on facing page. (Photo by Susan Kahn.)

Fontainebleau III
(detail)

1988; full piece (not shown): 11 in. by 16 in.; paper, pencil, thread; drawing, embroidery. (Photo by Susan Kahn.)

Suellen Glashausser's books link the present and the past, piercing the soft-focus images of interiors long since lived-in with tiny, stabbing stitches and pencil strokes. She also creates room-sized environments of cloth, paper, paint and wire, as freely wrought as the books, but monumental in comparison. She discusses her books:

> Artists' books are portable works of art, which bring the owner an intimacy and participation not available in other art formats. The reader/viewer forms connections from one page to the next as the story/image is revealed. For the artist, the random possibilities of turned and skipped pages give energy and flow to a work.
>
> Books and magazines are very familiar forms of communication. By taking this accessible shape, the book artist builds on an acceptance of image and works in a serial format. A history

of pictorial and literary books prepares the viewer to observe and read quickly or slowly from front to back or back to front.

My books are collages of found papers that are sewn together and bound. The paper itself, often used and crumpled, carries associations from its original use. Although rarely containing words, they do tell a visual story. Stitched edges strengthen every page and make visible the hidden stitching in all book spines. Stitching is used to attach and highlight images. Pencil marks often mingle with the stitches.

Fontainebleau III [detail on the facing page] is constructed from an old book of postcards. I use the most basic single stitch for every aspect of the book. Random stitches attach the postcards to the ground, anchor the tape and alter the images. Flower parts are stitched to the page edges, and the pages are stitched together. Irregular cross stitches appear on the page surface.

It's important to me to keep the stitches as simple and irregular as the pencil marks with which they often mingle. I look for the touch of the artist's hand in each of them.

In *Fontainebleau II* [the interior is shown above, the cover on the facing page] the individual postcards are stitched onto silk shoelaces, which are themselves stitched together as the binding. Architectural details on the cards are outlined with stitching, while the interiors are hand colored with pencil. The reverse of the stitching forms the back of every page.

JOAN SCHULZE

Urban Fish

1987; 25 in. by 37 in.; nylon, silk,
cotton, plastic, other fabrics;
layered construction, hand
embroidery, machine embroidery.
(Photo by Sharon Risedorph.)

Fabric fragments, rich passages of texture and
quiet spaces compose the embroidered collages
of Joan Schulze. Each appears to have been created in a moment of supreme play, the wind lifting
snippets of fabric and thread and placing them
just so. Each collage, however, takes its own de-

liberate time, and Schulze may spend hours adding and subtracting elements until she senses that the piece is complete. She explains:

> I'm always seeking composition; that's my first priority. I move things around until I get that sort of magic—I don't want to say "balance" because that's not a good word for what I do— until it "feels" right. I try not to put words to what I do compositionally because that can lead to a formulized style. But when I look at slides of my past work, I do notice common elements: I use a lot of diagonals; I do things in asymmetrical ways; I put an exciting color or rich texture off to the side. This means that I have somehow made that composition work, or that area would appear to fall off the piece.

Schulze tries to keep the designing process open to new possibilities and not repeat herself. She uses whatever techniques and materials she needs for a particular piece: quilting, painting on paper and fabric, dyeing, hand embroidery and machine embroidery, paper and fabric collage, drawing, photographs, even the snippets of threads and fabrics that fall to the studio floor.

With so many options, it takes time to start new work. Schultz moves around her studio spaces, putting away bits and pieces and pulling out others. She explains her procedures:

> I make a lot of postcards of anything funny that I clip from the newspaper, little stories that I find amusing or relevant. I use parts of my photographs that I didn't think were great as a whole. I may combine them with clippings or some of my drawings to make the postcards. It's a way of starting work, and very often it's the only thing I might do that day. I have used some of these postcards as a take-off point for other pieces. They really become drawings, like entries in a journal. I work on them until I find myself moving on to something else. Very often I start out this way, and by the end of the day, I can't even imagine how I got to be doing what I was doing.

Larger works evolve in a similar freewheeling way, beginning slowly and gradually building in intensity. Schultz starts a series of pieces by laying out several backgrounds at once. The ground fabric is often the wrong side of a thin cotton that she has used for a printing or painting demonstration. She begins with a standard size, often 11 in. by 14 in., plus about 4 in. all around to allow the work to grow. She rarely has a preconceived idea of what will emerge. "I go out to my storage room where the painted fabrics are, and I might spot some things that have possibilities. I won't know where I'm going with all this, but I gather it all up, sit on the floor and start playing, layering, checking things and putting them back. Perhaps I'll start on a second or a third or fourth piece. I work until something strikes a chord. And then I think, "Oh, that's something I saw in Japan," or "That reminds me of the Bayland walk I took the other day."

Having connected with an idea, Schultz begins to "push" the composition in that direction. "I think that what I'm doing is getting to a point of departure where the momentum of the work takes over. Then I work until I drop."

There are times, however, when a piece refuses to be so cooperative, and only time or a fresh viewpoint helps. Such was the case with *Urban Fish* (on the facing page), which began with a gift. On one of her trips to Australia, Schulze met Wendy Holland, an artist whose silk-screened fabrics she admired. She mentioned her appreciation to Holland, especially noting the fish she printed. Shortly thereafter, Schulze received a package containing many fabrics, each covered with "a life-time supply" of silk-screened fish. One fabric segment went into *Urban Fish,* a work that recalls the detritus collected near a dock. Bits and pieces of flotsam and jetsam form

Poems and pieces

Sunset From the Bullet Train
1988; 34 in. by 44 in.; cotton, silk, nylon, other fabrics; layered construction, hand embroidery, machine embroidery. (Photo by Sharon Risedorph.)

Poems are becoming an integral part of Joan Schulze's art. She says, "I used to wake up at night with an idea to work on, but now I wake up with words. I like the fact that a lot of the pieces I have done have a poem to go with them. It doesn't explain the work; rather, it extends the work. The work doesn't need the poem, nor the poem the work; but when they're together, they're interesting." The poems (at right) are part of the two works illustrated here and on p. 162.

SUNSET FROM THE BULLET TRAIN

Thoughts race fast
As the train and
Setting sun,
Time to reflect on
Rice fields
And exotic roofs
Mixed with sky.
A flash of temple gates
The land goes to bed
While I plan tomorrow
1988

URBAN FISH

pond layers
hide fish gliding
in a watery city

currents mix
and stir
this murky soup

bits of sky
spiced with gold
among flowers

caught among
drowning leaves
and rotting sticks
I stare deep
reflect
and dream
1990

floating layers, obscuring the depths. Schulze discusses the work:

> It's a special piece to me; it was one of those tough ones. The fish was always there, right from the start. I loved beginning it, when I was layering all the cloth, but then I got totally lost. I had it up in the studio for a long time, and I didn't know what to do with it. Then someone sent me some net, the kind that holds the freeway hills. It was great stuff. I had some other sort of netting, and I started using that, and the piece took off again. I was working with an architect at that time, and he came through the studio and commented that it looked like a city, and that was when I knew what it was. In fact, it really was a city; I just needed a word.

Words are important to Schulze. She writes poems connected to individual art works, which, in turn, add new meaning to the visual content of the work. "I stop frequently to write notes and combinations of words for possible poems or titles. Sometimes the words become more important, and I find that I have written a poem. Then I'll be working from the poem to the piece; and the poem will be finished, and the words will tell me what the piece needs in order to make it finished. They cross over a lot."

Occasionally, Schultz incorporates words or letters in the collages. In *Sunset From the Bullet Train* (on the facing page), a post-trip recollection of her experiences traveling in Japan, Schulze used fabric she had printed by rubbing it over inked wooden letters. She liked the resultant texture, and considered ways to change the Roman letters to resemble Japanese calligraphy. "I thought it was an amusing idea, since I saw sweatshirts and T-shirts in Japan with the most unusual combinations of English words on them. Maybe we do the same thing with Japanese calligraphy and don't know it." She cut the printed fabric in narrow strips and used it for a border. Strips of red and white fabric, which twist and turn in the upper left corner, also suggest calligraphic brush strokes. The poem, in this case, came first, and was written while she was on the bullet train.

Words are not only important for the ideas they convey and for the visual effects they produce, but also because they are usually printed in black, a color Schulze uses frequently. "Part of my use of black is because of reading. I deal with black and white a lot—photocopies, books, newspapers. The other reason, and I think this is totally subconscious, is that there are times when my work gets so subtle that people aren't going to come close to look. I use black to make them look. It marks the areas where I want them to come close. I've watched, and it works. So I think the other function of black, for me, is for contrast, forcing the viewer to get close." In *Sunset From the Bullet Train,* black is laid over brilliant blue spots, the only place in the work where these strong blues are located. Black marks the spot where the blues contrast with the predominating reds. Two black strips also serve to suggest train tracks, the horizontal lines forming a base for the wispy, speeding quality of the rest of the work.

Schulze is stimulated by travel. She makes what she refers to as "pre-trip pieces," anticipating what she will see. "Sometimes I really have it down, and sometimes I'm way off the mark." She takes a sketchbook with her to make notes and drawings. She doesn't refer to them much when she returns to her studio, but she has found, after the fact, that there were strong similarities between those sketches and a finished, post-trip work.

She always travels with a camera, "the best way I have of 'being there.'" The images help capture the essence of an experience. "If I weren't doing the photography, I don't think my work would be nearly as interesting. It has trained me how to look. Although I do drawings, I think the photography is a more accessible way for me to capture what I wanted."

Travel is important to Schultz's work, but so is being home in central California. One double-sided work, *Apparition* (at right), captures this duality:

> Side One, with the orange-triangle mountain area and the wild blue at the bottom became, as I worked on it, more and more an experience I had had in the Southwest. There were

foggy mornings, and incredible changes of light. At the same time, it also brought up memories of home and the Golden Gate Bridge, the sun hitting just a part of it, the rest in fog and very mysterious. On Side Two, there is just one tower of the Golden Gate Bridge and the rest is in fog. Beyond the fog are the leftover bits of sunset.

These two experiences turned into one, and now they're inseparable in my mind. I think that what happens is that when I'm away, my experience of home also gets tied in. These two parts of my being, at home and away, enrich each other. I titled it *Apparition* because these things are very fleeting, and to try to describe them is very difficult.

There is structure in the stripes, which Schulze says "brought the two sides together," a suggestion of architecture and stability, surrounded by changing fog, sun and mists.

Many of Schulze's larger quilts contain compositions on both sides, and can hang in the middle of a space, but working smaller pieces, such as *Apparition,* in a double-sided format is new for her. She finds that working both sides brings a depth to the idea that viewing only one side precludes. Although she has Plexiglas stands to allow for viewing both sides, she is amused that these stands create anxiety on the part of a potential buyer about which side to display.

Schultz is not averse to creating uneasiness in those who view her work, because she actively pursues risks herself. "I'm looking for a little anxiety in my work that almost makes it not work. I don't want it to be safe. If the work is just okay, if it just doesn't excite me, I get rid of it." When a work doesn't feel right, she cuts it up and recycles it, transforming these pieces into new risky ventures, adding and subtracting until the sum is a new visual poem.

Apparition, Side One

1989; 11 in. by 15 in.; cotton, silk; painting, hand embroidery, machine stitching. (Private collection; photo by Susan Kahn.)

Apparition, Side Two

1989; 11 in. by 15 in.; cotton, silk; painting, hand embroidery, machine stitching. (Private collection; photo by Susan Kahn.)

Embroidery is a labor-intensive technique, and it is painful to feel that precious time is lost when a work bogs down. Many artists get around this problem by working on more than one piece at a time, a tactic that allows them to get some emotional distance, as well as physical distance, from the work. On returning to it, new solutions to a problem may present themselves. This may mean ripping out, but that is all part of the artist's discipline. In the interim, time has not been squandered on, as one artist puts it, "the luxury of being stuck."

When a series is finished or an idea is explored to its fullest, the artist may feel emptied of ideas, blocked in a different way. This presents an opportunity, perhaps, for trying small exploratory studies or for playing with a new material, technique or idea to get the creative juices flowing again. Some artists use this time to finish up work that requires more technique than thought. Others catch up on books and magazines, aware of the stimulus they provide. Artists return to drawing, photography or even resort to cleaning their studios. Keeping the hands busy and the eyes alert allows for new ideas to tantalize and crystallize.

WORKING ON MULTIPLE PIECES OR SWITCHING TECHNIQUES

Dana Romalo Andrews: "When I get stuck, I take another work, or I draw or I write, but that's why I have several works going at the same time, including making beads out of threads. I also experiment with knitting, some of which is covered with embroidery, but the knitting shows through."

Arturo Alonzo Sandoval: "I work three or four pieces at one time; then when I need that moment of rest to look at a piece, I can proceed with another one that has already likely had a hiatus."

Terrie Hancock Mangat: "Usually I have all these ideas queueing up in my head, and the most important ideas push forward, so that's what I spend my time on. But sometimes I can't; they get to be too overwhelming, or for some reason I can't deal with them, or my mind blocks. If I get to that stage, I make a log cabin quilt, or I do the embroidered parts. I make embroidered things that are like warm-up exercises. They relieve my mind so that the ideas can come out again."

Mary Bero: "I switch to another piece and work on it. I pin the first piece up and look at it. Maybe I'll see things completely different from the way I was looking at it before, and perhaps I'll decide on a new approach. It's usually just getting that space and distance from the work."

Risë Nagin: "To get unstuck I sit in my studio and take different approaches. I just sit for a while and draw; sometimes that will get me unstuck. I also experiment doing small pieces with different materials. I look over my drawings, going through old sketchbooks to see what I did before. Sometimes there's something that I did that I see a better solution for, or something I wrote down and never explored."

DISTANCING AND ANALYZING

Susan Wilchins: "If there's a problem with a piece, I come back to formal issues. I usually look at the color contrast, areas of light and where they are placed. If the whole piece is not giving me an emotional response, I tend to throw the whole thing in a dye bucket, and take it from there. That's the thing I love about the process that I've chosen. You can always change the next time. That's a simple thing, but it's very helpful when you're stuck."

Caroline Dahl: "I've gotten stuck, and it's usually just a question of tacking the piece up, looking at it for a day or two and working it out."

Wilcke Smith: "If I'm in doubt, I need to ask questions about color, about value, about the totality. Is there something in here that I ought to get rid of? The relationship of negative and positive is so important. It's a good idea at the end to be very critical, almost as if a teacher were standing there, saying, 'First, let's talk about color. What have you done about color? Where are your dominants? Do you really have enough contrast here? When you put the work at a distance, is it going to carry visually?'"

B. J. Adams: "I hang the piece up, go away for a day or so, come back and hope to see the problems with fresh eyes. I'll turn the piece upside down, look at it in a mirror and try to get as far away from it as possible. If I have someone around, I get their opinion. Sometimes I rip out huge amounts of fabric. I listen to what I would tell my students, 'Look at contrasts, curves, lines, lights, darks, restful spots, rhythm and such—all those design nouns.'"

THE DISCIPLINE OF WORKING IT OUT

Deidre Scherer: "I work on more than one piece at a time, and when I'm stuck on something, I just move to another table and pick up something else. I've learned to do that because I rely on sales for a living. It's dangerous not to be working. If I'm not working, I'm not producing enough. I can't submit to a block; I've had them, but I've just worked through them, because otherwise I would be waitressing or something else."

Merrill Mason: "There's a whole issue about leaving something that's successful. You know that there's a kernel of something new, but you're leaving something successful; you dip lower in your curve, and end up doing work that you know is not as good as the last. It's hard to try to work that through. For me, with phenomenal luck, it takes six months, and usually a year. I feel rather insecure during that time."

Lloyd Walton Blanks: "If it's not right, all your wanting it to be right won't make it right, and it will need to come out. I control myself at times like that by thinking, 'Look at all the hours that are in the piece. Another week, another two weeks is not going to make a bit of difference.'"

ANALYZING YOUR WORKING PROCEDURE

Deidre Scherer: "Draw a sketch of how you work. Make it a diagram, or a graph or a circle shape, but actually visualize on a piece of paper how you work. Focus on a project, rather than a day. For example, the project will last a month. See each of the stages of that job. Go through the initial conceptions, material setups and whatever commitments you make whenever you set out to work, even when you take breaks and that sort of thing.

"Watch yourself go through all the different stages and processes and write them down and put down what length of time and even what emotions you experience. I found out when I did this that the worst block I had was when I was making a commitment to a project that would involve me for any lengthy time, even a week. 'Oh, a week of my life!' I would go up to it, fall back and reconsider, and feel like I was making no effort that day. I felt like I was running away from the commitment.

"Then there's a stage when you're singing along in the middle and you're humming, and another stage when you're trying to figure out whether you should stop, or should you have stopped two days ago. I've found that a drawing of how I worked was a real revelation."

CHALLENGING YOURSELF WITH COLOR

Susan Hoover: "This is an exercise I assigned my beginning students the first day of class, when I was teaching at the University of Northern Colorado in Greeley. It provoked a lot of groans and complaints throughout the semester, but eventually it led to lots of enthusiasm and group sharing. Ultimately, they learned a great deal about color: composition, variations/modifications, materials and textures.

"Make a list of the colors you love, the colors you like, the colors you look good and feel good wearing, the colors you dislike and the colors you absolutely hate.

"Then, the challenge is to create a sampler using the color you absolutely hate as the main color source (at least 75 percent). You'll most likely be surprised at the results and your response to the colors you use."

DESIGNING AGAIN AND AGAIN

Erma Martin Yost: "Jasper Johns once said, 'Do something, do something to that, then do something to that.' This has become one of the maxims by which I create. I have found in my own work and that of many students that the initial idea is seldom brilliant. It is only the germination of an idea, but much reworking can develop that kernal into something highly original. Below are some exercises for developing an idea.

"In a small white square about 3 in. by 4 in. make a simple line drawing, filling the space so that some lines and shapes touch the edges. Don't be afraid of how unoriginal or even foolish this may be, because you are going to transform it ten different ways:

1. Redraw the design as though it's being stretched on a huge rubber band.

2. Redraw the design as though it's being compressed in a vise.

3. Take a tiny section from any of the above drawings and enlarge it greatly.

4. With any of the above drawings do the 'three R's,' with tracing paper: *reflect* it, (that is, create a mirror image), *rotate* it four times around a single point and *repeat* it four times, two over two.

5. With tracing paper over any of the above designs, eliminate some of the lines to create some new, larger shapes. Add some new lines to divide other shapes.

6. Fill in some shapes solid black.

7. Reverse the black and white shapes.

8. Fill in some shapes with texture, actual or invented.

9. Trace your favorite composition so far, and paint it in one color plus white, creating as many tints as possible.

10. Do it again, with two colors plus white.

"The idea is to work quickly; don't let any one step get too laborious until you've created a design that you like and that's worth a lot of labor."

GALLERY

STEPHEN BEAL
Another Moment's Peach

1981; 23 in. by 24 in.; wool and cotton floss on canvas; needlepoint. (Private collection; photo by GSP.)

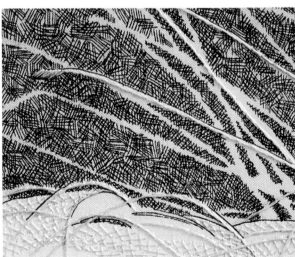

KATHERINE COLWELL
Three-mile Creek

1983; 5½ in. by 7 in.; ink and silk on silk; embroidered etching using stem stitch, herringbone stitch and satin stitch; detail at right. (Photo by Katherine Colwell.)

STEPHEN BEAL
It Takes the Day, Etc.

1975/revised 1987; 32 in. by 32 in.; cotton floss on canvas; needlepoint. (Private collection; photo by GSP.)

JOANNE A. LAESSIG
Loch Carron Cove

1988; 15½ in. by 12 in. by ½ in.; opaque glass beads on cotton; embroidery. (Photo by Jean Schnell.)

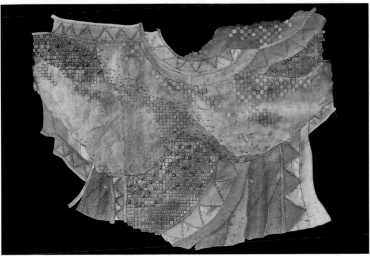

LISSA HUNTER
Earth Mantle

1986; 27 in. by 33 in.; paper, watercolors; stitching with cotton floss. (Private collection; photo by K.B. Pilcher.)

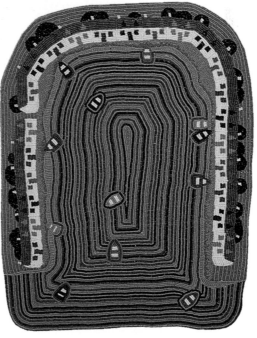

HELEN RUMPEL
Santorini Reflection

1985; 15⅜ in. by 12⅛ in.; silk,
rayon and metallic embroidery on
wool. (Collection of Warren D.
Rumpel; photo by Herb Lotz.)

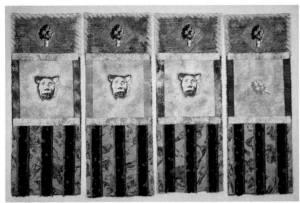

MARNA GOLDSTEIN BRAUNER
Carciofi alla Giudia

1990; 70 in. by 102 in.; Photo silk
screen, paint, dyes and pigments
on stamped on linen, beads, glitter;
embroidery, appliqué; detail at right.
(Photo by Richard A. Gehrke.)

JILL NORDFORS CLARK
Brugge Lace-Window Series #1

1988; 16 in. by 13 in.; needle lace
and machine stitching on handmade
paper. (Photo by Roger Schreiber.)

CAROL WARNER
Parrot Fish

1987-88; 5¼ in. by 5⅜ in.; cotton
threads on cotton, couching.
(Photo by Petronella Ytsma.)

MARION SPANJERDT
Midnight Magic

1989; 32 in. by 30 in.; cotton, silk,
metallic and synthetic fabrics;
machine appliqué, machine
embroidery; full piece at far left,
detail at left. (Private collection;
photo by Marion Spanjerdt.)

CELEBRATING THE STITCH

TERRIE HANCOCK MANGAT

Through the Looking Glass

1988; 60 in. by 60 in.; quilt: reverse appliqué, piecing, painted frame; life-size Alice: embroidery, painted canvas mounted on plywood form, appliqué. (Photo by Terrie Hancock Mangat.)

Three Barge Fireworks

Overleaf: 1987; 6 ft. by 9 ft.; assorted fabrics; reverse appliqué, piecing, strip piecing, embroidery, beading, painting, appliqué. (Collection of Esther Saalfeld Hancock; photo by Terrie Hancock Mangat.)

Like the magical world on the other side of Alice's looking glass, Terrie Hancock Mangat's quilts are full of surprises. Familiar objects are transfused with new meaning. Nothing is quite as it seems; it becomes "curioser and curioser." Mangat's quilts are autobiographical and contain their full share of strength and vulnerability, wit and whimsy, travels and travails. To look carefully at her quilts, to follow her stitches, is to share in Mangat's journey.

Each quilt takes time to read, since it is awash in embroidered, attached, painted and appliquéd details. The embroidery is intense and idiosyncratic, the style changing from deliberate smoothness to frank sloppiness, depending on the image Mangat is stitching and the point she is making. Faces, done in cotton floss, get careful, skilled treatment. The face of Alice, the free-standing figure in front of a framed quilt, in *Through the Looking Glass* (at left) is worked solidly on a heavy canvas, the embroidery modeling the features. There is a smooth transition between the embroidery and the rest of the figure, which is painted. Mangat's self-portrait, set low and to the center in *Shrine to the Beginning,* (on the facing page) is handled in a similar way, the delicate stitches applied as smoothly as paint. In all her quilts, each face is treated with respect, the stitches directed around the contours in a manner reminiscent of *opus anglicanum,* the high period of 12th-century English embroidery. These refined areas are in sharp contrast to the almost slapdash appearance of stitches elsewhere.

Mangat uses rough, imperfect stitches when she is attaching sections of painted linen or canvas to the quilt. This is appliqué that would horrify a fine technician and is one of the ways Mangat expresses her rebelliousness. "I stitch them on with great big stitches. It's really blatant; a childlike execution in a way. I sort of rebelled against that part of the quilt world where they want 11 stitches to the inch."

Mangat also adds "found" embroideries to her work. Embroidery from Mexico is cut up and used as a linear element in *Three Barge Fireworks* (on p. 174). In this case, the embroidery is treated like the many tokens and objects she attaches to her work.

Another function of the stitch for Mangat is to delineate detail, "making marks that seem best in thread." Rows of chain stitches become individual bristles in the paint brushes in *Sacred Heart Garden* (shown on p. 179). Stitches form flowers, stems or outlines around figures, a function they share equally with paint.

Mangat has been embroidering since she was eleven, when she spent summer afternoons stitching with the girl across the street. "I think everybody thought we were weird. We liked to embroider on hot afternoons." She has always loved fabrics and sewing, and she knew when she was quite young that she wanted to be an artist, "but I didn't think I would be an artist of fabric." She majored in art at the University of Kentucky, studying printmaking and ceramics, finding the textile classes either boring or pedantic. She started making traditional quilts as soon as she graduated from college.

While in Kentucky, Mangat met Mrs. Earl Clay, a maker of traditional quilts, and became fascinated with her work. "She put really strange fabrics together. They were wonderful, really unusual and different. She could take two pieces of fabric that no one in their right mind would consider and put them next to each other, and the overall scheme worked!"

In art school she had felt burdened by the weight of tradition surrounding painting. Mangat didn't know any traditional rules for quilting, and so she worked in an uninhibited manner. "I didn't have any expectations about how a quilt ought to look. I just started putting the pieces of fabric together to express an idea, and it could be any way it wanted to be. Because I started

Shrine to the Beginning

1988; 101 in. by 96 in.; cut-up painted canvas; embroidery, reverse appliqué, appliqué, beading, painting, embellishing. (Photo by Terrie Hancock Mangat.)

making quilts that way, it was easier for me. I didn't have to break any preconceived ideas about what quilts ought to be."

The first art quilt Mangat started was a map of the farm she and her husband lived on in Oklahoma. She put it away, unfinished, and worked on a series of traditional quilts. Seven moves later, the first quilt still wasn't done, and Mangat had completely altered her approach to quilt making. She decided to incorporate the unfinished quilt in a new work. This became *Shrine to the Beginning,* a monumental piece that includes her embroidered self-portrait with paint brushes and roses, a painted portrait of her husband (whose pose is reminiscent of the plastic statues of saints), brightly colored embroidered and appliquéd rocks, vivid flowers, and countless other absorbing details applied in one way or another. The house, barn and bright blue sky in the center are the portions of the early quilt around which the new quilt was constructed. "I put all these stones around it and made it into a shrine to the beginning, the beginning of my life; not as my parents' daughter, not as a student, but the beginning of my married life."

As she does on most of her quilts, Mangat combined materials with techniques to suit her ideas. "I sew together a bunch of fabrics for the foreground and then cut back into them for reverse appliqué. Sometimes I appliqué parts back into the hole I cut for the reverse appliqué. It gets to be many levels of both fabric and complications. Then I may embroider or paint onto that and maybe even sew on more canvas. I always trim back though, to eliminate bulk."

There are so many parts to her quilts that she works them in sections. She draws passages to be embroidered on small pieces of fabric and stitches them in spare moments, on trips, at the beach or while waiting during her daughter's lessons. The larger areas require uninterrupted blocks of time, which she reserves for the studio. Over time, "it all starts to come together as a quilt."

Mangat uses a variety of materials as her palette, choosing from beads and zippers, printed and painted fabrics, sequins, dime-store finds

An embroidered quilt from the heart

Terrie Hancock Mangat's highly personalized quilts, an amalgam of experience, ideas and materials, grow by an additive process. Her ideas unfold as she works. "The idea is in my head. Not doing much drawing ahead of time is what makes it easier to put the inner parts of myself into the quilt. Once you make definite plans for a quilt—the pattern, all the final decisions—it stops the flow from your heart. Then you make the quilt to fit the plan. But if you don't have that plan exactly in place, then you can keep letting it flow from your heart and changing it."

Sacred Heart Garden (at right) flowed directly from her heart. A child psychiatrist Mangat knew once shared an analogy with her about depression. He likened the inner self to a garden surrounded by a stone wall that protects it. Each stone is an important defense. If one stone ("you go to lunch when most of you wants to stay and work,") after another is removed, then a hole develops in the wall and depression can get in. Mangat tells the story:

"I thought about all the things that I felt I needed to protect in order to stay happy, certain things I have to do for myself or I get depressed; things like exercise, eating healthily and taking time for spiritual matters. I needed to take care of my relationship with my family.

"I thought about a garden and each one of those things as a plant. Beside the wall where some of the stones are pulled out is a big black plant of depression, painted with words like 'guilt,' 'greed,' and 'materialism.' There are good plants too. One has a hand in it, and there's a plant growing out of the hand that has watches on it. This is the 'time to make things' plant. There's an exercise plant, a spiritual plant and a plant with my parents' portraits, the plant of parental relationships. There's a plant for each of my children, one with soccer balls for my son and one with ballet slippers for my daughter.

"There are wild-looking plants, which I called 'free-to-be-me' plants. Then there are paintings of violets and zinnias, which I call 'free-beauty' plants. Violets are one of my favorites; they just come into your yard and you don't have to do anything. People try to poison them and get rid of them because they're so free. Zinnias are easy to grow and have great, intense colors. They represent things that come to you in your life; people you happen to meet; things that are wonderful and beautiful, and you don't do anything to them to make them happen; they just occur. It was a complicated piece to figure out. It's a very eclectic-looking quilt. Probably the composition is not the greatest, but I love that quilt!"

Sacred Heart Garden
1988; 96 in. by 91 in.; reverse appliqué, embroidery, beading, painting, sewn-on painted canvas, appliqué, piecing; detail below. (Photo by Terrie Hancock Mangat.)

and even a plastic saint here and there. Her studio is organized in such a way as to put all of these in easy reach. One long wall of boxes and cans filled with embellishment items faces a wall of fabrics sorted by colors. In the middle of all this sits Mangat, working with childlike enthusiasm, on big pillows on the floor.

Mangat feels that her early years of teaching art to elementary-school children helped to free her approach to materials. "Appreciating what kids did gave me the ability to take a lot more risks than I might have otherwise." She feels that using unusual materials helps to move the work out of the domestic category, out of the quilt world. She doesn't think of the objects or her work as "kitsch" or "camp." "It's not so tongue-in-cheek as that, because I really like the stuff. For me the zipper *is* the paint; all that stuff *is* the paint. It's the medium I use to express my ideas."

Tying together the disparate materials and techniques in Mangat's work is the quilting done by Sue Rule. The fine lines of stitches, each planned by Mangat with Rule, travel in many patterns and directions and serve as a cohesive element, providing structural strength and a subtle rhythmic background for the images and the abundance of embellishment.

Many of these objects and motifs have overtones of other cultures, which reflect what Mangat has absorbed and collected from frequent travels to Kenya, Mexico and the American Southwest. She is impressed with the color and rituals she finds, and compares them with those of her childhood experience:

> In other societies people are allowed to wail and express how they feel. I'm impressed by the intensity of their religious expressions. I find that very attractive, because I wasn't allowed to do it. We grew up having to make everything appropriate to what everyone else thought. We couldn't really share our feelings. Emotions were supposed to be "appropriate." I think middle-class America was like that. Part of the way my quilting evolved was that it was the only place where I could express myself the way I wanted to.

Early in her artistic life Mangat received a memorable commission and a critique. When she was in the first grade, she sewed a bag to hold her marbles and took it to school. One of the boys in her class liked the bag so much that he asked her to make him one too. She tells the story:

> I was flattered and said, "Sure." So I made him a marble bag like my marble bag. They were well stitched, but I put the seams on the outside, because nobody had ever told me to turn the seams to the inside, and I loved it that way. I went to school the next day, and he loved the bag and thanked me. Then he went home and his mom looked at the bag and said, "This isn't stitched right. I'll take it apart for you and sew it together the right way." So she took my marble bag apart and put the seams on the inside. The next day he came back to school and said, "My mom said you didn't do this right, so she fixed it."

Mangat is careful to listen to her own ideas about what is "right" now. She has since done a marble-bag quilt, depicting one bag with an exterior seam made of bugle beads, full of life; the other, a neat bag "sitting there like it's dead and all the fire is taken out of it."

Each of Mangat's works is so full of life that it is hard to imagine how she knows when to stop constructing the world on the other side of the looking glass, to know when the work is finished. "I just know. I think I have a good eye, and I just keep looking. I see things that need to be done. I put in little lines of embroidery that nobody else probably sees, but they're important to me. At some point I view it and say it's finished. The whole idea is there, and visually it starts to work. For me, it has to have all those little things of interest; it can't just lie there."

BETTE USCOTT-WOOLSEY

4/7 Woven, Needlepoint Rug

1977; 34 in. by 67 in.; wool on canvas; needlepoint. (Photo by Susan Kahn.)

A contemporary painter's sensibility and an admiration for the detail and care applied to traditional textiles are combined in the work of Bette Uscott-Woolsey. She comments on the merging of her interests and her training.

My formal art training is in painting, and my studies were primarily with painters exploring formalist issues, notably color, composition and gesture. My interest in embroidery developed in the late 1960s out of my concern with these formal elements as they related to the traditional textile arts: rugs, embroidery, tapestry and the like. I created a number of counted-thread embroideries and needlepoint rugs using traditional patterns as the starting point for color and spatial exploration.

In an effort to develop less geometric compositions, I did a series of gouache paintings, conceived as studies for carpets, standing screens and embroidered hangings. The embroideries that followed concentrate on the "brush" stroke created by the needle, the endless thread color mixing and blending possibilities, and the use of ornament as design, not embellishment. I chose the butterfly as an image because it is so naturally ornamental. My work tries to do two things—to have a highly designed look within a traditional framework, and to deal with more painterly concerns that are not native to embroidery. The technical elegance and design of historic embroidery is a high standard that I aspire to. However, I see my *Carpet Series* work (at right) as intentionally rougher and more paintlike.

Carpet Series #2

1988; 71 in. by 41 in.; wool on cotton; embroidery. (Photo by Susan Kahn.)

181

DANA ROMALO ANDREWS

Take to the Road

1987; 11 in. by 9 in.; cotton, wool,
silk and metallic threads;
embroidery on stretched canvas.
(Photo by Susan Kahn.)

Dana Romalo Andrews has lived a wanderer's life. Born in Romania and now an American citizen, she has traveled and lived all over the world with her husband, who was in the foreign service. She studied linguistics in Romania, painting in New York and Berlin and weaving in Germany. The constant movement and changing living conditions often meant adjusting to small spaces for brief periods. Thus, her looms became cumbersome to transport and set up, and painting took up too much space, so she began working in pen and ink and in embroidery. She continues to work in both media and paints occasionally. Drawn to embroidery for its portability and adaptability, she has come to appreciate it for its expressive possibilities.

Her dense but delicate constructions are formed by the life she has led. "The complexities of establishing temporary residences in various countries have created special conditions, affording many opportunities but also setting equally many limitations. These changes of environment, together with the way I have reacted to them, have influenced the evolution of my visual response to the world and determined the character of my work."

Change has taught Andrews the necessity of simplifying her needs and of setting limitations in her work. "My work and my life are sort of parallel. If I don't set limits I just get lost. In my work, if I take on too many colors or too many textures, I end up losing my sense of direction." By working within strict self-imposed limitations, Andrews is able to produce works of wondrous complexity. Though minute in size, her densely stitched embroideries are more commanding than works many times their size. "Focusing my attention on a limited area has led me to strive for a special kind of refinement, both in thought and in expression."

Andrews embroiders tangled webs, spun of strokes of pure color, which catch and hold the light or weave an impenetrable darkness. The stitches appear to have no visible means of support; in fact, she is getting so close to the essence of thread and stitch that some of her embroideries now have no ground fabric at all. In these works, Andrews is simultaneously constructing (by weaving of sorts) the ground upon which she is stitching. One reviewer likened her works to the encrusted remains of a well-used artist's palette. Andrews's embroideries are thick; stitching covers both sides of the work and extends up to and over the edge of the fabrics. Glints of metallics and silks play in the midst of humble cottons and linens. The works might suggest landscape or the play of natural light on indeterminate objects, but they also celebrate the thread and the very process by which they are made.

Andrews starts most work with a small piece of cloth, its edges left raw. Threads, usually small bits left from trimming previous work, are coiled and pinned to each side of the cloth. She couches them in place or uses a running or back stitch to secure them on one side, then repeats the process on the reverse. From there, as Andrews states simply, "It grows."

Small running stitches and back stitches are worked on both sides, the threads coming out and over the edges of the cloth, creating a dense thicket of stitches. Using no knots, she works the beginning and endings of the thread back into the mass of stitches. She doesn't use a frame either, so the finished piece is sometimes a bit askew. She comments that the works are like some Oriental rugs, without square corners. Finished works are suspended between layers of Plexiglas so both sides can be viewed.

Andrews says, "Whether in weaving or in stitching, I have used simple techniques as a means to convey my ideas in images. In stitching, I have used mostly the running stitch, often in combination with underlying threads or yarns. The advantage in this kind of technique has been that I could use stitches going in any direction, rather than the vertical-warp and horizontal-weft relationship that I had used when weaving." She began to explore the possibilities of double-sided work in the 1970s after an artist in Yugoslavia admired the back of her work. "There isn't a 'right side' and a 'wrong side,' but two sides to each work, and each side is different from the other." As her hands are occupied, her mind is free to wander:

> The methods I use are slow in execution and conducive to complex thinking. Through the complicated interrelation and webbing of the threads, I search for new images and relationships. As the work progresses, patterns and figurations emerge. Limitations and choices become a necessity. Relationships are formed, one thing leads to another, one thread calls for the next. Slowly the work acquires a reality of its own, certain vibrations and a specific density. I favor a certain ambiguity in the merging and melting of forms into one another, whereby the work can lend itself to different interpretations and can reveal new aspects each time it is viewed.

In some works Andrews has eliminated the background cloth completely. For these she lays a few coils of threads on a flat surface, and using a running stitch, plies her working thread through the coils until she has created a loose structure. She needleweaves on this surface to make soft, lacelike constructions. These works are difficult to display because they have little body, but she continues to explore the idea.

Andrews has an inquiring approach to each work and is not frustrated by the difficulty of working these bodyless forms. "I approach each work with anticipation and gradually get involved in its intricacies, dealing with possibilities and alternatives." Andrews becomes intimately involved with each piece. "Small thread works represent for me an ideal opportunity to create an extension to the existing world, such as I perceive it. By focusing the eyes and the mind on a very limited area, I enter a different space from the one around me, separate yet tangible."

Andrews speaks of the need for solitude when she works. "You and the work are, in a way, isolated from the world around you, and at the same time, you are creating something that is tangible, and that is an extension of the world around you." Her studio is an attic room in her home, and she finds it important to remove herself "not from the world, but from daily life and its problems" to work. "The work is so intricate and life is so complicated." She remembers living in Australia, where a young painter commented to her, "The trouble with you, Dana, is that you are too involved in life."

The strength in her work is achieved through balancing a life lived to the fullest and lengthy solitary labor. Andrews names each work with care, saying, "The titles I give my works are not arbitrary, but as necessary as titles to a book or a poem in the sense that they do relate to the content of the work." Some titles just appear; others come from a phrase in a book. She collects titles: "I have books of titles. I'll never in my life be able to do all the works from the titles that I've accumulated." She is careful, however, to choose purposefully ambiguous ones in keeping with the character of each work and out of respect for the viewers' varying interpretations. "Stitched works change with the light: daylight, cloudy day, rainy day, evening, artificial light. These forms change, and whoever watches them can interpret them in different ways."

Her titles suggest that her works are offerings, a contribution in return for what she has received: *Take to the Road, Small Song in the Cosmos, In Lieu of a Prayer.* And like her titles, the works are themselves lyrical, "like a poem." Each stitch, like each word in a poem, is deliberately made and delicately placed. Her quiet, attentive approach to making art involves her completely in listening to what the work needs next. She quotes art historian H. W. Janson, who wrote, "The making of a work of art has little in common with what we ordinarily mean by 'making.' It is a strange and risky business in which the maker never quite knows what he is making until he has actually made it."

Small Song in the Cosmos II, Side One and *Small Song in the Cosmos, Side II*

1989; 5¼ in. by 5½ in.; cotton, silk and metallic threads on canvas; double-sided embroidery; *Side One* at top, *Side Two* at bottom. (Photos by Joel Breger.)

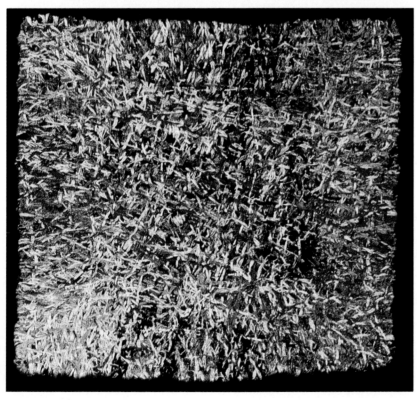

ELLY SMITH

Fred

1984; 24 in. by 18 in.; cotton floss
on cotton hardanger cloth;
counted-thread embroidery. (Photo
by Steve Meltzer.)

Almost 200 years ago, a young girl stitched the following sentiment into her sampler: "Patty Polk did this and she hated every stitch she did in it. She loves to read much more." For generations, alphabets, numbers, borders, patterns and intricate motifs have been stitched with zeal and determination in samplers, perhaps not always with the feisty belligerence displayed by Patty Polk. Samplers, originally meant for practice and copying a motif, evolved into examples of technical proficiency and an opportunity to instill lofty thoughts. Patty Polk was part of the independent wing of the sampler tradition, and so is Elly Smith.

Smith has been fascinated by samplers ever since she first tried a charted design as a young adult. Working the counted-thread motifs reminded her of the embroideries she had made as a child in Holland and the delight she took in the process. She began to do samplers for friends, researching appropriate motifs for each. This led to an interest in symbolism, particularly as symbols applied to samplers. Smith, a perpetual student who devours information about whatever interests her, realized that in researching the subject, she was reaching for the essence of samplers.

Smith's research took her back to Holland, where she studied historic samplers (see the sidebar on pp. 188-189). What struck her about these Dutch samplers was that, although they appeared cluttered at first, they were a visual delight, with "a wonderful sense of balance." She concentrated on "the scattering process, the misspellings, the design errors in the borders, the didactic epitaphs, and the avoidance of scale and perspective."[14] They were, for her, a "visual phenomenon."

Creating her own "visual phenomenon" became a goal, leading Smith to stray from the traditional sampler path in delightful ways. Her work incorporates many separate motifs (some appropriated from historic samplers), many secret symbols and, until recently, many quotes. "I'm moving away from the moralizers, although I know a lot of people have a need to read. They avoid the seeing process. If there is nothing to read in the piece, they'll read the little white tag, the title, the artist, the price of the work."

In one work, *Fred* (shown at left), Smith stitches a centralized figure. There are no words to reveal her message, but there are shared characteristics with samplers, including cross stitches, repeat patterns, hints of landscape and symbols, that reveal an extremely subtle political message. Smith reflects on her early childhood terrors of air-raid sirens and bombers overhead in Holland

Embroidery as the Leisure Art

1989; 27 in. by 57 in.; cotton floss on cotton hardanger cloth; counted-thread embroidery. (Photo by Steve Meltzer.)

during World War II, fears that recurred for her later in childhood during thunderstorms:

> *Fred* symbolizes the atom bomb exploding into an already actively destroyed, insipid yellow, war-zone wasteland. He represents an ideology, a mentality. He is conservative in appearance, a pin-striped suit and the bourgeois bowler hat (a touch of Magritte); he represents a national phenomenon. The chessboard behind his hat represents his structured attitude. I doubled one of his spectacle lenses to illustrate his uneven, unequal focus on reality. In his breast pocket are lilies of the valley, some shaped like hearts, a sardonic touch, because they are leaving him.

A gentler bit of communicating, though still a strong commentary, is stitched in *Embroidery as the Leisure Art* (shown above). While researching the history of embroidery, Smith noted that many authors quoted one another rather than doing original research. Then she read *The Subversive Stitch* by Rozsika Parker (see the Bibli-

ography on p. 225-227), a revisionist view of embroidery as it relates to feminist history. This scholarly study has led her to reassess the history of embroidery and the role of women in society.

For *Embroidery as the Leisure Art,* Smith visualized an idealized (and idolized) Victorian woman working on a sampler in her enclosed garden. Her lady doesn't look too comfortable in her enclosure; in fact, she looks a bit beleaguered and slightly disheveled. In the sampler, Smith quotes motifs from a 16th-century German sampler and the earliest-dated English sampler found in London's Victoria and Albert Museum. These works, which have lasted for generations, serve to remind Smith of the possible longevity of her work compared to her own relatively short life.

The angels with butterfly nets trying to capture winged clocks refer to thoughts about time and work. "People ask how long it takes to make one of these stitcheries. I don't want to know. I stitch to lose time." Smith does admit that this work was three years in the making, taking its own time to develop. She added one motif after another, continually concerned that the overall design would suffer. Then, as many embroiderers find, the work bogged down. There had been traditional references to begin the work, but it took a contemporary piece to suggest its conclusion. In an exhibition she saw a hanging designed with strong, colliding lines, convincing her to add some bold, broad dark lines in the central area where an arch is suggested. These lines completed the work.

Smith rarely strays from traditional materials and techniques, and her samplers quote freely from historic sources. It was a long time before she even allowed herself to add a backstitched line to her cross stitches. She appreciates the limitations imposed by working in this manner. She uses three-ply cotton floss on evenweave cotton hardanger cloth. Her materials are carefully researched, and she has stitched small reference samples of the over one thousand colors of thread available. To chart the counted-thread work, she uses a graph paper with 11 squares per inch. The grid adapts easily to her stitch, which crosses over two threads on the 22-threads-per-inch fabric. Although her sketches are charted on graph paper, Smith freely adds motifs as they occur to her in the process, graphing as necessary. After steaming, the work is stretched over an acid-free board and framed.

Smith's work is no less than a measured search for the meanings of embroidery, of limitations, of life and her role in it. She uses the work as self-revelation and self-expression, allowing motifs to emerge from her uncritical subconscious self, and saving the analysis for later. "I'm not always totally aware of the significance of the motifs, but I find my subconscious discovers the solutions for me. Explanatory notes get released at odd moments, like fleeting dream strands, and if I don't write them down, they get lost in the shuffle between thoughts of what to cook for dinner and what to do about the laundry." This thoughtful and thought-provoking artist, a modern-day sister of Patty Polk, offers us a new view of tradition, stitching samplers for the 20th and 21st centuries.

A Friesian sampler and a system for enlarging letters

Elly Smith's energetic research leads her in many directions. An interest in the lettering on a Friesian sampler led to a greater understanding of the culture that fostered the work. The women of Friesland, a northern province of Holland, created remarkably ornate samplers distinguished by small eyelets surrounding each letter. Smith shares her interest in samplers, the Friesian people, and a system for enlarging letters based on one 18th-century sampler (shown on the facing page):

"Of all the different translations of the word *sampler,* probably my favorite is the German version, which is *Stickmustertucher.* I like the way it rolls out of the mouth and the way the meanings are put together. The word *stick* refers to embroidery, *muster* refers to model or sample and *tucher* refers to cloth or fabric. The Dutch word for sampler is a rather disappointing *merklap,* literally translated as 'marking rag.'

"A 'marking rag' certainly doesn't describe the ornate Friesian samplers created in the 17th and 18th centuries, which are, to me, sampler work in its quintessential form. These samplers are attractive because of their finely balanced details. I love the ornate cauliflower trees that explode on the rectangular strips of linen. A closer look reveals tiny silk cross stitches done in green, brown, red and ocher.

"In this particular sampler, dated 1703, the center motif, a tree of life, is shaped like a capital letter Y with a small globe or sphere nestled in the upraised 'arms.' The arms appear to be the leaves of a palm tree, but they may be sheaves of wheat. Resting in the tree are a heart, some flowers and peacocks. Variations were created on these motifs by changing a pattern or by removing one portion and substituting another. These were called 'inventions' in the 17th century.

"I'm amazed by the manner in which such large (some as high as 5 in.) and seemingly awkward letters were balanced in these samplers. The intention seems to have been to cover every possible inch of fabric. These large letters, almost decadently rococo, reveal the Friesian love of ornament.

"The alphabet itself must have been revered in those days, considering how important and valuable it was to have

Friesian sampler, 1703; silk embroidery on linen. (Courtesy of Fries Museum, Leeuwarden, Holland.)

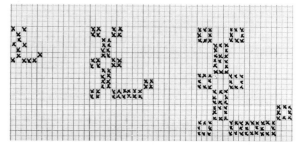

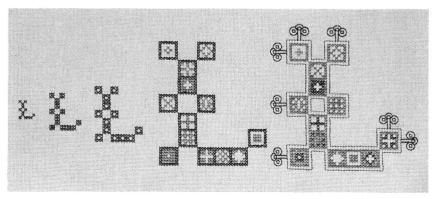

Based on her study of Friesian samplers, Elly Smith scales letters in her work to various sizes by first charting them on graph paper. Above (left), she begins by charting a fancy letter L, then enlarges it by quadrupling each X in the chart (middle). To again enlarge the letter, she doubles the four X's making up each square to form a larger square with an empty center. Below, Smith embroiders the charted letters, adding a final pair of even larger, embellished L's. (Photos by Susan Kahn.)

knowledge of the letters. One wonders if they were taken directly from the pattern books that were supposed to have been in circulation at the time. These samplers appear to have been made for both reference and practice. I wondered what such large letters were used for, and in Dokkum, Holland, I found the answer. There, in the upper rooms of an early 18th-century brick house, I was allowed to look through drawers and chests containing bed sheets and pillow cases. The bed sheets displayed the ornate letters I had seen on the samplers. Large central motifs flanked by equally large and ornate letters made a decorative and well-balanced appearance. Before a young girl married, it was of primary importance to embroider enough linens to fill up the linen cabinet. The cabinet itself was one of the most important pieces of furniture and was usually given as a wedding gift.

"I realized the importance of ornamentation to the Friesians when I viewed a typical 17th-century room in the Fries Museum. Luxuriant decoration is everywhere—from the blue tile-covered walls to the painted cabinets, the engravings on the silver and the elaborate designs of the Chinese porcelains. I can imagine the pride and strong self-identity of these people who were able to resist the Romans, the Counts of Holland, and the Saxons.

SUSAN DOWMAN WILCHINS

Dreamland

1988; 48 in. by 72 in.; fabric; dyeing, screen printing, piecing, appliqué, stitching. (Collection of North Carolina State University, gift of North Carolina Engineering Foundation, Inc.; photo by Jackson Smith.)

Susan Dowman Wilchins creates lush works alive with texture and color that reveal a poetic moment in time:

> I use fabric to write poems for which I have no words. All my art is an attempt to describe with fabric my intense visual experience of the Earth and its natural phenomena. Each series of work is inspired by specific sources, such as maps, aerial views of the Earth, microscopic photographs of living matter, patterns of sunlight through windows, and the natural carpet at my feet as I walk in the forest.

1989; 48 in. by 48 in.; fabric; dyeing, screen printing, piecing, appliqué, stitching; full piece at bottom, detail below. (Photo by Marc Wilchins.)

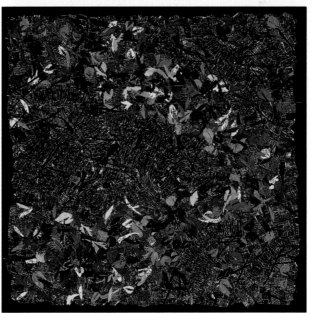

The work reflects the order that Wilchins sees in nature. The rich accumulation of a forest floor—leaf upon leaf, new, bright colors blending with those deepened and dulled by decay—is echoed in the bits of printed, torn and manipulated fabrics that make up her work. She explains:

The works are constructed through an accumulation of layers on the surface, a type of structure commonly found in nature. In its final form, my work provides at least two distinctly different visual experiences: a strong composition when viewed from a distance and a rich, textured surface crowded with color, pattern and energy when viewed closely. This dichotomy, which also occurs in nature, renders the familiar suddenly unfamiliar and allows the viewer new experiences and connections with the living world. I celebrate those dichotomies, which in Nature always lead ultimately to harmony: growth and decay, order and chaos, agitation and tranquility, the ordinary and the sublime.

Wilchins's art is romantic, expressive and generous in its wordless paeans to nature. But for all her visual orientation, she loves words. A voracious reader, she mentions that one of her favorite writers is Dickens, a master of detail. She admits to having written "bad" poetry when she was young, but now she says that she leaves composing good poetry up to her husband, a writer. Together, they title her works, revealing a mutual affection for playing with words, as in *The Shadows Know* (shown at right). They also share a love of music, particularly of opera, and she feels a connection between her work and the temporal qualities of music, which is "very of the moment, and that is exactly the way I think about my pieces."

Just as note upon note forms a musical composition, so too is Wilchins's process a cumulative one. An initial idea leads her first to screen printing. She mixes a variety of printing pigments in the colors she has chosen for her palette and photo-silk-screens multiple images made from photographs of natural objects, such as tree limbs and leaves, on 1-yd. lengths of fabric. She builds up to at least three layers of image in different colors on each fabric length, printing from 12 to 30 pieces of fabric for each completed work. Overlapping the images and the subsequent processes of tearing, piecing and cutting

Building a textile construction

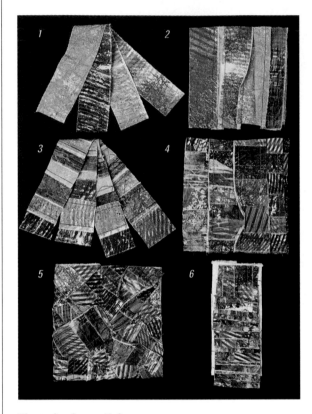

Photo by Susan Kahn.

S usan Dowman Wilchins transforms white cotton into multihued, multidimensional textiles by layering colors, cutting, seaming, recutting and resewing. She starts with 1-yd. segments of white fabric and applies multiple layers of screen printing. She describes the way she "builds" her textile constructions:

"First, I tear the printed fabrics into strips 1 in. to 1½ in. wide, which I arrange sequentially in groups according to the color effect I want to create [photo 1 at left]. The strips in each group are then sewn together side-by-side to form new 1-yd. sheets of 'cloth' with quarter-inch seams protruding from the printed surface [photo 2]. I then cut horizontally across each sheet of sewn strips to create a new set of strips, which I again arrange in sequence with cut strips from other newly cut groups [photo 3]. The fourth step in the process involves resewing this new

arrangement side by side, putting the seams on the surface. The result is a patchwork of multicolored prints. The exposed seams from the first and second sewings are perpendicular to the final vertical seams, and together they create a textured grid. These sheets of textured cloth are the basic constructions that make up the background of my pieces [photo 4]).

"I next cut sections of various sizes and shapes from the assorted groups of pieced fabrics and assemble them onto a sturdy, heavy twill-weave cotton backing, sewing them down by machine [photo 5]. Bunched and sewn assemblages are now sewn to this newly constructed fabric. They are linear segments, about 2 in. wide, cut from the gridlike fabric created earlier. These are alternatingly tucked and sewn to form a heavy, ridged texture [photo 6]."

will render them unrecognizable. As nature transforms a leaf to mold and soil, rocks and shells to sand, so Wilchins creates individual elements that will become part of a new whole.

Through a process of cutting, seaming, re-cutting and resewing, she deconstructs and re-constructs the fabrics, transforming them into a new cloth, composed on a heavy twill-weave cotton backing. She sews them in place with a Bernina 930 sewing machine, lowering the feed dogs and using the darning foot to ensure a stable stitch.

Once assembled into a composition, Wilchins puts her fabrics to another test by ma-chine-washing and drying them to "hasten the fraying of the fabric edges and to soften the surface." She keeps a large stock of previously dyed fabrics in solid, bright colors on hand, which she uses to complete the composition. She cuts these fabrics into small shapes, like recently fallen autumn leaves, and arranges them on the surface until the colors and distribution appears right. These shapes are machine-appliquéd in place, about ⅛ in. from the edges all around, thus creating additional texture with the raw edges. There is no neatening of the outer edges of the final piece; they are appropriately rough and ragged.

For Love Must Have Wings

1989; 48 in. by 72 in.; fabric; dyeing, screen printing, piecing, appliqué, stitching. (Photo by Marc Wilchins.)

Wilchins plans how the work will be finished before any assembly is begun. The twill backing is turned back and hemmed on all sides, with a 5-in. deep hem on the top for extra stability. Once all the pieces are sewn on, she sews a casing to the top. The casing has some give in it, so it is not flat against the back. It also has two breaks in it one-fifth of the way in from the side edges, at points that offer optimum support. She then slips a 1-in. to 1¼-in. flat aluminum rod into the casing. Holes drilled previously in the rod coincide with the breaks in the casing. The piece is intended to hang from two nails in the wall that match the holes in the rod. The works shift with time and settle, their ragged edges hanging softly against the wall.

This is physically demanding work for a woman who is barely 5 ft. tall. "The screen printing is heavy work and the dyeing is even heavier." Wilchins uses small screens, no more than 15 in. across, moving them frequently across the fabric, printing many small images. The manipulated fabrics on the backing become very heavy and need to be lifted as they are fed through the sewing machine. She thinks of a time when she may go back to weaving or another technique to "use a different set of muscles."

Wilchins works in a two-room studio in her home, each room about 13 ft. by 14 ft. A loom is stored in one room, along with a 4-ft. by 8-ft. table for her sewing machine, walls for pinning up work and storage areas. The other room has book shelves, a print table, a desk and filing cabinets.

This room is located next to a utility room with a washer and dryer and a stainless steel sink with a sprayer for dyeing. Wilchins elaborates on this setup:

> One of the reasons I like having my studio in my home is that I can print a layer, then run up to the kitchen and stir the soup. I don't want my art making to be separate from things I do in my daily life. The notion that we have to give that viewpoint up to participate in the art world is a total fallacy. It's just that we have to get critics to understand there are different approaches to making art.

Wilchins sees a link between her interests now and her training in art school. As an undergraduate at Indiana University, she studied gradational dyeing and overdyeing, which helped to strengthen her skills with color. In a design class she became fascinated with aerial photographs and wanted to weave this imagery. However, she felt constricted by the loom. "It didn't give me the freedom or the gestural qualities of line that I wanted to use." Instead, she did a series of small, satin-stitch embroideries that gave her the flexibility she needed with both line and color. She explains:

> It was about that time that I went to the University of Kansas for graduate work and I began to talk to [professor of art] Cynthia Schira about ways of using fabric more directly: coloring, dyeing and printing. I began to manipulate the fabric, not having seen anyone else doing it. I began to push it around, as well as working with the dyes and building up the surface. I was stuffing the pieces, and the things were sort of gross at that point. I was trying to push the ideas and to see how far I could get with them in a short period of time.

Wilchins focused on the ragged, raw edges and the way the colors moved across the face of the work. It was at this point that the idea for multiple screened images came to her. The use of aerial photographs as inspiration coupled with the multiple details seen close at hand fit well with Wilchins's ideas. "It is something about the clarity that the aerial distance offers. It gives you a new perspective on what is so close to you so much of the time. One of the things I like to work with in the compositions is to have it read one way from a distance and very differently up close; to have two different kinds of perception going on."

Wilchins uses only a minimal sketch prior to directly composing a work. She thinks about her idea as she prints the fabrics, then allows the prepared, torn and reassembled fabric to develop a life of its own. She reacts to the work as it grows, altering it as needed, keeping the development a natural, organic process. For commissions, when some sort of sketch is required, she has used pastels. She has also begun to do "soft sketches," sewing snippets of fabric in place, suggesting the finished "soft paintings."

One of the artists Wilchins most admires is Matisse. She has great appreciation for his use of pattern and color. Matisse was very aware of the influence of prior painters on his work, and, in turn, his own influence on younger painters. He was concerned that the work appeared to be created with such apparent ease, with so little labor, that it would give young artists the wrong impression. His comments in a letter, written in 1948, on the making of art are apt in light of the seeming effortlessness of Wilchins's finished works:

> I have always tried to hide my own efforts and wanted my work to have the lightness and joyousness of a springtime which never lets anyone suspect the labours it has cost.... This slow and painful work is indispensable. Indeed, if gardens were not dug over at the proper time, they would soon be good for nothing.... An artist must possess Nature. He must identify himself with her rhythms, by efforts that prepare for the mastery by which he will later be able to express himself in his own language.[15]

Laboring long hours to craft a moment in time, Wilchins expresses her visions of nature and, in her own language, aims to capture the mystery of it from afar and the wonder of it right under one's feet.

THERESE MAY

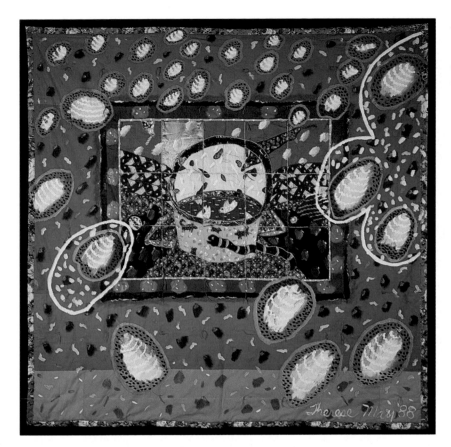

Painter, quilt maker and embroiderer Therese May creates exuberant works that are refreshingly witty and energetic, autobiographical and allegorical. She writes about her work:

> I started out as a painter, and then I switched to quilt making. Now, I paint on quilts. I'm basically an expressionist, and that's the way I sew, too. I start out with a drawing, which I use for a pattern to cut my fabric pieces. These are pinned to a muslin backing, and then I machine appliqué. I like to make use of the different colors of thread to build upon the image. I don't cut my threads; instead I let them form a networklike texture over the surface of the quilt.
>
> The images are composed of whatever seems to look good at the moment. For instance, I might think it would be fun to put a little animal here or there. Then later on, sometimes I find that my pictures can be interpreted in a number of ways. And so I can tell stories with them. This is the story of *Basket* [shown above]:
>
> Little white fish swim around inside the basket in the center. They've achieved something and they're protected from danger. Then there are big black monsters, and they're trying to get to the basket. They're not really dangerous, but they would like to get in because it's nicer inside. They don't really know how to get in, but they'll keep on trying until they figure it out.
>
> The snake is a symbol of power, and it's also trying to get inside just because it wants to give its power and love. On the very outside are big Easter eggs, and these still not only have shells around them, but they also have floating membranes surrounding them. They are still sealed inside, but these things have to be developed before they can come out.

LYNNE SWARD

Fragment-Series II

1987; 14 in. by 16 in.; cotton,
machine appliqué. (Photo by
Susan Kahn.)

Celebrations should have their lighter side, and Lynne Sward approaches the stitch, fabric and fashion with an attitude that is "tongue-in-chic." Her style is no style; she changes materials and techniques to fit her many interests, refusing to pin herself down. She memorializes textile icons (kimonos, copes and capes) by first miniaturizing them and then laminating them. Now she is redefining the hula skirt. She comments on her work:

> Sunsets (one of my passions—the others are chocolate and movies) are always different. Like sunsets, I find enormous satisfaction in challenging the viewer to discover new imagery and emotions each time my work is seen.
>
> I'm fascinated with miniaturizing large printed textiles and recreating new pattern designs. Thanks to the invention of the rotary cutter, I'm able to do this with reasonable ease and speed.
>
> *Fragments-Series II* [on the facing page] uses hand sewing and machine sewing over tiny cloth fragments layered onto muslin. This work pays homage to my mom, a great lady, who passed on several years ago.
>
> After designing clothing with a cut-cloth technique, it occurred to me that this "layered-fringed look" resembled a grass skirt. Thus was born my version of the hula skirt. *Hollywood Hula* [shown at right] is the third in a series, and its inspiration comes from my obsession with movies.
>
> The embroidery methods I use are not complex or exotic; my works generally contain a combination of straight-stitch machine sewing, hand quilting, appliqué and beading. I've long revered the marvelous artisans who, throughout the ages, have expressed themselves using thread on cloth. I'm a fan of all forms of embroidery; I strive to thread (tread) where no one has before.

Hollywood Hula

1989; 20 in. by 12½ in. by 24 in.; layered, fringed cotton blends, metallics; photocopying, laminating, beading, machine sewing and hand sewing; full piece at top, detail above. (Photo by Susan Kahn.)

MARIBETH BALOGA

Maribeth Baloga's work gives new meaning to the phrase "wrong side out." For her, embroidery has only a front and back, not a right side or a wrong side. She challenges our ideas of what is beautiful or perfect in embroidery, and what should be seen and what hidden from view.

After earning a graduate degree in textiles from Indiana University, Baloga moved to Los Angeles and began to look for a teaching position. A school of fashion design hired her to teach textiles, but she also had to teach a course in fashion history, which she learned on the job. She became intrigued by what an understanding of the history of fashion can do to augment the overall understanding of a culture, its politics and customs. She enjoyed seeing the slides year after year, and some of the images stayed in her mind even after she stopped teaching.

In addition to teaching, Baloga was also pursuing her own art work. For many years she had appreciated the reverse sides of her embroideries, admiring the apparent randomness and freedom of the stitches and knots, and wished to capture that quality on the face of her work. She decided to experiment using some of her old embroideries, cutting them apart and working back into the knots and threads on the reverse side with more stitching and colored pencils or paint. "It was hard to cut up what I had spent so much time on. But I'd been admiring the reverse side

Helen, Side One and *Helen, Side Two*

1989; 6½ in. by 7 in.; cotton floss on muslin; embroidery; *Side One* at top, *Side Two* at left. (Collection of Sandra and Rudy Kempter; photo by Susan Kahn.)

198

for years, and finally I couldn't not cut them up! My husband would have a heart attack every time I did it, and it became a family joke, surmising whether these were third-generation or fourth-generation embroideries."

Baloga's interest in fashion history and experiments in embroidery came together as two-sided embroideries depicting figures from the past, "portraits of ancient persons framed by information about the lands they inhabited and the gods they worshipped." She explains:

> I decided to do some historical portraits, and I started on the frames first. I was going to put all the information about the land, the occupations, gods and so on, in the frame with a portrait in the center. As I worked, I thought about the portrait and the fact that you really can't know someone who has already gone before. These days there are pictures, photographs and movies, but no matter how much you read or see, you really can't know that person. It's especially difficult when you're dealing with someone from the very distant past where there were no photographs and you depended on the local artist, if any, for information. It occurred to me that the image ought to be blurred for those reasons. As I worked I had the idea of the frame containing all the essential information and the portrait itself being a blurred image. It became a reversal of the traditional role of frame and portrait.

Baloga began with Helen of Troy and remembered that while reading the *Odyssey* in high school she had imagined Helen in flowing white robes. Based on her newfound knowledge of fashion history, she realized that "Helen was probably dressed in a rich, playful costume of embroidery and patchwork with pearls strewn in her hair. She reflected the whole culture to me." At the time, Baloga was interested in both Mycenaean and Minoan costume. *Helen* (shown on the facing page) has a decidedly Minoan stamp to her, and her portrait is placed on a back-

ground based on a Minoan fresco. Her portrait appears on the back of the work; the frame, incorporating figures and mazelike forms, surrounds the blurred image of Helen on the front.

During her research, Baloga chanced upon a photograph of a statue of a minor figure, Ebikhil, a temple guardian in the ancient city of Mari in Mesopotamia. "I picked Ebikhil because he wasn't a major figure; I didn't want a king or a god. I wanted someone who was sort of an everyman, important enough to have a little statue made of himself, but one whose name wouldn't come up often in a history of Mesopotamia." She was struck by the image and was intrigued by the sheepskin skirt he wore. She notes that in art of the period, these skirts are depicted in a stylized manner showing tufts of hair, and that some historians think the fleece was actually sheared into tufts.

Baloga based the pose in *Ebikhil* (shown on p. 201) on the statue, added ziggurats to the background and used vivid colors to bring this ancient presence to life. Initially she had picked the natural colors of sheepskin for the skirt, but "it had no energy at all," so she tried a lively combination of red and purple. Bits of red and purple also appear in the ziggurat and are echoed in the border on the reverse side. However, here they are quieter, muted by the large areas of off-white muslin that surrounds them.

By celebrating the integrity of both sides of an embroidery, Baloga's work challenges the time-honored tradition of hiding the "wrong" side behind a frame or backing. She appreciates the random energy of the reverse.

> The back is kind of a skeleton of the front; it contains all the information that's on the front, but in a different fashion. It contains the essence of the front, and it can tell you more than the front tells you. It tells more about the rhythm of the stitching, about the pattern. I look to the back to see if something is out of

whack in my composition. If I look at the front, the identifiable image gets in my way of seeing an imbalance or a color that isn't working. I turn it over and see the blurred area of stitching, and things just pop right out and tell me what is happening.

Technically, Baloga works with uncomplicated materials in a straightforward, traditional manner. She uses two strands of cotton floss for satin stitch and chain stitch, adjusting the thread to four strands for couching. She blends strands of color in her needle for shading, and stitches on a double layer of bleached or unbleached muslin. She uses an embroidery hoop, removing it frequently to hang the work on the wall to check the color and composition. She sketches in advance those elements that will be included in the frame and draws most of them on the fabric before she begins to stitch.

Baloga likes the direct control of the materials that embroidery provides. "You can put it in; you can take it out." She is working to loosen her hold on designing, taking care not to plan too much so there are mysteries to emerge and problems to solve as she works. "What I consider before I start is how big an area I want for the random threads on the back. For instance, in one recent work I started the knots much farther out than I usually do, because I wanted a broad area of loose threads. I'll think about things like that, little odds and ends like putting in sufficient threads to fill in the corners, but it's a very casual kind of approach."

The cut-up and reversed pieces that led to the two-sided portraits have spawned a companion series that establishes a link between ancient history and current technology. These nonfigurative works combine color photocopies of reverse sides of embroideries with actual embroidery and color-pencil drawings. Baloga has had access to, and much prefers, an older-model Xerox color-copy machine that doesn't produce a perfect photographic likeness of the embroideries. The appeal of these images is precisely that they are not perfect and are more like a "...caricature of the embroidery. They redefine the texture of the fabric. Strings become a whole lot more impor-

tant than they really are. Knots have more impact than when you actually look at the fabric."

Baloga combines the resultant materials in various ways: photocopies on paper with embroidery on fabric, color-pencil drawings and stencils on photocopies and embroidery on the paper photocopies. She has found a heavy 32-lb. copy paper that she can stitch into with little problem. She glues or stitches the paper onto fabric, depending upon the effect she wants to achieve. If the paper is to be flat, she uses glue; if the paper is to curve softly into the fabric, she stitches it.

In one series Baloga explored the idea of "shallow enclosures," such as flaps and pockets, combining reverse embroidery, photocopies on paper and color-pencil drawings in formal, geometric compositions. She had finished one of these works when she came across information on one of the last Sumerian kings, a beneficent young ruler named Gudea. She titled the piece *Gudea's Pocket* in his honor (shown on the facing page), despite the fact that Sumerian garments were probably not equipped with pockets. The pocket is suggested by three overlapping triangles of "reverse-type" embroidery applied over a fourth photocopied triangle. She has worked with color pencil back into the embroidered area to strengthen the color and has suggested threads by drawing into the margins around the copied image.

In exhibits of traditional embroidery, many judges insist on seeing the wrong side of the work in order to assess the craftsmanship of the embroiderer. There is no wrong side to examine in Maribeth Baloga's work, since it is an intriguing amalgam, revealing process as well as product. The skeleton of idea and technique is simultaneously exposed and fully clothed, completely open for inspection.

Ebikhil, Side One and *Ebikhil, Side Two*

1988; 6½ in. by 6½ in.; cotton floss on muslin; embroidery; *Side One* at left, *Side Two* at bottom. (Photos by Susan Kahn.)

Gudea's Pocket

1987; 8¾ in. by 8¾ in.; Xerox color photocopies, color pencil, fabric; embroidery. (Photo by Maribeth Baloga.)

B. J. ADAMS

Shoowamaze

1989; 43 in. by 49 in.; striped
fabrics; machine embroidery.
(Photo by Breger & Associates,
Kensington, Maryland.)

"Why do I do what I do?" exclaims B. J. Adams. "Because I have to. I just love it. I can hardly wait to see what will happen!" Her mind is quick, full of questions and eager to explore solutions to the problems she likes to generate in her work. She seeks multiple solutions, often working out a series of possibilities before either settling on one to develop or discarding the whole lot, because another, newer question seems more interesting. "I've come up with a lot of ideas that, I think, other people haven't thought of, but I haven't gone on with them, because I get bored doing the same thing again and again. I'd like to see what someone else would do with it in a series."

Her interest in generating new ideas and new solutions to compositional and technical problems makes Adams as enamored of the process of exploration as of the finished art work. She is an innovator, an inventor of possibilities and an explorer of techniques and materials.

Adams began as a painter. "My paintings from 30 years ago were from another person. My fiber work of 15 years ago was from yet another person. Then I was looking for industrial materials and new ways to use traditional techniques." These materials were primarily plastic tubings, which she sculpted into monumental wall and three-dimensional works, using coiling, twining and other techniques out of the basketry tradition. She also made high-relief wall pieces combining padded appliqué and hand embroidery with handspun or heavyweight yarns.

In the 1980s Adams began to use more machine embroidery, still with an emphasis on texture, but with finer materials, which she manipulated after they were gathered on a pleater machine and combined with broad bands of machined satin stitch (see the detail of *Kage Hinata* on p. 205). A new group of highly graphic, hard-edged works grew out of her interest in what the machined satin-stitched lines would do.

In these works, complex grids move in and out of the space, and many are portrayed with raw, pure, high-intensity color. Her move from soft, flowing lines and even softer fabric forms to strong linear, optically bewildering images is not as great a leap as it may seem. Before Adams was a painter, she studied mathematics. She has always fancied mazes, games and puzzles that challenge her analytical mind.

One of the puzzles Adams has created for herself, one of the problems she loves to solve, is how many ways she can use striped fabrics. Over the years she has explored manipulating stripes in multiple ways: pleating, tucking, folding, cutting across the stripes and resewing them, and creating areas of solid color by obliterating a second or third color in folds. Striped materials play a subtle but essential role as background for her latest pieces, and while they are not easily discernible in the finished work, they control much of the play of light and shadow within it.

Stripes combined with an interest in architecture to generate this series. For many years, Adams has enjoyed photographing reflections, distortions of line and shape in the windows of contemporary office buildings. An exhibition of Shoowa design at The National Museum of African Art, part of the Smithsonian Institution, was the catalyst which brought these divergent interests together. Here she saw distinctive and different possibilities for line, distortion, movement and pattern.

The Shoowa people are a small tribe from the Kingdom of Kuba, part of Zaire. "Their embroideries are intricate designs in earthy colors, usually only two or three. I saw basic geometric motifs developed into complex patterns; I saw so much more depth to geometric pattern." These mazelike designs, moving from small to large, unpredictable shapes, and distorted lines (see the sidebar on p. 204) clicked with Adams's passion for stripes and the architectural images she had

Shoowa design

B. J. Adams's designs are inspired, in part, by the raffia textiles created by the Shoowa people of the central African nation of Zaire. The Shoowa, part of the larger Kuba group, farm, hunt, fish and raise livestock. Their embroidered palm-fiber fabrics are considered the finest of the Kuba people and are an integral part of their community.

The embroidered panels are used primarily for ceremonial clothing worn at masquerades and initiation rituals, and displayed at funerals. The women's wraparound skirts can be many feet long and boldly patterned. In the past they were used for trade, and now, through missions and craft cooperatives, they are also made as small panels for export.

The labor is divided by gender: men cultivate, collect, prepare and weave the raw materials; women dye the cloth and raffia yarn and do the embroidery. In the afternoon, after returning from work in the fields, the embroiderer sits outside in the shade and works. She keeps the cloth wrapped in a cover, steadying the panel on her lap. She doesn't turn the panel to change direction of the motif, but changes the direction of the stitching when necessary.

Two stitches are used by the Shoowa women. One, similar to stem stitch, is referred to as "overstitching"; the other is a "plush stitch." For this stitch, a bundle of raffia fibers is inserted under a single thread in the weaving and is cut with a small knife, leaving two short tufts remaining. There is no knot to hold them in place. They can be arranged very closely to create a velvetlike pile or spaced apart to produce small dots of texture.

The geometric designs the women stitch are variations on a single motif, or mazelike diagonals or interlocking designs. There is enormous variety of scale within the work, with sudden shifts into new patterns and surprise interruptions in an expected repeat. However, there is no planned drawing on the cloth. The embroiderer works spontaneously with only a mental plan of the design. Taking months or perhaps years to complete, a panel is a symbol of prestige for an affluent or royal man whose many wives and concubines will produce many embroideries. (See the Bibliography on p. 225-227 for titles on the Shoowa and African textiles.)

Shoowa textiles. Although the sizes vary, these small raffia textiles generally range from 16 in. to 21 in. (Courtesy of Douglas Dawson Gallery, Chicago; photo by Douglas Dawson Gallery, Chicago.)

Kage Hinata
(detail)

1987; full piece (not shown): 30 in. by 60 in.;
pieced, stitched and manipulated fabrics; hand
appliqué, machine appliqué, embroidery.
(Collection of Eda and Steven Baruch; photo by
Breger & Associates, Kensington, Maryland.)

Order Into Chaos

1989; 11 in. by 13 in.; fabrics;
machine embroidery. (Collection of
Anne and Eastman Hatch; photo by
Breger & Associates, Kensington,
Maryland.)

accumulated. The works that have resulted from these inspirations sparkle with high-energy, incandescent color. Lines—in tandem and converging, forming new shapes, heading off on their own, straight lines generating curves, angled adventures—lead the eye on a merry chase around the work.

Architecture, Shoowa and stripes are the visual ingredients of Adams's work, but there is also a technical component. In the 1980s, when Adams was making textured manipulated fabric and machine-embroidered pieces, she purchased an Adler industrial sewing machine, which could make a satin-stitch line up to 1cm wide. She learned the advantages and disadvantages of using an industrial machine. The solutions to some of the technical problems with the machine contributed to the way this series came about. She learned which materials work best with the machine and what the possibilities were in the varied-width line it could produce.

The machine works best on heavy fabric, so Adams uses canvas as a backing. And since the machine runs very fast, Adams cannot use the machine embroiderer's standard method of placing the fabric in a hoop to stretch it. Thus, to keep the fabric from puckering, she uses the large, full-size pages of the woman's fashion journal, *W*, as an additional support on the back, ripping the page away from the back of the work when it is complete. She notes that the ink on *W* does not come off on the work. If she is doing a smaller piece, magazine pages also work well.

Adams cannot design these pieces as she is sewing, because she can see only about 2 in. of fabric behind the presser foot. She therefore sketches, generally on graph paper, then marks out the design on the canvas. She overlays the canvas with striped fabric and runs the machine stitching diagonally across the stripes. "I used the stripes as a guideline for a couple of pieces, but with the stitches all going in the same direc-

Sequentially Random

1989; 12 in. by 12 in.; fabrics; machine embroidery. (Collection of Camille and Alex Cooke; photo by Breger & Associates, Kensington, Maryland.)

tion, the base fabric began to get out of shape. So I started stitching across the stripes to counter the pull."

Adams graduates the thread colors from light to dark or from warm to cool, and bemoans the fact that she is limited by the colors she can find in commercial sewing and machine-embroidery thread. "I never have enough colors of thread to go through all the gradual changes I want. I have to adjust to that, and sometimes that adjustment becomes a more interesting spot." She changes the top thread frequently, but the bobbin stays the same. The top tension is loosened slightly so that none of the bobbin thread will be drawn to the surface.

Adams has found that the wide satin stitch shows the machine to its best advantage, but there must be a tiny space between the rows, of $\frac{1}{16}$ in. to $\frac{1}{8}$ in., since the needle cuts the thread of the adjoining row if it comes too close. Adams has turned this to her advantage in the design by incorporating colors and shapes from the background fabric into the composition. "In planning the background colors, contrasts become important. When I stitch with one color thread across a contrasting color background, changes occur and a double image eventually becomes apparent. I'm looking for these interesting changes—one color over multiple colors, many colors over many colors. There are so many variations possible." The wide black-and-white striped fabric at the top of *Sequentially Random* (shown on the facing page) asserts itself in the spaces, suggesting a striped shadow. Like rests in music, the unstitched spaces punctuate the rhythm of the work.

Whatever the background fabric, whether printed with curves, stripes of varying sizes, colors, or intensities, there are multiple choices for Adams, who thrives on generating new options. For her, making art is a circular process, not one that progresses in a straight, unswerving line. A diagram of her thought process would look more like the layout of the central nervous system than the orderly connections of the bony structure. There would be strands of her long-time interest in line, off-shoots of a sense of movement and direction and emphasis on stronger and graduated color, which is currently replacing the former focus on texture.

As new questions arise, new ideas are generated and new limits, albeit temporary, must be set. "There are always so many choices. That's where I need discipline. I have a hard time narrowing myself. I find hundreds of questions, mostly, 'What if I did this or that?' 'Why is it done that way?' 'What is the back like?' 'What if it were cut up or gathered or pleated or manipulated in some other way?' I might spend days—I could go on forever—doing little studies, details. I can do a series in my mind so fast, that I don't ever need to complete it."

This highly energized artist, whose words often flag behind the rapid pace of her emerging ideas, has a favorite quote from the painter Jacob Lawrence, which she feels describes herself well: "All artists are constantly looking for something, and they don't always know what."

Curving a right angle

When stitching the concentric squares in one piece from her *Shoowa* series, B.J. Adams saw curves beginning to emerge at what were supposed to be right-angled corners. The long, gentle curves occured as she worked toward the center of the square, and progressively narrowed the width of the satin-stitch rows on opposing sides of the square while keeping the width of the lines constant on the other two sides (see *Order Into Chaos* on p. 205). She decided to push this effect in the next few pieces. "It's these unexpected surprises," Adams says, "that keep me interested in any series."

Having accidently discovered these curves formed by straight lines, she decided to try another way to create a curved line. In this second method, used in *Sequentially Random* (shown on the facing page), she took advantage of the background fabric that is seen between each row of stitches. "In *Sequentially Random* I used a red, glittery obi fabric with a wave design as part of the background. Following one of the waves, I changed the color of the sewing thread on the surface for emphasis. It's a more subtle curve, but it's there." The bits of red and gold showing through the spaces between the stitching lines suggest the curve. Using strong contrasting colors of thread emphasizes this effect.

The obi fabric had waves woven in it, but in other works Adams has cut different background fabrics into curving shapes to achieve a similar effect.

CURVING CORNERS

Constant-width rows of stitches

Progressively narrowed rows of stitches

Gradual curve

Adams achieves a subtle curve at the points where the progressively narrowed rows of satin stitch meet in Order into Chaos.

SUSAN HOOVER

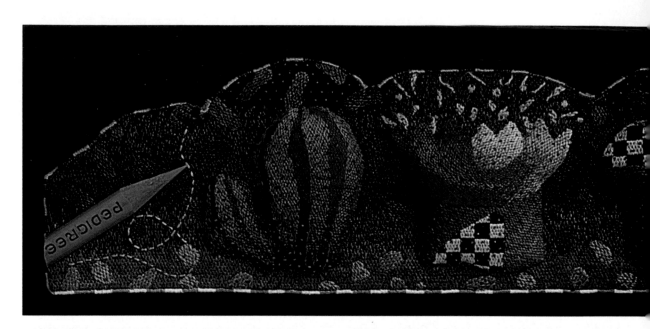

Pukki's Picabian Plain

Top: 1986; 2½ in. by 10¼ in. by
¼ in.; cotton floss, color pencil cut
lengthwise; cotton fabric; raised or
stump work, long and short stitch,
couching. (Private collection;
photo by Susan Kahn.)

Hackettian Ishkabibble #5

Above: 1989; 2 in. by 8 ½ in.;
cotton floss on cotton-blend fabric;
embroidery with long and short
stitch, couching. (Photo by
Susan Hoover.)

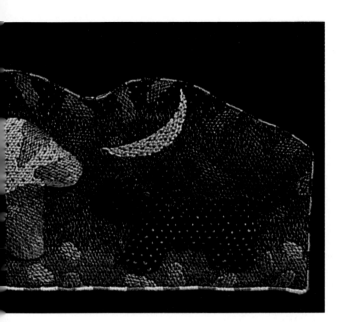

formidable, awe inspiring. I'll never forget the image and experience. Picabian, by the way, refers to the artist Picabia, who dedicated an art work to his lady friend's pet dog.

The stitches in this piece are long and short stitch and couching. The raised forms, the cactus and two mushrooms, were applied as raised or stump work. These forms were embroidered separately and then attached to the main fabric background. Just before putting the final couple of stitches into the seam, I gently pushed some fiberfill underneath the forms and then finished sewing the seam.

The materials used are cotton embroidery floss and a color pencil cut in half lengthwise. The color pencil is part of the design solution: it's raised and says "Pedigree," referring to the Scottie dog on the opposite end. It is also a pun on the signature: a color pencil for drawing versus a needle and color thread for embroidery, one and the same.

Hackettian Ishkabibble #5 (at bottom, facing page) is the story of gardening in my backyard. It's a bug's perspective of what's happening in the grass and what I'm up against. Worms and slugs are my worst problem. Yes, worms! Early in the summer they come out at night and pull the young plants down into their holes. There are other insects that pillage during the night, but I haven't discovered them yet. "Hackettian" refers to Hackett Avenue where I live. "Ishkabibble" is a slang term introduced by the comedian Fanny Brice, meaning "I should worry?" This is the fifth in the series, which is an ongoing process.

Susan Hoover was trained as a weaver and has produced both large-scale architectural works that portray her city environment and miniature brilliantly colored, abstract silk tapestries. In conjunction with her weaving, she has always enjoyed making embroideries. These works reflect her home environment and have, as she says, a "cozy quality." She enjoys working in a folk-art manner, depicting pets, plants, birds and bugs, using these images and personal symbols to tell her own contemporary folktales. She explains the techniques, materials and titles of the works, revealing her fascination with the world around her:

Pukki's Picabian Plain [at top, facing page] is based on a photograph I took in the great eastern plains of Colorado when I first moved there from Milwaukee. I had stopped for gas and photographed my Scottie dog, Pukki, sitting in the sand between small cacti and sagebrush outlined against the big sky. Suddenly it occured to me how foreign and alien he looked in this new environment. And how foreign *I* felt! It was a real geographical shock, very

PEGGY MOULTON

For many years Peggy Moulton explored technique and process, working with color-copied paper and fabric, weaving, plaiting, stacking and pinning together dense, richly colored complex constructions. Many of these small works had the appearance of highly magnified cross-sections of textiles; others referred to traditional textiles, such as Oriental carpets or log-cabin quilt designs. Her recent works retain the stacking element, but the serious and sophisticated nature of their predecessors has given way to loosely constructed, lively and rollicking images. She writes about her new work and the reasons behind the change:

> I began working with stacked fabric and embroidery as comic relief from the tedious plaiting I had been doing for almost ten years. The inspiration for change came from my studio cat, who often sleeps on the work table. I began by cutting freehand cat shapes from fabric and placing them on various plain and patterned fabrics, stacking the fabric until the combinations of colors and patterns pleased me. I tried to achieve a quick, spontaneous, perhaps naïve feel. None of the edges are turned under, and the shapes are uneven. The embroidery adds to this spontaneity with its quick and simple stitches. I use only the single straight stitch with an occasional French knot. The stacked-fabric technique allows me to work with bright colors, to mix patterns and to use hand embroidery—my favorite ways to express my artistic sense.

Cat Dance

1989; 12 in. by 14½ in.; silk, cotton, blends, sewing thread; stacking of fabric, embroidery; full piece at top, detail at left. (Private collection; photo by Kirby Moulton.)

One of the distinct pleasures of a creative activity is getting lost in the work, although it could be argued that getting "found" would be more apt. Whatever the term, there are moments, sometimes hours or days, when there seems to be nothing else in all creation other than the maker and the work.

Discovering a balance between keeping a tight rein on the work and allowing it to find its own way is one of the fascinating challenges of making art. There is no right way of doing this; what is correct is what works for each individual.

One artist calls this balancing act "listening" to the work. The listening process is continuous, from the originating idea, through the multiple stages of its making, to knowing when to stop.

LISTENING TO THE WORK

Lee Malerich: "My work and I have a symbiotic relationship. Sometimes I believe that we exist for the benefit of each other; at other times, I believe we exist despite one another. In either case we travel along together."

Jan Kozicki: "This dialog has many stages. The one I worry about the most is what I call the comfort zone. I have been there before. It is so easy to stop here where it is safe. I always go further. Am I destroying, or getting a new high? Sometimes it turns out okay. Sometimes someone else thinks so too."

Nancy Erickson: "It's boring if you already know the answer. I don't have answers. I really don't."

Renie Breskin Adams: "Ideally, if you can relax and sort of let it come out, art does have a life of its own separate from the artist. That's how the piece develops."

Joan Schulze: "The number-one consideration is that the work has to feel right. All the parts have to have a meaning to the whole. I've cut out really elegant parts of a piece because it didn't fit with the rest. It also has to connect with an experience I've had or intend to have; I don't do anything that doesn't connect with who I am or what I have experienced or what I think about."

KNOWING WHEN TO STOP

Maria-Theresa Fernandes: "It depends on what you want to get. To overdo a piece is terrible. You can do a finished piece in a few minutes."

Patricia Malarcher: "An old painting teacher said that a work tells you when it is finished."

GETTING LOST AND FOUND IN THE WORK

Maria-Theresa Fernandes: "Really, you have to be happy to work. You're in a world where you don't even notice anybody else. I think that you grow through your work and vice versa."

Renie Breskin Adams: "When I'm involved in this process, and this must be true for other artists too, it's a way of forgetting myself. You really do go some place else while you're working, and it's sort of nice."

Connie Lehman: "Making narrative art, especially drawing, is my way of marking time, sort of a life diary. The cast of characters is long and changing. Even if the drawings never become embroideries, I can go back to them and remember fascinations of the past and how time was put to good use. If the viewer becomes involved, I have achieved a double success.

Deidre Scherer: "You're still talking primarily about a visual experience. You're connecting the visual with some other places than your thinking side. You connect them with your hand and gut and diaphragm and heart. If you're saying, 'I love you,' and it's coming from the heart, it sounds different and feels different than if you say 'I love you' and it's coming from your head. Both are valid, but very often what we visually perceive ahead of what we actually end up with isn't the better of the two."

Joan Schulze: "I can't talk about the work while I'm doing it. I may write poems and I may put some notes down, but I never really know, until it's almost over, where the work is going. Sometimes I don't know even then; it may take me a long time to figure it out before I know. That's nice, because I like talking to a very deep part of myself. I like finding things out. I don't have to know everything all at once."

PRACTICING THE EXPRESSIVE QUALITIES OF COLOR

Susan Dowman Wilchins: "In helping to develop a sophisticated ability to use color, one of the most useful projects I've found involves matching from a specific source.

"First, select a color photograph from a magazine or book, preferably one that can be detached and examined closely. This works well with photographic sources that are suitably complex — that is, having at least eight to ten distinguishable colors.

"Second, make an analysis of the color structure of the photograph, including a listing of the colors used and noting their placement in the composition.

"Third, using paint (or dyes or print pigments — more challenging and more to the point with those interested in working with fiber media), mix the colors present in the photograph, being as precise as possible, making allowances for the change in media.

"Fourth, transfer these colors, in the same proportions as they appear in the original source, to a composition of your own devising.

"Last, begin to experiment with the same palette and altering the proportions of the colors. The real advantage comes in doing multiple examples and comparing them. The evaluation part of this exercise is essential.

"You could also attempt to do this with yarns (although the crossing of fibers in the woven structure requires another level of complexity in predicting the results) or with fabric swatches (if a large variety is available). If you're

trying to master color, being able to control it from the mixing stage on becomes vital.

"I've used variations on this idea in almost every class I have taught, and I find that it immediately does several things. It makes students more aware of the subtle color differences around them. It makes them ask questions about the relationship of color to composition, and it forces them to acquire good technical control of the color medium in which they're working. I stress that it is an exercise only. There is no creative problem-solving going on here.

"When you begin, then, to talk about these sources in terms of evocative characteristics or the color relationship and can begin to transfer that information into your own work, then you're really starting to obtain a high level of ability. Color then becomes a very powerful communicative tool. Although my students often chuckle at me when I say this, I really believe that color is power. It really is one of the first things that people respond to when they're confronted with an object."

PLANNING FOR LIVING

Barbara Lee Smith: "Write your own obituary. There's nothing like thinking about your life's ending to concentrate your energies on the importance of living. What are the goals you want to meet, the work you want to create, the places you want to see, the relationships you want to remember? Be specific, but also be fanciful; think of 'impossible' things. They may not be as impossible as you think.

"Now reread what you've written and focus on what you can accomplish within the next year or five years. Put your notes away in a safe place, and return to them in a few years. You'll be surprised at all you've already accomplished. You may want to add some other goals. And, having focused on your life ahead by looking back on it, you'll have established priorities which will affect your attitude toward your work in the present."

WRITING A PERSONAL ART HISTORY

Arturo Alonzo Sandoval: "I ask my students to write their personal art history. What I hope for is that they'll go all the way back to their childhood and include all of the art imagery they created and the art experiences they had contact with, including art museums, family or friends who shared art creations with them, or what they did in school with teachers or by themselves.

"I ask them to do this because I believe that each individual has the ability to be creative and that their personal life experiences, especially those where some art making was involved, can contribute to their present imagination and creative spirit. I have found in teaching that some students feel at a loss for ideas as an inspiration for art making. Therefore I encourage them to explore their own lives for a foundation of ideas which were, perhaps, laid before them as children and adults. The results are very informative, and the students have expressed how much they rediscovered."

GALLERY

MARIO RIVOLI
Mexican Jacket

1989; 30 in. by 24 in.; celluloid, Bakelite buttons, ribbons, felt soft toys on wool Mexican tourist jacket (ca. 1940), old jewelery; sewing. (Courtesy of Wittenborn & Hollingsworth, Ltd., Los Angeles, and Julie: Artisans' Gallery, New York City; photo by Tohru Nakamura.)

"If objects have a life of their own, I give them a stage. Assemblage has always been a conscious aspect of inspiration for the flotsam and jetsam of emotion. The influences that affect my art draw more and more on long loving friendships, the quick daily throughts that make me say 'ooh' or 'aah,' and the compulsion to pick up a rusted bottle cap. My art is up for interpretation—I like that—and it always triggers some chord, which makes me secretly pleased."

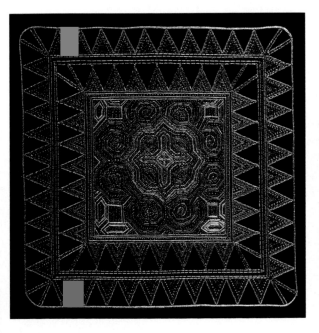

ROBERT BURNINGHAM
Cross

1985; 15 in. by 14 in.; beads, silk, cotton floss, metallic threads; stitching; full piece at far left, detail at left. (Photo by Robert Burningham.)

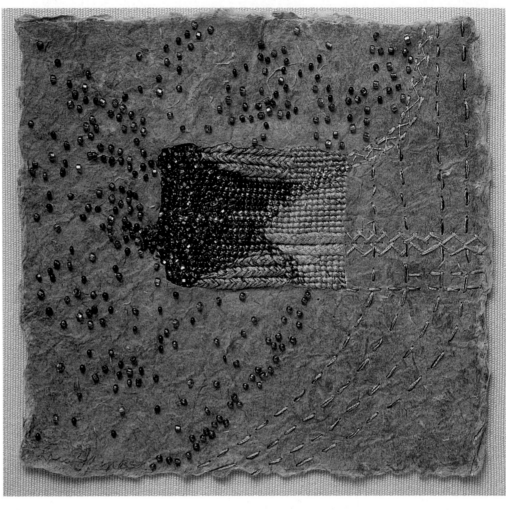

LOIS JAMES
Untitled Green

1987; 10 in. by 11 in.; handmade paper, beads; needlepoint. (Photo by Gene Ogami.)

CINDY HICKOK
Forty Days...

1988; 8 in. by 8 in.; rayon thread; machine embroidery on water-soluble film that dissolves in hot water; the remaining embroidery is sandwiched between Plexiglas. (Photo by Sandy King.)

JUSTINE K. VAUGHN
First Annual Valentine

1988; 12 in. by 12 in.; cotton fabrics, ribbon, metallic thread, silk ribbon roses, safety pins, porcelain lace embossed buttons; hand dyeing, piecing, quilting, embellishing. (Collection of Kathy Zielinski, Rockford, Ilinois; photo by Cleaver Photography.)

BEVERLY MOOR
Reflections: Fragmented Landscape

1988; 33 in. by 46 in. by 4 in.; handmade painted papers, Mylar, heat warped and laminated plastic; machine embroidery with unclipped threads. (Photo by Jack Grossman.)

LUCY A. JAHNS
Cadence

1989; 33 in. by 53 in.; dyed fabric; machine embroidery, machine appliqué. (Photo by Lucy A. Jahns)

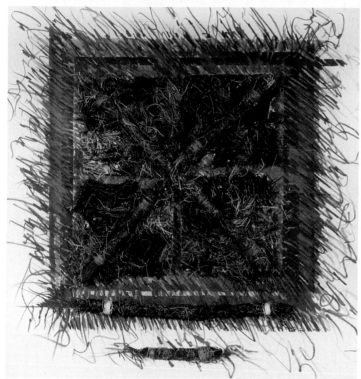

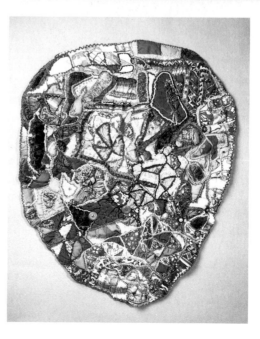

BARBARA MANGER
Combo-Combo I

1983; 18 in. by 18 in.; Prismacolors, thread, bamboo; drawing, stitching, wrapping. (Private collection; photo by Eric Oxendorf.)

ELIZABETH SCOTT
Broken Heart

1989; 32 in. by 30 in.; fabric, fibers, beads; hand stitching. (Photo by John Dean.)

GLOSSARY

Although most terms have been defined in the text, a few that refer to printing, painting or sewing techniques used in combination with embroidery may be unfamiliar. These terms are briefly explained here as they relate to embroidery.

Acrylic matte medium/acrylic gel medium: Synthetic adhesives often used in collages. Translucent when applied, these polymer resins dry clear.

Appliqué: Attaching one piece of fabric, usually by hand or machine sewing, to the surface of another piece of fabric.

Artist's linen: Unprimed linen, usually intended as a base for painting. Available at art-supply stores, this linen is used as background for embroidery and also for mounting and framing a work.

Counted thread: Any embroidery technique that relies on counting the number of threads in the background fabric to determine the placement of stitches; generally associated with cross-stitch embroidery.

Cyanotype: Blueprint printing; a photographic reproduction rendered as white lines or shapes on a blue ground.

Discharge printing: "Printing" fabrics by removing areas of previously printed or dyed color using chlorine bleach or a commercial color remover.

Fiberfill/quilt batting: Generally refers to soft polyester fibers used to provide padding within a work or when mounting the work. In sheet form, often with a glazed finish for ease in handling, fiberfill is called quilt batting. Cotton and silk batting is also available.

Gesso: A water-based primer resembling a thick white paste, used to coat and prepare a canvas for painting.

Gouache: An opaque watercolor paint; often used for preliminary studies.

Ground: The background fabric on which embroidery is worked; also used to refer to the background of a design (as in figure and ground).

Hue: The name of a color (for example, red or green).

Maquette: A small model of a finished work.

Monofilament: A single-filament, synthetic thread; generally associated with the clear "invisible" thread used in garment construction or quilting, or with fishing line.

Piecing: Sewing fabrics together, usually by machine. Strip piecing, as used in Seminole patchwork, is made by sewing long strips of fabric together to make yardage from which new pieces can be cut and, if desired, pieced again.

Reverse appliqué: Layering of two or more fabrics and cutting through one or several of these layers to reveal the colors beneath. Traditionally, the edges of reverse appliqué are finished by folding them under and hand hemming them. Machine satin stitch or zigzag stitch can also be used to secure fabrics. The technique is associated with molas, which decorate the blouses made by the Kuna Indians of the San Blas Islands, near Panama.

Screen printing: A method of printing color on fabric using a rigid frame to hold a stencil in place and a squeegee to pull fabric paint or dye across the screen in one stroke, forcing paint or dye onto the fabric.

Top stitching: A slightly longer than usual machine stitch that is generally used in clothing construction, worked near the seam line or the edge of the garment.

Transfer printing: Printing, generally applied to synthetic fabric, using inks or crayons that are first applied to paper and then heat-set on the fabric.

Value: Refers to the amount of light and dark in a color.

STITCHES

There are four basic classes of hand embroidery stitches: flat, looped, knotted and composite. And there are almost as many methods for making these stitches as there are people who have made them. In order to keep things as simple as possible, a stitch is defined here under its most commonly used name. A slight variation can mean a name change, but if the variation does not really alter the character of the stitch, the name change is not mentioned here for the sake of simplicity.

The following stitches are some of the most basic. You will find cross-references to several other stitches discussed and illustrated in sidebars in the main text. For information on various machine stitches, see the sidebar on pp. 38-40. For additional stitches and variations, refer to the excellent books on technique listed in the Bibliography on pp. 225-227.

Back stitch (flat): A linear stitch, often varied by whipping over it with a second thread.

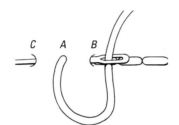

Come up at A, go in at B, out at C. Repeat, going back in at the end of the previous stitch (A).

Buttonhole (looped): A versatile stitch used to create a line or edging, which can be worked in a curve or circle or in rows to fill spaces. It can be spaced or worked solidly and can be worked in rows either left to right or right to left. When working the buttonhole stitch, be sure to throw the thread ahead of the needle as you work.

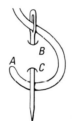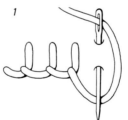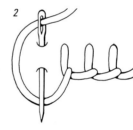

The thread must be held under the needle as the needle is drawn through the fabric from B to C.

This stitch can be worked left to right (1) or right to left (2).

Buttonhole stitch, detached (looped): See p. 54.

Ceylon stitch (looped): See p. 117.

Chain stitch (looped): A linear stitch that can be worked as a single stitch (known as detached chain or lazy daisy) for patterns like seeding, in a single row for outlining or in multiple rows for a solid filling.

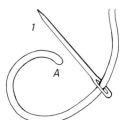 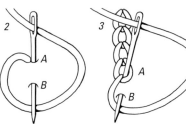

Detached chain used in a pattern.

Detached chain used as seeding.

Bring the needle out at A. Form a loop with the thread and hold it in place; put the needle back in at A and draw through at B, keeping the loop under the needle to form the first chain. Subsequent

stitches begin within the previous loop. Worked singly and tied with a small stitch, it becomes detached chain stitch or lazy daisy.

Coral knot stitch (knotted): A stitch used for straight or curved lines and for filling. Worked either left to right or right to left, the knots are made at a right angle to the stitched line. They can be spaced closely or far apart, worked singly or in patterns.

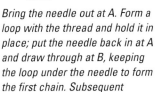 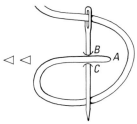 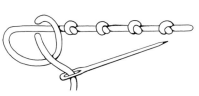

Bring the needle up at A, lay the thread in the direction of the line to be covered and hold it with your nonstitching thumb. Make a small stitch from just above the line (B) to just below the line (C) and loop

the thread under the point of the needle. Draw the thread through the fabric, gently encouraging it to form a knot. The space between B and C determines the size of the knot.

Couching (composite): Stitching one or a group of threads to the surface of a fabric with another, usually finer thread (called the "couching" or "working" thread). The couching stitch can be either almost invisible or worked in highly decorative patterns.

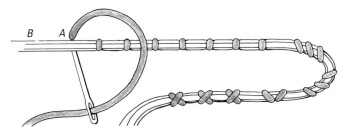

A single, thick thread or a bundle of threads can be couched, spacing stitches close or far apart or working them in decorative patterns. To couch, lay the thread(s) on the fabric or bring them up one at a time from the

back of the fabric. Then, with a separate couching thread, come up at A over the thread(s) being couched, down into the same hole at A and out at B to begin the next stitch.

Cross stitch (flat): A counted-thread stitch. Half-crosses are worked in one direction and then completed by a second half-cross worked at an angle in the opposite direction.

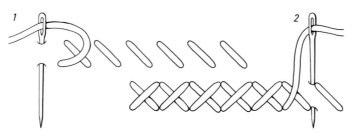

For a smooth appearance it is important to work all stitches in each step at the same angle.

French knot (knotted): A stitch used either singly to produce a small dot or massed in multiples to create texture or pointillistic shading.

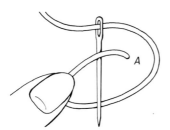

1. Bring the thread out at A and hold gently with your thumb. Slide the needle under the thread without piercing the fabric.

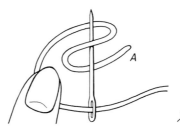

2. Loosen your grip on the thread slightly to allow the needle to rotate 180°, and pull the thread through. Sew into the center of the

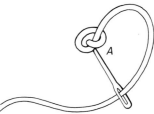

knot and pull the thread through to the back of the fabric to complete the French knot.

Herringbone stitch (flat): See p. 29.

Long and short stitch (flat): A method used to produce a smooth-textured surface; it is frequently used for shading. As its name suggests, the first and last rows within an area are stitched with alternating long and short straight stitches. All the rows in between are of equal-length stitches, adjusted where necessary, to fill a given shape. It is important to work this stitch with the fabric stretched taut in a hoop.

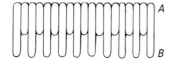

With the fabric stretched in a hoop, work the first row, alternating long and short stitches, coming up at A and down at B.

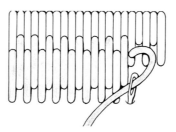

For the second row, and for all rows except the last, work stitches of the same length, positioning them as shown. Note that each stitch pierces the stitch just above it, splitting it from below and creating a smooth surface.

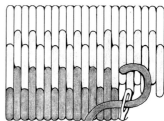

For the final row, work the stitches like the initial row, but reverse the long and short lengths. Adjust the stitches for irregular shapes and keep them the same length as the other long and short stitches as much as possible.

Needleweaving (composite): See p. 52.

Running stitch (flat): The most basic of stitches, a simple in-and-out line. This stitch can be worked in patterns, running evenly or unevenly for a rhythmic line. It is also used as the standard quilting stitch. In machine embroidery, a single line worked with no stitch-width change is referred to as "free running stitch."

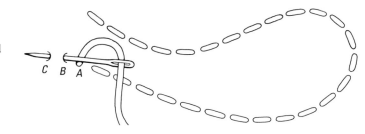

Satin stitch (flat): A smooth band of parallel stitches worked evenly side by side, with the thread covering both the back and the front of the fabric. You can slightly pad the edge of a shape by first working a row of stem stitch, back stitch or chain stitch around the shape, then satin stitching over this edging stitch. (See also p. 29.) Machine-embroidered satin stitch is formed when any width of zigzag stitch is worked close together (set the stitch length between 0 and ½).

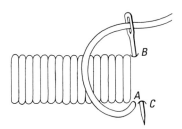

Working with the fabric stretched in a frame, draw the needle up at A, straight down at B, then straight up again at C, next to A. (For clarity, the diagram shows the needle stitching B-C as one step rather than two, as it is actually stitched.)

To use satin stitch to fill in a shape, outline the shape with back stitch, chain stitch or stem stitch.

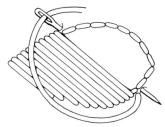

Cover the edging stitch completely with satin stitch, working the stitches at any angle you like. When working a large area, begin the satin stitching in the middle and work to one end. Then return to the middle and work the to other end. This keeps the stitches angled consistently.

Seed stitch (flat): Single, tiny stitches scattered erratically or in patterns to add dots of texture or color to the fabric surface. This can be worked as a single stitch or made thicker by adding a second stitch on top of the first, either in the same holes or at a slight angle to them.

Seeding (flat): Scattering tiny seed stitches across an area to add texture. (See also Seed stitch.)

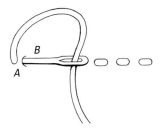

Basic seed stitch is worked by bringing the thread up at A and down at B (1). This stitch can be made thicker by repeating the stitch in the same hole or by overlapping the first stitch at a slight angle, from C to D (2).

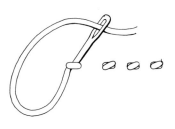

Stem stitch (flat): A slightly raised, linear stitch also known as outline stitch or crewel stitch, whose reverse side is back stitch. (See also p. 117.)

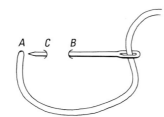

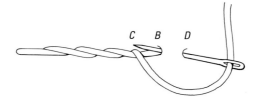

Bring the thread up at A, down at B and up again at C, halfway between A and B.

Continue the stitch by going down at D and up again at B. Note that the stitch taken is always half the length of the finished stitch. Be consistant with the working thread, keeping it always below or always above the line of stitches.

Tent stitch (flat): A counted-thread stitch, one of the most basic in needlepoint, which is worked over counted threads of an evenly woven ground fabric. To cover large areas, work the stitch diagonally to avoid distorting the background canvas. This stitch is best worked with a blunt tapestry needle.

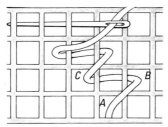

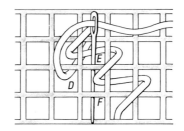

1. Starting in the lower right area to be covered, bring the needle up at A, cross over one intersection of threads, insert the needle at B and bring it behind two vertical threads and out at C. Continue to the top of the area. Keep the needle horizontal when working from lower right to upper left.

2. To work from the upper left down, turn the needle, not the canvas, bringing it out directly below the base of the last stitch worked (D). Cross over one intersection of threads, insert the needle at E and bring it down behind two horizontal threads and

out at F. Keep the needle vertical when working from upper left down to lower right. Continue over one, under two to the bottom of the boundary.

Whip stitch (composite): Whipping over a baseline stitched in stem stitch, back stitch or chain stitch causes the line to look like a raised cord. Best worked with a blunt tapestry needle, whip stitch allows a second color or texture to be introduced with the whipping thread. In machine embroidery, whip stitch occurs when the tension on the bobbin thread is much looser than that on the top thread, causing the bobbin thread to "whip" around the top thread that appears to be lying on the fabric surface. (See also p. 40.)

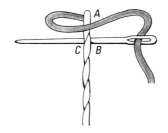

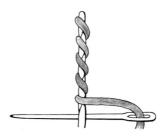

Work a baseline of a flat stitch (stem stitch is shown here). Then begin whip stitching around the baseline, bringing the thread up at A behind the line and stitching from B to C behind the line, without piercing the fabric.

Continuing to whip stitch around the baseline produces a raised, corded effect.

RESOURCES

The sources of supply below include some of my favorites and others
highly recommended by colleagues and friends. You will find many
additional mail-order sources of fabric and other embroidery and surface-
design supplies in *The Fabric & Fiber Sourcebook* by Bobbi A. McRae
(Newtown, Conn.: The Taunton Press, 1989).

Thread, Fabric and Sewing Supplies

Aardvark Adventures
P.O. Box 2449
Livermore, CA 945511
(800) 388-2687, (415) 443-2687

Britex by Mail
146 Geary Street
San Francisco, CA 94108
(415) 392-2910

Clotilde, Inc.
1909 S.W. 1st Avenue
Ft. Lauderdale, FL 33315
(305) 761-8655

G Street Fabrics
11854 Rockville Pike
Rockville, MD 20852
(800) 333-9191, (301) 231 8998

Joan Toggitt
35 Fairfield Place
West Caldwell, NJ 07006
(201) 575-5410

LACIS
2982 Adeline Street
Berkeley, CA 04703
(415) 843-7178

Madeira Marketing, Ltd.
600 E. 9th Street
Michigan City, IN 46301
(219) 873-1000

Nancy's Notions
P.O. Box 683
Beaver Dam, WI 53916
(414) 887-0690

Speed Stitch
3113-D Broadpoint Drive
Harbor Heights, FL 33983
(813) 629-3199

Sureway Trading Enterprises
826 Pine Avenue, #5
Niagara Falls, NY 14301
(716) 282-4887

Testfabrics, Inc.
P.O. Box 420
Middlesex, NJ 08846
(201) 469-6446

Things Japanese
9805 N. E. 116th Street
Suite 7160
Kirkland, WA 98034
(206) 821-2287

YLI
45 West 300 North
Provo UT 84601
(800) 854-1932, (801) 377-3900

Printing and Dyeing Supplies

Cerulean Blue, Ltd.
P.O. Box 21168
Seattle, WA 98111
(206) 443-7744

Createx Colors
14 Airport Park Road
East Granby, CT 06026
(800) 243-2712, (203) 653-5505

Dharma Trading Company
P.O. Box 916
San Rafael, CA 94915
(800) 542-5227, (415) 456-7657

Quick-Way Color Copies
100 E. Ohio Street
Chicago, IL 60611
(312) 943-3662

Rupert, Gibbon & Spider, Inc.
P.O. Box 425
Healdsburg, CA 95448
(800) 442-0455

Beads

Ornamental Resources, Inc.
Box 3010, 1427 Miner Street
Idaho Springs, CO 80452
(303) 567-4987

Art Supplies

Daniel Smith
4130 First Avenue South
Seattle, WA 98134
(800) 426-7923, (206) 223-9599

Archival Supplies

Light Impressions
439 Monroe Avenue
Rochester, NY 14607
(800) 828-6216

Books

Hard-To-Find Needlework Books
Bette S. Feinstein
96 Roundwood Road
Newton, MA 02164
(617) 969-0942

New World Books
2 Cains Road
Suffern, NY 10901
Write for information on how
to order.

You may find the following list of journals and magazines useful in learning more about contemporary embroidery.

American Craft
American Craft Council
40 W. 53rd Street
New York, NY 10019

Art Today: The Magazine of New Art Forms & Design
WEB Publications, Inc.
650 Westdale Drive
Wichita, KS 67209

CEG Ments
Canadian Embroiderers Guild
Box 541 Station B
London, Ontario N6A 4W1
Canada

Embroidery
The Embroiderers Guild
Apt. 41 A, Hampton Court Palace
East Molesey, Surrey, England
KT8 9AU

Embroidery Canada
The Embroiderers
Association of Canada
Connie Wolks
13791 101A Avenue
Surrey, British Columbia V3T 1M4
Canada

Fiberarts
50 College Street
Asheville, NC 28801

Flying Needle
Council of American Embroiderers
P.O. Box 8578
Northfield, IL 60093-8578

Needle Arts
The Embroiderers' Guild
of America
335 W. Broadway, Suite 100
Louisville, KY 40202

Ontario Craft
Ontario Crafts Council
Chalmers Building
35 McCaul Street
Toronto, Ontario M5T 1V7
Canada

Ornament
P.O. Box 35029
Los Angeles, CA 90035-0029

Quilters Newsletter
6700 W. 44th Avenue
Wheatridge, CO 80033-0394

Surface Design Journal
Surface Design Association
4111 Lincoln Boulevard, Suite 426
Marina del Rey, CA 90292

Threads magazine
The Taunton Press
63 S. Main Street
Box 5506
Newtown, CT 06470-5506

Treadleart
28534 Narbonne Ave
Lomita, CA 90717

American Craft Council
Membership Department
P.O. Box 1308
Fort Lee, NJ 07024

American Needlepoint Guild
P.O. Box 3525
Rock Hill, SC 29731

American Quilter's Society
P.O. Box 3290
Paducah, KY 42002
(502) 898-7903

Canadian Crafts Council
M. Joan Chalmers Cultural Centre
189 Laurier Avenue East
Ottawa, Ontario K1N 6P1
Canada

Canadian Quilters' Association
P.O. Box 326
Grimsley, Ontario L3M 1MO
Canada

Center for the Study of Beadwork
P.O. Box 13719
Portland, OR 97212
(503) 249-1848

Conseil des Arts Textiles du Quebec
811-A Ontario East
Montreal, Quebec H2L 1P1
Canada

Council of American Embroiderers
P.O. Box 8578
Northfield, IL 60093-8578

The Embroiderers' Guild
of America
335 W. Broadway, Suite 100
Louisville, KY 40202
(502) 589-6956

Ontario Crafts Council
Chalmers Building
35 McCaul Street
Toronto, Ontario M5T 1V7
Canada
(416) 977-3551

Surface Design Association
4111 Lincoln Boulevard, Suite 426
Marina del Rey, CA 90292
(213) 392-2274

Surfacing, The Textile Dyers and
Printers Association of Ontario
Box 6828, Station A
Toronto, Ontario M5W 1X6
Canada

BIBLIOGRAPHY

Embroidery Design, Technique and History

Ambuter, Carolyn. *The Open Canvas*. New York: Workman Publishing, 1982.

Barton, Julia. *The Art of Embroidery*. London: Merehurst, 1989.

Bath, Virginia. *Needlework in America*. New York: The Viking Press, 1979.

Beany, Jan. *The Art of the Needle: Designing in Fabric and Thread*. New York: Pantheon Books, 1988.

Best, Muriel, and Vicky Lugg. *Design Sources for Embroidery*. London: B. T. Batsford, 1988.

Best, Muriel, Vicky Lugg and Dorothy Tucker. *Needlework School*. Secaucus, N.J.: Chartwell Books, 1984.

Box, Richard. *Drawing and Design for Embroidery: A Course for the Fearful*. London: B. T. Batsford, 1988.

Campbell-Harding, Valerie. *Flowers and Plants in Embroidery*. London: B. T. Batsford, 1986.

de Dillmont, Thérèse. *Encyclopedia of Needlework*. Mulhouse, France: D.M.C. Library, no date.

Enthoven, Jacqueline. *The Stitches of Creative Embroidery*. New York: Reinhold Publishing, 1964.

Feisner, Edith Anderson. *Needlepoint and Beyond*. New York: Charles Scribner's Sons, 1980.

Field, Peggy and June Linsley. *Canvas Embroidery*. London: Merehurst, 1990.

Harbeson, Georgiana B. *American Needlework*. New York: Bonanza Books, no date.

Howard, Constance. *Inspiration for Embroidery*. London: William Clowes, 1966.

———. *The Constance Howard Book of Stitches*. London: B. T. Batsford, 1979.

Jerstorp, Karin, and Eva Köhlmark. *The Textile Design Book*. Asheville, N.C.: Lark Books, 1988.

Karasz, Mariska. *Adventures in Stitches, and More Adventures, Fewer Stitches*. New York: Funk & Wagnalls, 1959.

Krevitsky, Nik. *Stitchery: Art and Craft*. New York: Reinhold Publishing, 1966.

Laury, Jean Ray. *Applique Stitchery*. New York: Reinhold Publishing, 1966.

Mayer-Thurman, Christa C. *Raiment for the Lord's Service*. Chicago: The Art Institute of Chicago, 1975.

Messant, Jan. *The Embroiderers' Workbook*. London: B. T. Batsford, 1988.

Parker, Rozsika. *The Subversive Stitch: Embroidery and the Making of the Feminine*. London: The Women's Press, 1984.

Rhodes, Mary. *Ideas for Canvas Work*. McMinnville, Ore.: Charles T. Branford, 1970.

Springall, Diana. *Design for Embroidery*. London: Pelham Books, 1988.

Van Dommelen, David B. *Decorative Wall Hangings: Art with Fabric*. New York: Funk & Wagnalls, 1962.

Wilson, Erica. *Erica Wilson's Embroidery Book*. New York: Charles Scribner's Sons, 1973.

Whyte, Kathleen. *Design in Embroidery*. McMinnville, Ore.: Charles T. Branford, 1969.

Machine embroidery

Bennett, dj. *Machine Embroidery with Style*. Seattle, Wash.: Madrona Publishers, 1980.

Campbell-Harding, Valerie, and Pamela Watts. *Machine Embroidery Stitch Techniques*. London: B. T. Batsford, 1989.

Clucas, Joy. *The New Machine Embroidery*. New York: Sterling, 1987.

Dodson, Jackie. *Know Your Bernina*. Radnor, Pa.: Chilton, 1987. (Other brands of machines are also available in this series).

Fanning, Robbie, and Tony Fanning. *The Complete Book of Machine Embroidery*. Radnor, Pa.: Chilton, 1986.

———. *The Complete Book of Machine Quilting and Appliqué*. Radnor, Pa.: Chilton Book Co., 1987.

Harker, Gail. *Machine Embroidery*. London: Merehurst, 1990.

McNeill, Moyra. *Machine Embroidery: Lace and See-Through Techniques*. London: B. T. Batsford, 1986.

Skjerseth, Douglas Neil. *Stitchology: Sewing Machine Tune-Up Guide*. Seth Publications, 1979. (Available through sewing-supply catalogs.)

Related Techniques

Bath, Virginia C. *Lace*. Chicago, Ill.: Henry Regnery, 1974.

Digby, John, and Joan Digby. *The Collage Handbook*. London: Thames & Hudson, 1985.

Johnston, Meda Parker, and Glen Kaufman. *Design on Fabrics*. New York: Van Nostrand Reinhold, 1967.

Larsen, Jack Lenor. *The Dyer's Art: Ikat, Batik, Plangi*. New York: Van Nostrand Reinhold, 1977.

Nordfors, Jill. *Needle Lace & Needle Weaving*. New York: Van Nostrand Reinhold, 1974.

Proctor, Richard M., and Jennifer F. Lew. *Surface Design for Fabric*. Seattle: University of Washington Press, 1984.

Wada, Yoshiko, Mary Kellogg Rice and Jane Barton. *Shibori: The Inventive Art of Japanese Shaped Resist Dyeing; Tradition, Techniques, Innovation*. Kodansha International; distributed by Harper & Row, 1983.

Color, Design and Drawing

Albers, Anni. *On Designing*. Middletown, Conn.: Wesleyan University Press, 1961.

Albers, Josef. *Interaction of Color*. New Haven, Conn.: Yale University Press, 1963.

Cobb, Virginia. *Discovering the Inner Eye: Experiments in Water Media*. New York: Watson-Guptill, 1988.

Edwards, Betty. *Drawing on the Right Side of the Brain*. New York: St. Martin's Press, 1979.

——— . *Drawing on the Artist Within*. New York: Simon and Schuster, 1986.

Itten, Johannes. *The Art of Color*. New York: Van Nostrand Reinhold, 1961.

——— . *The Elements of Color*. New York: Van Nostrand Reinhold, 1970.

Lambert, Patricia, Mary Fry and Barbara Staepelaere. *Color and Fiber*. West Chester, Pa.: Schiffer Publishing, 1986.

Lauer, David, A.. *Design Basics*. New York: Holt, Rinehart and Winston, 1979.

Wong, Wucius. *Principles of Color Design*. New York: Van Nostrand Reinhold, 1987.

Contemporary Fiber Art

Constantine, Mildred, and Jack Lenor Larsen. *Beyond Craft: The Art Fabric*. New York: Van Nostrand Reinhold, 1973.

——— . *The Art Fabric: Mainstream*. New York: Van Nostrand Reinhold, 1981.

Dale, Julie S. *Art to Wear*. New York: Abbeville Press, 1986.

Editors of *Fiberarts* magazine. *Fiberarts Design Book*. New York: Hastings House, 1980.

Herman, Lloyd E. *Art That Works: The Decorative Art of the Eighties, Crafted in America*. Seattle: University of Washington Press, 1990.

Hutchins, Jeane, ed. *The Fiberarts Design Book II*. Asheville, N.C.: Lark Books, 1983.

Manhart, Marcia, and Tom Manhart, Eds. *The Eloquent Object*. Seattle: University of Washington Press, 1987.

Matthews, Kate, ed. *Fiberarts Design Book Three*. Asheville, N.C.: Lark Books, 1987.

Mayer-Thurman, Christa C. *Claire Zeisler: A Retrospective*. Chicago: Art Institute of Chicago. 1979.

McMorris, Penny, and Michael Kile. *The Art Quilt*. San Francisco: The Quilt Digest Press, 1986.

Milwaukee Art Museum. *Fiber R/Evolution*. Milwaukee: Milwaukee Art Museum and University Art Museum, University of Wisconsin-Milwaukee, 1986.

Morgan, Kathleen Nugent. *Lenore Tawney: A Retrospective*. New York: Rizzoli, 1990.

Quilt National. *Quilts: The State of an Art*. West Chester, Pa.: Schiffer, 1985.

Rhodes, Zandra, and Anne Knight. *The Art of Zandra Rhodes*. Boston: Houghton Mifflin, 1985.

Rowe, Ann Pollard, and Rebecca A. T. Stevens. *Ed Rossbach: 40 Years of Exploration and Innovation in Fiber Art*. Asheville, N.C.: Lark Books, 1990.

Smith, Paul J., and Edward Lucie-Smith. *American Craft Today: Poetry of the Physical*. New York: Weidenfeld & Nicolson, 1986.

For Inspiration

Adams, James L. *Conceptual Blockbusting.* Stanford, Calif.: Stanford Alumni Association, 1974.

———. *The Care and Feeding of Ideas.* Reading, Mass.: Addison-Wesley, 1986.

Buzan, Tony. *Use Both Sides of Your Brain.* New York: E. P. Dutton, 1974.

Flack, Audrey. *Art and Soul: Notes on Creating.* New York: E. P. Dutton, 1986.

Flam, Jack D. *Matisse on Art.* New York: E. P. Dutton, 1973.

Henri, Robert. *The Art Spirit.* Philadelphia: J. B. Lippincott, 1960.

London, Peter. *No More Secondhand Art: Awakening the Artist Within.* Boston: Shambhala Publications, 1989.

May, Rollo. *The Courage to Create.* New York: W. W. Norton, 1975.

———. *My Quest for Beauty.* Dallas: Saybrook Publishing, 1985.

Meurant, Georges. *Shoowa Design: African Textiles from the Kingdom of Kuba.* London: Thames and Hudson, 1986.

Munro, Eleanor. *Originals: American Women Artists.* New York: Simon and Schuster, 1979.

National Museum of African Art, Department of Education and Research, Smithsonian Institution. *Discover Shoowa Design* (pamphlet). Washington, D.C., 1989.

Picton, John and John Mack. *African Textiles.* London: British Museum Publications, 1979.

Richards, M.C. *Centering in Poetry, Pottery and the Person.* Middletown, Conn.: Wesleyan University Press, 1989.

Rilke, Rainer Maria. *Letters on Cézanne.* Edited by Clara Rilke, translated by Joel Agee. New York: Fromm International, 1985.

———. *Letters to a Young Poet.* Translated by Stephen Mitchell. New York: Random House, 1987.

Truitt, Anne. *Daybook: The Journal of an Artist.* New York: Pantheon Books, 1982.

NOTES

1. Pierre Daix, "Dread, Desire, and the Demoiselles," *ArtNews,* 88, no. 6 (Summer 1988): p. 133.

2. Cassandra Langer, "The Art of Healing," *Ms. magazine,* (January/February 1989): p. 132.

3. Lloyd Walton Blanks, "Color Blending in Needlepoint," *Threads* magazine, 10 (April/May 1987): p. 28.

4. Reprinted from *Cruisin' at the Limit. Selected poems 1968-78,* D. R. Wagner (Fallon, Nev: Duck Down, copyright 1982), p. 76, by permission of the publisher and author.

5. Reprinted from *Cruisin' at the Limit. Selected poems 1968-78,* D. R. Wagner (Fallon, Nev: Duck Down, copyright 1982), p. 94, by permission of the publisher and author.

6. Tom Lundberg, "Informed Sources," *Surface Design Journal,* 13, no. 4 (Summer 1989): p. 24.

7. See note 6.

8. Glennis McNeal, "Tom Lundberg: Where Symbol is Prominent," *Flying Needle,* 16, no. 3 (August 1987): p. 15.

9. Lloyd W. Blanks, "The Respondent: Lloyd W. Blanks," *Handmade Accents,* (Spring 1989): pp. 23-26.

10. Lloyd W. Blanks, "Color Blending in Needlepoint," *Threads* magazine, 10 (April/May 1987): p. 24.

11. Doris Walton Epner, "Lloyd Walton Blanks: Front Gallery Series and Other Works in Wool," *Needle Arts,* 16, no. 4 (Fall 1985): p. 14.

12. See note 10.

13. Lloyd W. Blanks, "Color Blending in Needlepoint," *Threads* magazine, 10 (April/May 1987): p. 27.

14. Elly Smith, "Reinventing the Sampler," *Threads* magazine, 21 (February/March 1989): p. 27.

15. Jack D. Flam. *Matisse on Art* (New York: E. P. Dutton, 1978), pp. 120-121.

Artists appearing in this book

Selected index